More Advance Praise for
Goddess Initiation

"*Goddess Initiation* is a detailed path to deepen the divine within, and to gain wisdom through insights and practical workings."

— Z. Budapest, author of *Summoning the Fates*

"*Goddess Initiation* [is] a thorough, powerful, and structured program of self-discovery . . . As in her first book, De Grandis combines a playful writing style with a keen insight into the processes necessary for true spiritual growth. Her program is safe for the inexperienced seeker, yet has enough substance to be challenging and insightful even for those whose spiritual journey is well underway. *Goddess Initiation* is a valuable healing tool, for women and men of any spiritual path."

— Carl McColman, author of *The Aspiring Mystic*
and *Embracing Jesus and the Goddess*

Acclaim for Be a Goddess!

"Francesca De Grandis has given us an inspirational bridge between ancient wisdom and our current life. Her guide to self-healing is profound."

— Lynn Andrews, author of *Medicine Woman* and *Love and Power*

"I loved it . . . An important book . . . A well-written and superb step-by-step introduction to Celtic Shamanism . . . lovely rituals . . . a smart and cogent introduction to the old religion, by someone who has learned wisdom the hard way: by putting in her time."

— Margot Adler, author of *Drawing Down the Moon*
and *Heretic's Heart*

"[*Be a Goddess!* is] destined to take its place on the shelf beside Starhawk's *The Spiral Dance* and Margot Adler's *Drawing Down the Moon.* . . . it is the book about Wicca and the Celtic mysteries which will be the standard for women and men of the twenty-first century."

—*Wisewoman*

"Astounded me no end . . . subtle and profound . . . The exercises are well planned and effective. The amount of hidden deep-level knowledge in this book is staggering. I recommend this book very highly, not only to beginners but to advanced practitioners as well."

—*Covenant of the Goddess Newsletter*

"[*Be a Goddess!*] represents the culmination of a lifetime's effort . . . unique and personal . . . Francesca De Grandis's work is in the greatest of wisdom literature traditions . . . rich and wise work."

—*Earthwisdom*

"Do let Francesca weave her spell on you. The wisdom she so generously shares can help us all become even more of the magnificent (sex) goddesses we already are. She turned me on to some beautiful rituals. I was inspired."

—Annie Sprinkle, multimedia sex artist,
    sex magic workshop facilitator

"Ms. De Grandis takes the reader to the realms of the village healer . . . The techniques described in this essential book allow anyone—and I really mean *anyone*—to gain the wild, natural power of the Goddess. The simple yet potent magic contained herein can help you to achieve the things most wished for in your life."

—*The Witch's Web*

"I don't usually endorse books, but I'm endorsing *Be a Goddess!* For an in-depth, intelligent, and ethical look at a fascinating magical path, you couldn't do better."

— Anne Newkirk Niven, editor of *Sagewoman*

". . . a dynamic and charismatic writer . . . a comprehensive training program of self-healing and transformation that helps you open to the ecstatic power of nature's forces . . . will appeal to anyone, male or female . . . a strong and wise instructor . . . this book is a real blessing."

— *Magical Blend*

"A teacher of mine said that the genders merge wherever there is great power or great ecstasy . . . in sensuality, shamanism, and spiritual transformation. That being so, *Be a Goddess!* should be required reading for anyone interested in any of these paths!"

— Hal Zina Bennett, Ph.D., author of *Zuni Fetishes*

"Of value to both beginners and advanced practitioners . . . great opportunities for growth, healing, and spiritual development . . . [De Grandis is] a true Shamanic teacher . . . This book is easy to bless. It'll bless you too!"

— *Goddessing Regenerated*

"I really look forward to recommending it to everybody . . . this work is powerful, deep, delicious, and enormously nourishing and empowering. Do it!"

— Susun Weed, author of *Wise Woman Herbal for the Childbearing Year*

Praise for Francesca De Grandis

"De Grandis teaches others how to have great sex, spiritual power, and enjoy the world, too."

—*Complete Woman*

"[A] group studying the writings of Francesca De Grandis or Thomas Merton could provide a wonderful and vibrant community."

—*The Aspiring Mystic* by Carl McColman

"Francesca the witch is wholesome, of all things. She is friendly. She is nice. She is one of those newfangled good witches, the kind that are not supposed to exist, the kind that wreck Halloween for everyone."

—*San Francisco Chronicle*

Goddess Initiation

Also by Francesca De Grandis

Be a Goddess! A Guide to Celtic Spells and Wisdom for
Self-Healing, Prosperity, and Great Sex

Goddess Initiation

A PRACTICAL CELTIC PROGRAM FOR SOUL-HEALING,
SELF-FULFILLMENT, AND WILD WISDOM

Francesca De Grandis

HarperSanFrancisco
A Division of HarperCollins*Publishers*

Material in this book has appeared, perhaps in different form, in: The Third Road®
training material; *The Wiccan and Faerie Grimoire of Francesca De Grandis* (an on-
line publication); *Her Winged Silence: A Shaman's Notebook; Reclaiming Newsletter;
Eye of the Day's Newsletter; Covenant of the Goddess Newsletter;* and in lectures—and
rituals—throughout the United States and Great Britain. The Third Road® is a reg-
istered service mark owned by F. De Grandis.

This volume's stories and characters are fictional, and resemblances to persons
living or dead are merely coincidental. The two following exceptions hold: the author hopes that she herself exists; there *are* some true tales within, about people who
gave their permission.

This book's program is not a substitute for psychological treatment or for medical care by a physician. Users of this book are responsible for the results of their
usage.

FIRST EDITION

Library of Congress Cataloging-in-Publication Data
    De Grandis, Francesca.
        Goddess initiation : a practical Celtic program for soul-healing,
    self-fulfillment, and wild wisdom /Francesca De Grandis.—1st ed.
            p.   cm.
        ISBN 0–06–251715–5 (pbk.)
        1. Magic, Celtic.   2. Goddess religion.   I. Title.

    BF1622.C45 D42   2001
    133.4'3'089916—dc21   2001024371

01 02 03 05 06 ❖RRD(H) 10 9 8 7 6 5 4 3 2 1

This book is for Kush, my friend and former professor, for the following reasons:

He spends as much time between an electron and a nucleus as I do.

His belief in me has been a mainstay, without which The Third Road® Institute would not have come into existence and with which I am more able to continue to teach and write.

The unusual (to put it mildly) wild and woolly place that Kush has made for himself is a viable position in which he provides tremendous service to others and is happy. This inspired me to follow my own unique, bizarre, and risky vision of making a full-time commitment to teaching shamanism.

Souls like Kush's are humankind's salvation, yet the work of such souls goes largely unnoticed.

This book is also in memory of Roger Stafford (1940–2000). He tried to be himself and help others.

Finally, this is for the entire Stafford/De Grandis tribe, which is made up of remarkable individuals. I love you all. Members Hannah and Kaya: you are two of the five reasons that I was put on this planet.

Contents

Table of Rituals, Spells, Prayers, Spiritual Exercises, . . .

Please be creative by applying these rituals (spells, prayers, spiritual exercises, . . .) in ways not mentioned in this book. It is impossible to list all the benefits this book's exercises offer, and in fact they offer what might seem an impossible amount of self-healing, prosperity, and great sex.

Flour Ground from Stars: A Vision and Invitation

I am a Pegasus—Goddess's winged horse. Come fly with me. Or if you travel instead on four powerful wolf's legs, I invite you to run along the plains with me. I love to gallop as much as I love to fly. Our legs can keep pace with each other's. Or do you enjoy your human form alone and want to find its every power? I will take my human form, and we can break bread made of flour ground from stars.

Do you say, "How can I come? I have no magic, no power"? Come, you belong here with us. You will be surprised. So many ways one might *be;* come with me whatever you are, or come find out who you want to be. Come to me in your glory. Or come to me thinking you know nothing other than shame and confusion, and you will find that you know all that God does. Come even if thinking, "I cannot join you, I do not have what it requires. I wish I did, but I don't!" Yes, you do, I can see it, and I will show it to you.

Come play with me and discover the secrets that you suspect are revealed in your unremembered dreams, the secrets that you know will make all the difference. Secrets that are the keys to love, power, and happiness.

The Goddess will hold us all within Her wisdom and do everything that is needed for our well-being.

So be it.

The Road to a Magical Gateway

Past all our doubts, angers and fears,
there stands a gate we can pass through
to enter into a circle of love.
Your heart's desire waits there for you.*

These are song lyrics I wrote for an initiation. (Wait, some of you skipped over those song lyrics and didn't read them! I saw you with my psychic powers! Okay, yes, I'm joking; I have a ridiculous sense of humor. The Goddess does too. I hope you have fun with us.) A Celtic shaman seeks a spiritual path that is uniquely personal and interprets life in his or her own way instead of being told what to do or think. *Self*-initiation is a logical step in this *self*-determined search and *self*-defined lifestyle, creating a *self*-expression that is crucial to any person's quest—whether spiritual or mundane. That self-expression is the essence of *Goddess Initiation*.

As is *Be a Goddess!* (my first book), this book is both a self-help program and a shamanic journey. I hope that through it you will find and celebrate your truest self—you at your best and happiest—and learn to follow your star, either for the first time or better than ever before. The

---

*From my musical album, *Pick the Apple from the Tree*

book's quest toward initiation into full power will come about through a traditional Celtic shamanic healing and empowerment.

Adele Learns to Follow Her Star

When Adele came to study with me, she worked as an administrative assistant. She was good at her job, but it left her feeling empty and unfulfilled. One evening, while I was teaching a class in which she was enrolled, I happened to say, "The Goddess does not demand we suffer unnecessarily to earn spiritual brownie points." Adele smiled tentatively and asked, "Does that imply that She feels it is okay if I find a job I enjoy?"

I responded, "She'll think it is *great!*" Adele tilted her head to the side, got a thoughtful look in her eye, and pressed her lips tightly together; she was clearly considering my words but did not yet look fully convinced. The lesson came alive for her when she performed the ritual "The Goddess's Garden of Earthly Delights." (You will learn this ritual in your fifth month's lesson.) During this rite, Adele actually experienced the Goddess's desire for her to enjoy life and could believe in her heart that she had the Goddess's blessing on her attempts to improve her life. This, along with the rest of the semester's shamanic lessons, helped her thoroughly bolster her self-confidence and become clearer about her career goals. She soon gained employment that was meaningful to her, as a fund-raiser for a battered women's shelter.

The book's series of lessons will lead you along the path of power, a road on which you can better define your life goals, create a life that is uniquely fulfilling, and live according to your hopes and dreams.

This shamanic training leads up to and culminates in a self-initiation, which is a lesson unto itself, as well as a sacred gate: pass through it into the circle of love that is humankind woven with Goddess woven with Cosmos. This circle raises all people to their fullest self-expression and most spiritual, joyous selves. The lessons of *Goddess Initiation* will teach you how to:

- Heal your inner blocks to both worldly and spiritual happiness
- Create a spiritual path that is down-to-earth and meets your deepest needs
- Attain personal satisfaction, career success, and romantic fulfillment
- Gain the full power of the human spirit and of shamanism
- Increase your creativity
- Discover your innate wisdom
- Find your inner god(dess) through loving care of yourself. It is a core belief of mine that we are all already gods. But we all don't realize it yet.
- Do spells to gain life's blessings: fun, romance, prosperity, job satisfaction, and contentment
- Have more passion

"Have more passion" refers not only to sexual passion. Some people don't know what they want to do with their lives because they cannot get in touch with the passion that strongly motivates one toward a particular career, hobby, or other goal. This book will help you find hidden passions within you, the enthusiasm that lets you know what means the most to you and helps you commit to those things.

For the purposes of this book, *shamanism, Celtic shamanism, Goddess Spirituality, Wicca, witchcraft, Faerie Tradition, Faerie magic, Fey magic, The Third Road*®* (I will explain the latter term shortly), and similar terms are synonymous. In the same vein, words similar to *priest(ess), shaman, Wiccan, witch, minister, mystic, Faerie shaman, Faerie witch, Celtic shaman, pagan,* and *magician* have the same meaning in this text. Because this book is written for both women and men, the terms *priest* and *priestess, he* and *she, her* and *his,* etc., will be used interchangeably. By the way, an initiation is not needed to do spells or be a witch.

Each and every one of us is a priest, so this book can be used by anyone. A Faerie shaman defines pagan priesthood not necessarily in terms

*The Third Road®, and variations thereof, is a service mark owned by Francesca De Grandis.

of overt ministry such as leading rituals, performing weddings, spiritually counseling others, or teaching people magic. A priest might focus instead on the subtler forms of service that anyone can—and everyone hopes to—perform: being a caring, sensitive person in one's daily life and pursuing one's true destiny, through which one makes one's life meaningful.

You will discover your own definitions of priesthood. For example, one reader's priesthood might mean being a stay-at-home mother who devotes her time to raising her children, while another reader might minister by recycling or saving the rain forests. My ministry may be writing books about Wicca and then seeing they are published, but yours may be writing extraordinary poetry that you do not wish to publish. Priesthood will be defined in a practical way that is accessible to anyone. Thus any reader of this book can find self-fulfillment by using her innate powers and wisdom to serve others and enjoy self-expression as a "priestess" to family, friends, community, and earth. Whatever your ministry is, it expresses the hope and inspiration of your inner god(dess) to others, thereby increasing your own self-love.

More About the Gifts of the Shamanic Quest

Like those in *Be a Goddess!*, this book's lessons are built along the lines of classical shamanism with some significant adaptations. This makes it a multifaceted program suitable both for those who need and those who do not need the completely unmitigated rigors of a full classical shamanic training. Let me explain.

The village shaman of the Celts was a person who overcame a shattering inner and/or outer life change—a major life trauma such as rape or the violent death of a family member—and through this accomplishment gained happiness, wholeness, mystical powers, and an ability to heal others. However, the healing that the shaman went through in order to gain selfhood was in some ways as dangerous as the original trauma.

Well, I saw spiritual seekers rightly drawn to shamanism because it clearly holds out an important promise whether or not they are trauma survivors. Shamanism calls to many types of people; they know it has special gifts to offer them. They might intuit that the Goddess offers solace in the warm sun on their face and that they are Her precious beloved. They might hear wisdom in the rustling leaves of an oak tree. But I watched these seekers sometimes use more dangerous shamanic techniques without knowing how dangerous they actually were—methods such as calling on a spirit whose power to heal is equaled by his power to wreak havoc when an untrained person summons him.

Often, these seekers were not trauma survivors and did not need rigorous work to heal themselves. Or even if they required major healing, they often did not need to use the more dangerous techniques to achieve profound well-being.

I also saw people who were not using shamanic methods to their fullest advantage. For example, my friend Antoinette kept performing prosperity rites to no avail. Deep down she believed herself unworthy of abundance. I pointed this out and taught her a ritual to clear away her inner block to drawing abundance into her life. Suddenly her spells worked. (I will teach you why and how to clear the blocks within you to effective spell casting.) All these observations started me on a long journey; in 1986 I began to create a new shamanic system. Years of research and development went into creating a safe, effective program for change.

The program is multifaceted. The lessons in *Goddess Initiation* are derived from that curriculum, which has helped already-happy, successful people find even more self-fulfillment and vibrancy in their lives. In addition, trauma survivors and members of the recovery community—those recovering from alcoholism or its accompanying family dysfunction or from incest and other forms of childhood abuse—have found crucial healing and inspiration through the material. The lessons have been constructed so that each person gets what they need from any, and every, part of the training.

So, whether you need in-depth inner change or simply want to improve an already-happy life (or both!), I will provide you with the tools to:

- Improve your relationship with your significant other
- Overcome problems in your present life caused by childhood difficulties, whether those obstacles are large or small

- Take pride in yourself and your accomplishments and have a healthy ego so that you take care of yourself, express yourself, and trust yourself. A healthy ego is good and necessary as long as it has checks and balances.
- Enjoy success in both your personal and professional life
- Find a spirituality rich with depth, power, and creativity
- Revel in great sex

Though you need no previous study to do the training in *Goddess Initiation*, you'll discover that it can help you take the next step if you enjoyed the training in *Be a Goddess!*

In this training, you will meet my mom and dad. Perhaps you already know them—the Goddess and God? If you are like the Celts and me, you view the Goddess and God as your mother and father. But if you don't or are new to pagan religions, don't worry. I am not about to tell you that you must embrace these deities or else. That is not how pagan religion works. We do not coerce, and our Gods (*Gods* is the plural term for deity whether male, female, or both) are not sadistic tyrants who threaten us with eternal suffering if we don't follow their path.

If I do something that hurts me or others, the Goddess offers Her gentle healing and teaches me how to be the kind, generous, giving person I naturally want to be. When I rebel against that natural inclination, that innate goodness in all of us, She is as patient as is needed to show me how to improve myself. For example, I was miserable because I felt life was not giving me enough. Over time, the Goddess showed me bit by bit how it was my unhealthy pride and lack of gratitude that were causing the problem: I was demanding more than was my due and so stopped enjoying the bounty and pleasures already available to me. This behavior was not kind to myself. And sometimes I still am recalcitrant about acting on that information, but She tells no priest to scold me. Instead, She patiently teaches me, by waiting until my own misery motivates me to get my ego in check and revel in the pleasures She gives me every day. Thus I find my inner goodness.

Slowly but surely, over years' time, the Celtic Gods have taught me to celebrate everyday life with sacred playfulness and to enjoy worldly possessions and my body. They have provided me with heaven on earth, this lush, gorgeous planet. My Divine Parents are understanding, compassionate, and forgiving. They are not gods one cowers before. In fact, I can ask them to protect me from the bullies of this world; they will encourage you to develop inner strength so that you will not be a doormat.

Lest I oversimplify, they are gentle gods only when allowed to be so. They can also be harsh. Just as you can learn life's lessons the easy way or the hard way, so too the Gods will teach you how to be happy the easy way if they can, the hard way if they can't. All loving, responsible parents know they have no choice but to do things the hard way if that is the only way to teach their children what they need to be whole, content, and safe. If parents don't accept this responsibility, their children will not only be unable to become happy, well-adjusted adults, they will grow up without the tools they need to survive the adult world.

Though in this book I often mention the Goddess without the God, if She is involved, He likely is too. They are in love, so you don't see much of one without the other. I often call the Goddess "God" as in "God Herself"; when I use *God* specifically for the male deity it will be apparent.

The lessons herein are a shamanic training; you can become a shaman. Through this quest you can come to define your own goals—instead of being motivated by what the neighbors think—and be responsible for your own soul. I am often asked, "Can someone who is gay (or male, young, black, Christian, rich, poor . . .) be a witch?" Everyone is welcome!

In fact, I ask you to feel free to be *more* of who you are, not less, and the system in this book was created to help you do so. My students learn to become, not something foreign to their true and intrinsic selves, but more and more themselves, to cherish and draw on the wonderful traits they already have, both those they already use and those that are too hidden to use yet. This is what it means to become fully self-realized, and it's a great thing. Though one of course wants to change inner blocks that make one unhappy, people are often unhappy because they are trying to change the wonderful, unique, and essential parts of themselves.

For example, Joseph came to me for spiritual counseling (which in my case can also be called shamanic counseling, a psychic reading, or psychic counseling) because he felt ashamed at the anger he felt toward his girlfriend, Denise. For years, wanting to do everything in his power to please her, he had sacrificed all his own wishes. He let her pick all their social activities: she enjoyed movies, he preferred camping. She chose their dining habits: she liked eating out, he reveled in barbecuing and had a talent at the grill. She even selected his clothing. By the time he came to me, he wasn't enjoying life, resented Denise for her control of him, and was disappointed in himself for feeling that way. He believed that a warm, caring person discounted all his own needs and dreams in favor of his beloved's.

It took time, but in increments I was able to convince him otherwise, through dialogue and rites such as those you will learn in this book. Once, I asked him, "Have you ever asked Denise to go camping? Perhaps she would feel flattered by your desire to share your passion for the great outdoors with her." Joseph enjoyed life more when he learned to alternate doing things Denise's way and doing things his way. And he had some delightful surprises. For example, Denise preferred restaurant dining partly because she hated to cook but loved sampling new dishes, so Joseph's constant innovations when barbecuing became an added treat for her when they camped out!

A crucial part of a Faerie shaman's path is her initiation. By doing the lessons in this book, you can gain one type of shamanic initiation. Bit by bit, what an initiation truly is will be explained as you follow the lessons presented.

The shamanic journey is the path to a Goddess Initiation (also called a shamanic initiation); the journey and initiation are inseparable and draw forth your deepest, happiest self.

Shamanism rests not on hierarchically imposed dogma but on personal experience and revelation. I do not need a priest to tell me how to live my life, and anyone can talk directly to God.

The search for God and self—the pursuit of one's own personal truths—can *feel* like a solitary struggle. I hope this book provides all the tools you need to feel supported and inspired as it leads you to your own unique revelations and truths.

There are other types of shamanic initiation, but this book focuses on *self*-initiation. For an advanced spirit it can be the highest degree of empowerment, and for a novice it can be the vital beginning, but it is always a logical step in the *self*-determined search of your own shaman soul.

The Fey Folk (also called "the little people" or "Faeries") have touched The Third Road® with their magic. (The Third Road is the shamanic system taught in this book. I will talk more about that name later.) The mystery and wild spirit of the Fey Folk have always inspired humankind to work toward their dreams and goals. Faeries whisper encouragements and rhymes into the ears of poets, helping them write their poems. Faeries block the path you are walking on with logs, to encourage you to take another road along which your dearest wishes can be fulfilled. They steal your eyeglasses when you plan to read but need instead to sleep. They fill you with self-confidence through their secrets and Faerie dust. Their power will help you in this training.

The Third Road

I call the system of shamanism I developed The Third Road® because I need a spiritual path that embraces many so-called opposites. I need to honor the mundane as divine and the sexual as holy. I must understand service to others as care of myself, and care of myself as love of others. I must know humility to be self-love, not self-abasement in which I feel I deserve God's contempt. You might avoid confusion when reading if you know that my shamanic institute in San Francisco is also called The Third Road—named after its curriculum—as is the community that has sprung up around the material.

The Third Road carries on the tradition of classical shamanism. Adaptations are an essential part of traditional shamanism. The Third Road system is based on many years of experience, and I use it both as a spiritual counselor and as a teacher of Wicca.

I first worked professionally as a spiritual counselor in an old-fashioned occult shop. There never were many of them, and despite the metaphysical boom of recent years, there are still only a few traditional, cozy, dusty, weird, and mysterious shops.

The store was in a predominantly African-American neighborhood and catered to practitioners of traditional Voodoo as well as to college students who were moving into the area and bringing their newly discovered interest in Wicca along with them. (Despite its reputation, Voodoo is a legitimate and ethical, not to mention profound and beautiful, religion, based on ancient spiritual teachings from Africa.)

I learned that the folks who came to me for counseling didn't need my high-sounding spiritual theory or feminist rhetoric. They needed help with their everyday lives: love, money, marriage, and health! So when I created the shamanic system I teach and the healing techniques I use when I counsel—both of which inform the curriculum in this book—I tried to help people with those same important concerns.

For example, Isabella came to me because she was not earning enough to pay her bills. I told her not to worry and to trust God. But that alone, though high sounding, was hardly enough of a remedy. I also showed her that part of "trusting God and not worrying" was facing bravely the challenging pursuit of her goals. We faced that challenge together: I helped her see that her fear of success kept her from striving toward her cherished career goal. I taught her a ritual to remove that fear. Then I used my intuition to help her work out a practical plan for taking control of her life and increasing her earnings:

She was a single mom, but her mother watched Isabella's three-year-old son while Isabella worked at her nine-to-five job. A class in computer technology would help Isabella obtain the higher-paying job she needed, but she felt that being away from her son during her workday *and* while attending night school would amount to deserting him. I asked God to show us another option, to show us what She wanted for this devoted mother. God told me to tell Isabella, "There is funding for single mothers trying to pursue better careers." Free of her fear of success, Isabella followed up and discovered a grant that covered her tuition and some of her bills, allowing her to work part-time, attend school, not do "without," and spend sufficient time with her son.

It was concern for my counseling clients as well as my observation of the misuse of shamanic techniques noted earlier in this book that started me writing a body of liturgy and rituals in 1986. I sought out, as well as constructed, theological, philosophical, and ethical paradigms to accompany these rites. I also developed a new way to use energy, based on a vision I was given of a style of energy usage that would give people who applied it both spiritual health and an effective, safe way to do spells.

You Possess Profound, Unique Genius

There is a dire problem in this country: we are told that there are few geniuses, few people creative enough, deep enough, committed enough to make up their *own* lives. The media tells us that there are only a few "stars," a special elite. This is a travesty! We are all shining, unique stars.

This book focuses on helping you make up your own world, in other words live *your* ideal life, as well as celebrate the distinctive way you go *about* creating a unique life.

For an actress that path might mean performing in comedies and helping people laugh at themselves. For another actress, that might mean inspiring people with *dramatic* performances. For a computer scientist that could mean choosing a high-paying day job in order to finance his art form—playing in a salsa band—during his leisure hours. For another computer scientist that might mean deciding that how she creates new software *is* her most precious art form. For a parent that might mean determining that the best way to raise her children is to bring them up on a farm, because her own youth in a rural area so strongly shaped her life for the better. Everyone makes up their own world according to their gifts.

One of my gifts is the ability to create an entire spiritual tradition. So doing that is part of my personal tale. (You will learn later that for some people, part of The Third Road is synthesizing other people's work into a personal path for themselves—a great way to create their own world. Third Road is a tradition in which you get to be eclectic!)

While the life *you* create and the way you go about creating it may be very different from mine, I believe that all our tales are special, and when *anyone* tells their story, it helps others blaze their own unique path. So below I will tell my tale in more detail.

One can tell special things about oneself in a way that is not part of the snobby, hierarchical star system! We can tell our stories without setting ourselves apart and above—"Aren't I different?"—by acknowledging that we are all alike, side by side. My tale of creating a tradition is not unusual. We are *all* doing what I did—making up our own lives, whether it is what one teaches or what spirituality one practices or how one raises children or views the world. We are all trying to be creative in our approach to modern life, whether in how we get the kids off to school on time or how we make investments. We all possess profound genius. I hope my story, told with pride, seeker to seeker, one peer to another, will help you say, "Wow, someone is like me, someone else is doing what I do," so that you feel encouraged and realize you have others by your side.

In addition, I hope that in hearing the eccentric *means* by which I created my world, you might better trust your own odd means, such as your own unusual modes of perceptions and ways of discovering truths. Believe in the unique steps you need to take to create the life of your dreams.

The Third Road material came from the deepest, most personal part of me, so creating that material is a prominent part of my most personal story. And with that, more history of the curriculum as a way to tell my tale:

Someone once called me a wise woman. It is an inaccurate term. All I do is share the *Goddess's* wisdom. She tells me things and I teach them to people at The Third Road institute. Or if I am counseling a client, I tell them what She says to do about their problems. The years of research and development needed to create my shamanic system were not spent in a library.

They were spent in part by studying with teachers—mostly Victor and Cora Anderson—who taught not from literary sources but through a lineage of oral tradition. I completed a rigorous seven-year training to become a traditional spiritual healer and Celtic shaman. It was glorious. I love to rock back and forth in a rocking chair while I teach—rocking chairs are so magical—therefore I was delighted when I discovered Victor also adored rocking chairs. I sat many a day with Victor and Cora, he and I rocking away, as on two giant birds that carried us through the magical realms that we both so treasure, while Cora, seated like an implacable monolith on her couch, kept us on course with her steadfast common sense.

My research with the Andersons, as well as other teachers and colleagues, influences all my teachings. I will always be indebted to all of them for this. But there was a far more important source: the Goddess. I spent seven years in a contemplative life during which a major portion of my time was spent in trance, as I meditated on my goals for clients and students and received a great deal of the material I teach. God gave me rituals, prayers, healing techniques, magical techniques, philosophical constructs, and other information that make up a large part of the system I now teach. This other information even included insights into physics, since physics, magic, and God are all interwoven. I constructed a great deal of material in trance.

Some of what is presented in this book as traditional shamanism Third Road style is what I was taught, but a great deal, whether ritual, ancient Celtic worldview, prehistoric cosmology, or so on, is as I decided it must have been. We can all trust ourselves this much. If you can't yet, I promise you: it is possible. I later found this material described in other sources as traditional shamanism, but I already knew it to be so: the Goddess told me. I knew my "new" material was "old." While I take a healthy pride in writing the poems that make up the liturgy in this book, I do not ignore the source of all poetry and creation, the Goddess as the Muse. In the story of my particular life, the Goddess is a central figure.

The Goddess is all-powerful. And because so much of what I am given comes from divine source, you get what *you* need. People from all walks of life—lawyers and bike messengers, psychologists and trauma survivors, Christians and witches, and everyday people wanting inner transformation and spiritual depth—have studied with me. A mayor, a professional actress, many a busy mother, and other folks who don't like to waste any time in their busy days have found that whatever they need to enjoy and transform their life, the Goddess can guide them to. She will do this for you as you work your way through this program.

The god of chaos walks hand and hand with the goddess of order and organization. For this reason we need all the gifts of the self—mind, heart, logic, fantasy, and everything else. When creating a system of self-healing, though much of my research was done in the other "realms"— meditating while God gave me information or being in trance so I could observe psychic phenomenon—it was precise, exacting work.

For one thing, it took years of rigorous, disciplined exercises to develop the sharp psychic perception needed to perceive, and thus be able to research, what happens in the psychic realm, such as how a given ritual might affect a person's self-confidence, happiness, or serenity.

Furthermore, I could not create the curriculum only through right brain, intuitive, or creative work. I logically analyzed the data received in meditations, refined that material, then showed it to my teachers for their input. A shaman learns to combine logic with intuition, poetry with physics, and heart with mind. In fact, a shaman also finds the logic *in* intuition, the poetry *in* physics, and the mindfulness of the heart. This book will, sometimes subtly, help you integrate these seemingly disparate parts of the self.

The aforementioned bringing together of what seem contradictory positions is one reason I called my system The Third Road®: to represent a path that always falls somewhere between the cracks of reality. Or at least what is considered reality when we—as many of us sometimes do—become blind to the finer distinctions in life. The system or tradition of Celtic shamanism called The Third Road® teaches us a world in which the antics of clowns are seen as well organized, and fools somehow sing in glorious, perfect harmony. Such is the magic of the Fey Folk.

In a sense, this book's lessons are not from me but from a tradition that, coming through me, is above and beyond me. The lessons came from something far bigger than my human efforts, no matter how diligent those efforts have been. The Goddess, as a never-ending source of all we need, will tell us anything we need to know about shamanism in the lessons in this book.

A quick word before the next chapter: *Goddess Initiation* is derived from a specific part of The Third Road material: a system developed both to deepen The Third Road core shamanic training and for all others who seek self-empowerment. This multilayered program not only is accessible to and geared toward novices but is also advanced and sophisticated enough for adepts (advanced practitioners).

Whoever you are, whatever your goals, the shamanic path is challenging. But it is well worth the effort. The pursuit of shamanic wisdom can change you and your life in ways that you might have longed for deeply but never thought possible. You *can* take this wondrous journey,
you can take all the power and love the Goddess offers you,
you can take the simple next step,
which is to turn the page.

What to Expect in This Shamanic Training

Practice, not theory, is the heart of spirituality. Instead of teaching a spiritual premise that you don't then know how to use, each lesson will show you how to apply the book's spiritual themes concretely and specifically to change your life for the better.

Some people believe that depth in Goddess Spirituality can be demonstrated only through theory or academically based analysis. *Goddess Initiation* will contribute an alternative view: that true depth of Goddess Spirituality can also be found through daily *practice,* much like the richest kernels of Buddhism. In fact, the Buddha refused to discuss theology or cosmology with his students.

It is through taking hands-on spiritual *action* that people can heal their spirits and find a balm for deep psychic wounds and thus achieve extensive personal growth, self-love, and the ability to embrace life as a divine gift.

I am devoted to helping people heal themselves. The degree of my commitment may be over the top, but sometimes that's what it takes to change this world. You can rest assured that your best interests are foremost in my mind, and I am right there with you as you embrace spiritual growth. Each step of the way, this book will support you. If you want support beyond what the book provides, this book will show you ways to get it. Yours will not be a lonely, solitary struggle. The lessons will show you how to become nourished and inspired by others whenever you need.

A story about theory versus practice: One day I was writing a lecture I was going to give that night in class. Then I went shopping at the supermarket. As I pushed my cart I turned from one aisle into another and found myself blocked by an elderly woman whose back was to me.

I said, "Excuse me." No response.

"Excuse me." Again, no response.

Realizing she must be hard of hearing, I made my third request much more loudly. However, I could tell that my voice was also curt with a sense of utter annoyance.

Flustered, the old woman turned to me and with a sincere apology moved her cart out of my way. I was sorry that I had given in to my impatience.

My point is not that one should never be annoyed. The Goddess does not expect us to be perfect. No matter how hard we try, we get annoyed and otherwise fall far short of our goals. We are on this planet to strive toward better ways of being, but God only expects us to *strive*, never to *achieve* a saintly way of being. This is not a race in which the stragglers get sent to hell! The Goddess is compassionate; She is understanding about the mistakes we make.

My point is that in the supermarket I was struck by the contrast between the lecture I had been writing and my extreme vexation at being momentarily blocked by a shopping cart. I had forgotten that ultimately it is actions, not words, that count.

Healthy humility, which is not the same as self-denigration, helps me see when my actions fall short of my spiritual beliefs. Then my actions can change and I no longer cause pain for myself and others. I do not take to humility naturally. I resist it. In that supermarket, I didn't like seeing the discrepancy between my lecture and my annoyance. But what a gift Goddess gave me: when I thought, "That woman should know that there are others in the aisle," God instantly gave me the momentary humility to see my reaction as unbridled annoyance. I had been filled with self-righteous feelings of spiritual superiority, when in fact *I* needed to know there were others in the aisle! I am not saying She made me feel like a bad, bad person—my god doesn't do that—but She did give me that moment of humility.

By the way, I believe in a healthy ego and that it should get as big as it needs to. But it must be balanced by healthy humility.

This training will show you how to face your attributes that you want to run from. You'll learn to view them without shame, without thinking yourself bad. You'll be free of whatever keeps you from acknowledging the traits that hurt yourself or others.

Spirituality is practical. This book presents methods that you can use to change the way you actually live. It contains tools to help you clear away inner blocks to serenity, self-confidence, and happiness. It will show you how to open your heart to be of service to the community. The book also offers techniques with which you can find your deepest self and that sure inner voice that tells you how to grapple with life's challenges and opportunities. Practical is not the same as shallow and unimportant.

Few of this book's practices require props and long preparation, such as shopping for candles. These are spiritual practices that are easy to do at home, on the bus, or maybe even on a business trip. A seeker can often just read them, then use them! You will not be frustrated by spiritual procedures too cumbersome to weave into your day. Spiritual practices that demand anything other than the doing of the process itself—for example, memorization of a prayer—are not always useful. For spirituality to help us, it must be something we can actually get *done*. So you needn't be intimidated by the thought of spirituality; you *can* care for your spirit.

This book's year-long program for finding one's destiny is an in-depth shamanic training leading one through the traditional steps to initiation. The book has monthly lessons. Each month has its own chapter and includes weekly assignments to be done during that specific month's time in the order laid out within that lesson. Please don't worry about trying to get big, mean assignments done. Though the thought of doing spiritual practices can be intimidating, the assignments are simply easy-to-use tools for happiness.

The lessons are constructed so that someone can reasonably sustain and enjoy the journey over a year's time. The book will explain how you can work at your own pace and why any pauses you find yourself needing, no matter how long their duration, might be a crucial part of your training.

Each month's lesson is structured according to the best way to convey that specific lesson. Instead of proceeding through a typically logical progression, the training will twist and turn and travel through what may *seem* a maze. But the seeming chaos of shamanic lessons has an inexorable logic that carries us deep into the ancient cells of our bodies so that we discover our secret powers to make our lives whole and wondrous.

You will learn the basic magical (or, if you prefer, *psychic;* I often use *psychic* and *magical* as one and the same) skills of shamanism. Assignments are often accompanied by instructions in the magical techniques needed for the assignment in question. By and by you'll learn how these instructions can be applied to other rituals. It will be obvious when certain instructions for one sacred technique are applicable to others; other times I will point out exactly why and how to use those instructions for other rituals. The chapters also include sections called "Francesca's Helpful Hints for Better Magic," which teach all sorts of tricks. By the end of the training you will have learned, in small, easy increments, the basic magical and ritual techniques necessary to be a true shaman.

I hope you find shamanism's direct exploration of its sexual Mysteries playful and fun, and thus draw on the healthy romance and sexuality of the Goddess culture. Some people wrongly associate Wicca with man hating. I want to be a goddess who attracts, loves, and honors men. Another woman may want to be a goddess who attracts other women. Whatever your sexual preference or gender, be assured that the Goddess hates no one. She welcomes those who are heterosexual, lesbian, gay, bisexual, women, men, transgender, or intersexed. All people are mirrors of Her. (*Transgender* is used as an umbrella term that includes men who dress as women and vice versa; folks who have surgery to change gender; and those who keep their given body but have a different gender identity. Some individuals born as hermaphrodites prefer to be called *intersexed* people.)

Throughout this book are helpful hints about avoiding self-sabotage on one's journey to both mundane and spiritual success and riches. I know I am not the only person who, when trying to improve her life, is sometimes blind to her mistakes that are actually making life worse. This training will help you avoid such blunders.

My friend Phoebe Wray says that a good teacher helps students realize that what they are already doing is the right thing. This book will lead you to, or strengthen, your own unique revelations and truths. I want to help you become what every moviegoer longs to be: a hero in his or her own life, gaining the things in life and in self that come not from gurus but only from one's own efforts and unique style of seeking and living. In this manner you can find your own way of greeting spirit, of dancing with God, of the self-initiation that's inevitably a part of such a process.

Initiation isn't always a rite. It can be the moment when a harried wife suddenly realizes she has had enough and therefore creates a sane, nurturing schedule for herself. Initiation can be giving birth to a child or getting married or even falling down the stairs drunk and thus realizing one is an alcoholic and sobering up. We all have a journey that is truly our own and truly personal. When we learn, to *whatever* extent we are able, to honor that journey and embrace it, we find the heart of spirit, become true shamans if we so wish, and fully reap the wondrousness of being human. Our spirituality then fulfills the deepest part of our souls, without denying us the worldly satisfactions that range from enjoying great food to sharing great sex. This program will help you, if you so choose, to create a wondrous, self-defined spirituality.

How to Use This Book, or Ways to Become Really Happy

Trust that no step is too small or too irrelevant to create big changes in your life. When you improve one part of your life even the tiniest bit, everything else about your circumstances is also nudged forward. Whatever bit of self-confidence we gain improves our life, career advancement, ability to parent effectively and with peace of mind, and so on, all simultaneously. A person is of a piece: you are not a machine made up of isolated components but a living organism in which no part of you is cut off from the rest of your being, and no part of you can be changed without all of you being affected. Nowhere is this more evident than in personal fulfillment and growth. *Anything* you use in this book will improve your sex life.

Since every little thing we do to improve our life will accomplish far more than we may understand at the time, just trust each of the little steps I assign, and that *anything* you accomplish will make a difference. *Anything.* I emphasize that because in nineteen years as a counselor, no matter how often I say this to people, some of them will still answer, "But this case is truly different. My improvement really is too small to make a difference in my life."

You may not see immediate results from your efforts. Remember that living a full life is a skill one must develop. No one looks great in their first dance class and might therefore think they are wasting their money on leotards. Try living fully for a while and see how it goes. In fact, don't worry if at any point in the training it seems like not much is happening.

From here on, it would be helpful for you to know that I often use *prayer, meditation, affirmation, spiritual exercise, exercise, spiritual practice, psychic practice, practice, ritual, service, magical spell,* and the like interchangeably. I call them all *sacred techniques.*

Sound spirituality often doesn't look like much on the page. Actually do the exercises in this book, because the proof is in the pudding—oh, I love the truth in those old fashioned clichés.

The training in *Goddess Initiation* is effective and safe if done at the pace recommended, in the order given, and without adaptation. I implore you to abide by this because I want you to get the many benefits possible from this training, avoid serious pitfalls, and not accidentally hurt yourself with the awesome, unusual power that this system calls forth for you. It can be overwhelming or unnecessarily problematic to experience the powerful emotional and psychic changes of the training too quickly or outside the context of the training done as given. Even the fabulous concrete results of this training can be a challenge! And magical accidents can happen when the training is not used as instructed.

There are, of course, exceptions to using the book exactly as directed. They are discussed in this chapter and in later ones when relevant. Down the line, I will also show why even an adept should do the training as given instead of forfeiting useful, safe results by, for example, thinking his many years of magical experience allow him to skip over—or speed up—parts of the lessons.

Each week includes not only assignments but "lectures." The lectures are less about intellectual comprehension than experiential absorption. Therefore, they should be read over a year's time for full impact and so you don't feel overwhelmed with material that can powerfully affect you in ways you may not notice. This book is a year's worth of transformation; the premises stated in the lecture portion of lessons aren't always properly absorbed until one has done the reading and exercises that lead up to them. Those who can be most healed or empowered by a lecture may reject its power until they have done the work preceding it.

Do each week's lesson as a whole: before doing an exercise or assignment, read the text that comes before it, both the instructions specific to the exercise and the general lecture for that week. They are often related in important if not immediately apparent ways. Do this reading within the same week you do the exercise(s).

In other words, do no lesson until you have done all the lessons preceding it.

It will be easy for you to see what you need to accomplish each week. Every month's assignments includes clear instructions as to which week of that month said assignment should be done. A "Table of Assignments" at the end of each month lists that month's assignments week for week, providing an easy review.

When I say "this month's lesson," I am not referring to a specific month of the year such as December or June but to the month-long span of time over which each lesson is to be done.

I give assignments as if there are only four weeks to a month. Adjust accordingly, and don't worry needlessly about being absolutely precise. For example, if work for January bleeds a bit over into February, remember that the sun is far away yet still warms us; nature is not as precise a calendar.

Though I give many exacting instructions concerning your training, I really want you not to be rigid about following these instructions (or call them *disciplines*); for example, you can peek ahead and read the next whole month or the whole book. You can always go back and read each lesson again as you "do" it.

The healthiest way to pursue the *discipline* of shamanism is like the healthy way to try to achieve your moral and ethical standards:

- Avoid unhealthy worry or perfectionism.
- Do your best to follow the discipline as instructed or achieve the moral goal you believe in. That is very important.
- But know it is *just as important* to view these disciplines and standards as goals one must strive toward but *can never achieve!*

You may find the training easier if once a week you devote a full evening to it, as if you and I were in an actual class that night. Whether working alone or with a group, you needn't work without a break. I stop my three-hour classes after an hour and a half or two hours, for about ten minutes. We might have a cup of tea to see us through the rest of the evening. By taking good care of ourselves and not working too hard, we honor ourselves as sacred. Besides, if you push too hard in your shamanic endeavors, you get exhausted, and then what spiritual good can you do yourself or anyone else? Not to mention that you'll lack the get-up-and-go for powerful spells!

You may want to set the same evening aside each week for class night. We schedule time for work, for taking clothing to the dry cleaners, for doing the more time-consuming housework. Unless you schedule time for your weekly class, it might be hard for you to find the time to do it. Make your spirituality and happiness a priority.

Doing the training with a friend or group can build power. If you have no suitable local pals, e-mail is a fabulous way to share the training simply with occasional notes asking things like, "How did you feel after this week's lesson?" or "Do you agree with page 26 where Francesca wrote . . . ?" Or share thoughts like, "Until I read this I thought I was the only person who believed (fill in the blank: I was a Faerie, magic isn't just a metaphor, Wicca could be practical, discipline and freedom are not mutually exclusive but support each other . . .)" or "Sometimes

I think this training is just dumb!" Yes, this too is a healthy thing to express!

You might benefit greatly by chatting on the phone occasionally with that friend long-distance. You're worth the price of that phone call!

If you are lucky enough to have a local friend(s) with whom to do the training, you may want to meet once a week or once a month, perhaps reading the lessons out loud, doing the rituals together, and discussing the process.

Third Road 101 is not the same as other Wicca 101s or Shamanism 101s. An adept doing this training needs The Third Road basic building blocks on which to build more advanced work as the year unfolds. Some of The Third Road only *appears* the same as other systems. Please don't skip a sentence or exercise that contains something familiar, *even* if you have read something similar in *Be a Goddess!* Pursue this training experientially: over time you'll find subtle, critical differences and can learn new, important facets of the gems you already knew. Also, adepts who use the system as given find that the more experienced you are, the deeper and farther the training takes you.

Not to mention that we all need spiritual basics repeated over and over. I can get carried away thinking how very spiritual I am and need a friend to remind me of things like "You're working too hard, take more time for yourself! Remember, you can't help others 'til you help yourself."

Like all of us, I have times when I am besieged by serious problems, feel miserable, and am sure there is no light at the end of the tunnel. At such times I need friends who will listen patiently to my complaints and be nurturing, but I also need someone to tell me, "Yes, I realize your problems are a handful, honey. Anyone would be upset by them. Yes, I'm glad you feel you can vent to me about them. But without suppressing your feelings, you can still look at the bright side; you've forgotten one of life's spiritual basics: a positive attitude."

At which point I can tell myself, "I've gone through far worse than my current situation with far more serenity, and maybe I can regain peace if I try to be grateful: I am still able to do the work that means everything to me. I enjoy teaching and counseling; they are my favorite activities. I felt wonderful in the last class I taught, I laughed a lot with my students and helped them gain a few new insights."

Thank goodness for such friends. It is easy for me to forget the basics or start to delude myself that a spiritual exercise is beneath me, so I need constant reminders.

These rudiments may be simple, but they can be the hardest of all spiritual actions to take. We must challenge ourselves to automatically incorporate these basics into our daily actions. There is nothing greater than their power.

Third Road magic is a technically oriented system—like tai chi (an energy system of healing), martial arts, or ballet—so, spirituality aside, we must keep coming back to certain essentials if we are to do an authentic magical *training* rather than just have techniques in our head. This is a virtue of repetition.

Jim: True Adepts Follow Instructions and Face Their Shortcomings

Jim Hogg is an old-time Wiccan, an accomplished practitioner of tai chi, and a sought-after teacher of that form. He has a lot of wisdom about spirituality and psychic matters. His letter to me illustrates some of my points about using the book as given and represents a lesson in and of itself:

> You said in *Be a Goddess!* we should do its lessons at the pace designated, and skip none of the assignments. I thought, "This book is nothing *really* new. After all, I'm an adept; Francesca *said* so last time we spoke! All her warnings weren't meant for *me.*"
>
> So I read the book at my own pace, doing whichever exercises seemed interesting. I got to the lesson that said that adepts in your classes found great value in the basic lessons. I thought, "Okay, maybe she *did* mean me." I decided to start over, keep to the pacing you advised, and do even the exercises I didn't *think* were all that new or interesting.
>
> At this point I still didn't think the warnings applied to me. The night that I decided to go back and start over, I did a variation of

"The Laws of Nature" prayer* [a prayer in *Be a Goddess!*] as I lay in bed with the lights off.

Wondering if I had set the alarm, I got up in the dark with my glasses off to check it. Then I noticed an orange glow above my bureau. I thought, "What can that be? What if it's something Fey? I just did that prayer!" I looked closer but couldn't figure it out. I finally ended up ten inches away and still was clueless. So I reached out to touch it—and got burned!

It turned out my wife, Karen, had left a stick of incense burning, and I'd seen and touched the glowing ember at the end! Then I "got" it. I can't begin to count how many times I've seen stick incense burning. This time, however, I was seeing it in a new way, a way I wasn't used to. Not only was it mysterious, but because I didn't recognize it in this context, it was actually a little dangerous!

Since that experience, I've done the lessons the way the book tells me to. I've gotten a lot out of it. And none of my efforts has caused any more burns! Your book didn't cause the burn; adepts need to be willing both to be open and to seeing things new ways. Not to mention honoring the power of following instructions.

I find it interesting that Jim discovered his shortsightedness once he decided to do the lessons as given. I often can't see a shortcoming of mine until I both am open to the possibility that I might have that shortcoming and I take a spiritual action to address it—for example, meditating or asking a friend if I have that shortcoming. Of course, as in Jim's case, the very action I am resisting is often the one I have to take.

---

*"The Laws of Nature" is part of a body of poetry, in the form of prayers, liturgy, lore, and lecture, which I wrote and in which I included my philosophy. My material has been passed down in oral tradition, and some of it adapted in *Goddess Initiation* and *Be a Goddess!* Despite all the material I publish, I will not publish most of my work; some shamanism should only be passed on orally. But you can find much of the oral material I created, because it has come to be considered "standard" Wicca in many Wiccan traditions. For example, lines of poetry I wrote, such as "A healthy priest(ess) makes all things sound" and "Your will through mine," are now thought to be standard Wiccan expressions.

. . .

This book and *Be a Goddess!* are both complete trainings unto themselves. After finishing the program in either book, you have a complete working system with which to improve your peace of mind, create great sex, find self-esteem, and enjoy the good things in life. You will be practicing shamanism! Yet you can continue to enhance your life and reap enormous benefits if you use both books; they offer different rewards, and each has an abundance of material not found in the other. Also, each training works with the other, deepens the experiences resulting from the other, supplements the other, and broadens the scope of the other.

In asking you to not worry if the rules for this training differ from those of other trainings you have had, I extend that to other trainings with me. For example, *Be a Goddess!* asks you not to even read its lectures without doing a prefatory rite; I don't ask that in *Goddess Initiation*.

Though the lessons in *Goddess Initiation* are set up to be done within a year—thirteen months, actually, to include some essential, fun followup work—it is nevertheless an integral part of self-initiation that everyone pace these lessons differently, so you may want to go more slowly. Perhaps after three months of lessons, you get a new job that takes all your time for a while. Or you fall in love and want time to enjoy your new lover. Or you divorce and are overcome with grief at the loss of your marriage. Don't think you have stopped the training: life and the training are one and the same. For a shaman, life is not separate from spirituality. And, I give you assignments, but life's challenges, joys, and obligations are assignments that come directly from the Goddess. If you can't do the book's lessons for a bit, eventually pick up where you left off. Or if it seems more appropriate, start over.

A last thought about doing the training as given: only you know what is best for you.

Self-Initiation:
The Journey into Full Power

What challenges must be faced before initiation? What are the joys and pitfalls of the journey into living fully and with the fullest magical power? What dangers exist? What abilities, assets, and responsibilities are gained? Your lessons with me answer those questions.

For now, I am going to avoid defining initiation the way a dictionary would. One can understand initiation better if one doesn't start with formal definitions.

Initiations take many forms. Performing in a concert can be a initiation, as can growing a garden or going to a job interview. (No, you don't have to bring a rattle and shake it over your prospective employee's head!)

Geraldine: A Young Woman Initiates into Adulthood

When Geraldine prepared for her first job interview at age eighteen, in the summer before her freshman year of college, she was a nervous wreck. An extraordinarily pretty woman, she feared no one would take her job skills seriously.

Her family had always focused on her looks, praising her sharp sense of fashion and canny ability with makeup. No matter how well she did in school—and she did quite well—the praise she received for her academic achievement paled next to the attention that her family lavished on her looks. Years after the tale I am telling you, Geraldine visited with me and revealed that she had come to understand that her mom,

Beatrice, had been quite unpopular as a teenager. Beatrice had feared that her daughter might suffer the same loneliness. When Geraldine turned out to be beautiful, her mother viewed her physical attractiveness as a preventive against possible loneliness. Relieved and delighted, Beatrice constantly told Geraldine that one's looks are the most important thing one has. But at the time of this story, Geraldine did not yet know Beatrice's history or its full import.

Geraldine enjoyed being pretty and planning her wardrobe. But more, she loved organizing events and people. As a child, she put on plays in her backyard, using her innate warmth and enthusiasm to organize the neighborhood children into an acting ensemble and cajoling some of them into helping with costumes. An imaginative girl, she outlined plots for her playmates, the exact tales needed to spur them on: her friends acted out Geraldine's stories, using their own imaginations to improvise their parts. Even as a child, Geraldine sometimes knew just what part to give her friends to bring out the best in them. She even managed to occasionally get adults to pay a dollar for the privilege of watching these shows.

Whenever Beatrice attended these plays she would remark on how pretty her daughter looked, never the other apparent skills Geraldine demonstrated in these theatrical ventures.

In her early teens, Geraldine organized fellow classmates who were academic achievers into a tutoring group that helped students who were struggling with their studies. Beatrice warned Geraldine that "being bright" scares boys away.

Luckily, Geraldine was born with determination and more than a fair amount of self-confidence. Her mother's limited perspective didn't necessarily stop Geraldine from using her organizational skills in ways she enjoyed. And luckily her peers saw her for more than her looks, which bolstered Geraldine's confidence.

But often nameless fears made her back away from social or academic groups or creative projects that she wanted to be involved with.

She gained entrance into an excellent college and started looking for a summer job before she left home in the fall. However, as I pointed out when counseling her, deep down she was feeling that, since her mom had not valued her fine mind and ability to meet challenging goals, neither would anyone else in a position of authority.

A well-known author in Geraldine's neighborhood put word out that she needed an office assistant. Geraldine wanted the job but became paralyzed with fear. She was convinced there was no way to get the job. But, hoping against hope, she came to me for counseling.

I suggested Geraldine view the job interview as an initiation. We did a ritual as follows: Once she felt comfortable and relaxed and her eyes were closed, I suggested, "Geraldine, imagine the job interview is a gate you are standing at. It is a gate into your adulthood, into living life the way you dream. Once you've got that picture somewhat in your mind, then imagine: Who is standing at that gate telling you to not walk through it?"

Geraldine said her mother stood there. Then Geraldine added, "But I know Mom is wrong. I've always known I have more value than my mother told me. So why should she be in my imagination telling me to turn away from my destiny?"

My intuition was that some part of Geraldine had in fact accepted her mom's beliefs. Geraldine's attempt to fly from the nest necessitated her breaking free of those beliefs yet brought those very same ideas forward in a way that was sabotaging her. I told her this and then led her in a ritual that you will learn in this book, a ritual to rid oneself of self-defeating beliefs. Then we did a meditation in which I said, "Imagine you are telling your mom that you love her but you have your own life to live now. Then walk through the gate." She enthusiastically used my suggestion.

The next week, Geraldine went to the interview and was offered the job. Thus encouraged, she later went on to eventually become a high school principal, a career she had always dreamed of.

Geraldine's entire experience was an initiation. One initiates *into* something, in her case into adulthood. Of course, the job interview alone was not sufficient, but it was *part* of her initiation into adulthood, part of the total process. Or you might see the interview as one of many initiations into adulthood. Her experience had other earmarks of an initiation: there was a challenge to face, in this case her own self-defeating belief; and the experience brought her further along the path toward her dreams, destiny, and happiness.

An initiation needn't have any ritualized elements. If, instead of coming to me, Geraldine had gone to a therapist who helped her jump through the same hoop (or "gate" if you think of it in shamanic terms) and there had been nothing in their process resembling shamanism—only straightforward psychological tools—it still could be called an initiatory experience. Initiations happen whether we name them or not. They are a natural part of life.

Giving birth can be an initiation, and it is seen as such in many cultures. Facing pain to bring new life into the world is an initiation like nothing else is! Birthing is one way a woman might understand how powerful she is.

Unfortunately, nowadays, some medical attitudes toward childbirth seem more aimed at disempowering women than helping them find their strength. A woman is often laid flat on her back, a position many people think makes delivery harder than is necessary. The prospective mother is told by the best authority she has access to—her doctor—to assume a passive, somewhat useless position, while the doctor appears to take over and be responsible for the entire process.

I am not saying doctors are useless or unnecessary in the birthing room. And doctors who practice as I describe may do so with the best of intentions. In fact, the customs I criticize are not as prevalent as they once were. However, as a medical doctor told me with disgust, in Victorian times a physician was taught that during a woman's pregnancy he should, in one of his internal examinations of her, pinch her cervix and tell her that because he had done so her labor would go well, even if he could not make it to her delivery. What an awful lie, to so rob a woman of her power, to hide that she—not he—is giving life! That terrible lie also conceals that a woman has awesome powers perhaps unknown to her until she draws on them during the immense challenge of childbirth, awesome powers that henceforth she can draw on to face all of life's challenges.

It could be argued that the physician's untruth relieved any worry the patient might have had. But it also made her think of herself as powerless and that the process of childbirth was not her own but rested *entirely* in the hands of her doctor. This anecdote may be Victorian, but much of its mind-set influences medicine today. While some women prefer other equally potent means of claiming their power, childbirth does that job extraordinarily well. By teaching a woman she is of little consequence during what can be one of the biggest empowerments she might ever have, medical practitioners are perpetuating a horrendous double whammy: loss of power the seeker may need to face life's challenges coupled with a great wounding. When you are at a stage in life when you are about to find more power, gain a greater sense of personal worth, and embrace your deepest self, and another person robs you of that chance, a deep wounding may result.

Later, this book will offer a healing to those injured by being robbed of their chance to be strong or gain strength at such a crux in their lives. And a pregnant woman can, just by doing the lessons in this book, gain power from her pregnancy and obtain what she wants from the initiatory gate that labor provides.

Initiations come in numberless types, and an initiation is not actually a moment in time—one event or rite—but a process that spans time both before and after "the big moment." This span of time can sometimes be very lengthy. Initiations that usually do not involve ritualized elements include: getting a driver's license, having one's first date (first menstruation, first drink), or buying a new home. Others may include risking violence and possible death as a soldier or political activist; risking job loss, public censure, or death by standing up for one's rights in the battle against sexism, racism, religious intolerance, or homophobia; or rescuing someone from a burning building.

Some nonritualized initiations are spectacular, others are not. Some are common to many of us, such as the long arduous challenge of taking care of a parent who is chronically ill or coping with the death of a wife or husband. Some are experienced—and needed—by a rare few. But they all provide us with chances to grow strong and learn to love and be loved whether we view them as initiations or not. Magical forms of initiation—not all of which need a year's training and preparation—are just as numerous and diverse and range from the difficult to the gentle experience many of you might have with this book.

Don't waste your time and perhaps cause yourself a real tragedy by looking for challenges just because they *seem* powerful or smack of the drama of a movie script. One gets lost, hurt, or distracted from one's true power by wanting to be the "Oh, Great Shaman." The real challenges that make you a true shaman will come your way, believe me! The Goddess will send you the ones *you* need in order to gain the most power possible.

When people go through initiations, their experiences range from the mild to the horrendous. Initiation can be brutal. Don't close the book right here! Keep reading. If you are struck by an upsetting life event such as a job loss or heartbreak or, God forbid, the death of a loved one—initiation needn't be a ritual and can happen whether you choose it to or not—I want you to have the guidance this book offers instead of going through hard times or a tragedy unaided. I hate needless suffering, and going through a hard time without support means suffering needlessly. There is enough unavoidable suffering in life.

When you endure a major challenge or tragedy, you experience things like fear, emotional confusion, constant worries, negative thoughts, and emotional flip-flops ranging from anger to grief. If faced, these hurdles *initiate* you into new power, and you can emerge stronger and happier than some folks can ever believe possible. You may even become strong and happy for the first time. During this process, old wounds might come forward so that they can finally be healed, the way Geraldine's initiation—her job interview—brought forward her fear that no employer would value her organization skills.

I've gone through very hard experiences without guidance and support. (I'm not going to tell you those stories; I need privacy to continue healing. Please respect your own need for privacy, cherishing yourself by giving yourself what it takes to feel safe and be whole.) I wish I had received assistance and nurturing at those times. That is one of my reasons for writing this book: to show you how to meet life's breakthroughs—whether you call them initiations, challenges, or destiny—with minimal suffering and in a way that can bring you many gifts. Through life's initiations you can receive gifts of happiness, abundance, a feeling of fellowship with others, and a feeling that you have found your place in the world.

Initiation is not rough for everyone. Don't be drawn and hence trapped by the glamour, drama, and supposed nobility of needless suffering and thus create an unnecessarily difficult path for yourself. We will do a ritual soon that will help you refrain from creating problems in your life and in your initiation process. The rite will also help you overcome any fear of personal growth you might have as you take this shamanic journey. If you are using other activities to grow—such as Buddhist meditation or psychiatric counseling—alleviating that fear will also enhance those processes.

A Witch Seeks a Uniquely Personal Path and Vision

A witch seeks a uniquely personal path and vision. *Self*-initiation is a logical step in this self-determined search and can happen at any stage in it. In fact, many self-initiations can happen.

Initiation is only one step on the path of power. The path itself is to become responsible for one's own soul and to define one's own priesthood. These issues are crucial to, and the essence of, any quest. Let's break down this paragraph using Geraldine as an example.

Initiation is only one step on the path of power. Geraldine's counseling facilitated something larger than her one job interview. It helped her move along her path. Her journey would lead to, among other things, eventually becoming a principal, which was one of the ways she could best find and express her power and unique gifts. Her job interview—initiation—was only one step on that path of power. After she was given the job, she had to keep it. This meant she had to learn how to balance her career with her busy social life. She continued her counseling with me in order to overcome these challenges. Over the years, I accompanied her through several more steps along her journey to power, which included finishing her college thesis, which she found overwhelming; coming to believe that a woman needn't choose between career and motherhood; and writing as well as publishing her first article on education, an accomplishment that she dearly longed to achieve but found herself unable to even start.

The path itself is to become responsible for one's own soul and to define one's own priesthood. In choosing education as a career, Geraldine was responsible for her soul by making her own moral decision: she felt that children need the best possible education available and that it was her job to help that happen in whatever way she could. She didn't abide by her mother's words, which were that the right spiritual action was to get married and spend all her time and energy taking care of a man. Facing up to her first job interview, to her doubts about her value to an employer, and to her mother were some of the ways she lived by her chosen moral values. This was also the case when she married a man who supported her career.

We could say that in becoming a principal she chose education as one of the realms of her "ministry." Principal as priestess! Mothering and writing could be viewed as other aspects of her priesthood, though in fact Geraldine never thought of these activities as a priesthood, and I did not call them such in our work together; she is neither a pagan nor thinks in terms of ministry. (Though I teach paganism, I counsel clients from a wide diversity of religious and spiritual walks of life and work with them according to their beliefs.) Yet Geraldine illustrates true ministry by being a great example of someone following her star, finding self-fulfillment, and serving others.

These issues are crucial to, and the essence of, any quest. One is missing the point of any quest, spiritual or mundane, and will likely fail, unless one strives to:

- Think for oneself
- Be responsible for one's spiritual condition through analysis and action instead of being a mindless follower

- Let the power, wisdom, and sweetness of God shine in oneself so that one can accomplish and enjoy the special things one is put on this earth to do

By phone, I counsel people all over the world, and I receive letters from any place you can imagine. I have learned that innumerable people in geographical and other types of isolation suffer deeply from thinking they are the only one who believes leprechauns are real (likes sex, wants to stay single, hears the ocean sing, has sexual feelings for members of their own gender, is a teen Wiccan, believes life is here for the living, deems being an artist a worthy career goal, or was born with a man's body but feels they are really a woman, and on and on). The variations are endless.

Yet *none* of these people is alone in their attitudes, desires, inclinations, beliefs, experiences, and choices. I know, because after all this time I have met many people who (take your pick) believe in Faeries, hear the ocean sing, are teen Wiccans, and so on.

Even when you experience—think, choose, want, do—things that you consider even weirder than my above examples, you are still not the only one. There are zillions like you. Honest. You *are* unique, but you are not the Lone Ranger! People constantly think their ideas (poems, habits, beliefs, experiences, . . .) are weird. Then they tell me their idea (poem, habit, belief, . . .), and it is something I have heard a million times or that makes lots of sense to me.

Don't get me wrong. Every person on this planet has incredibly unique thoughts, desires, beliefs, and the like, but there is not much a person need think is *weird* about himself or herself. As long as nothing immoral is involved—as long as you are hurting no one—there is nothing to be ashamed of in this life. If you are a happily married woman who is committed to monogamy and have occasional sexual fantasies about women yet no real plan to act on them, then so what? And if you find the right people, they will not mock your unique ways. They will likely say, "Wow, I do that myself. I thought I was the only one." Or, "Gee, I had an experience like that, but your poem helped me see it really clearly for the first time."

No matter how far out you may consider yourself to be—and I consider "far out" a compliment—other people can relate to you. When teaching classes, I am amazed and blessed by the enormous creativity, uniqueness, and distinctive way of viewing life that almost *every one of my students shows.* This has been the case since I started teaching in 1986, and I have taught a lot of people. Everywhere around you are likeminded souls just as unique as you. I didn't believe this for a long time, but as a teacher I was in a wonderful position to have been taught differently by my students. And since I am so odd by mainstream standards, people feel free to tell me all sorts of things they would tell no one else.

When we honor that others can, and long to, define their own personal morals and priesthood, whether they define it in pagan or any other terms, we find community support for our own quest. Thus we meet company along the way and are freed from loneliness. If you still think you are "the only one," that's fine. Really! I ask you merely to be open to the idea that you share community more than you think. That is a first step. Consider it an informal and optional first assignment.

When we understand that others are just as wonderfully creative and unique, it does not stifle our own specialness but supports it.

Jeanne's Creativity Blossomed When She Honored Others' Creativity

Jeanne has a singing style that is all her own. But it was hard-won. She, like many people with enormous, unique talents, suffered for two reasons. She kept running up against teachers who stifled her approach. Her vocal coaches focused on making her sound like everyone else. In addition, Jeanne made it difficult for herself; she had to fight so hard to maintain what was special in her style that eventually she wouldn't listen to any input, even ideas from her latest teacher, Thom, who suggested ways that she could get better in touch with her own approach.

Jeanne came to me for counseling because she had something to express in song, and yet it wasn't escaping her lips very often. I intuited that she was angry because no one had ever supported her own special way of singing and that though her anger was perfectly healthy and appropriate, it controlled her so much that she thought any input, discipline, or changes would stifle her.

Anger is a funny thing. Sometimes it spurs us onto success; sometimes it defeats us. She felt her anger was good, so we left it at that. I showed her one of this book's techniques for clearing away inner blocks. You will learn it as part of the ritual "Eagle Birth" in the tenth month's lesson. She used the technique to cleanse herself of defeating beliefs so that she could use her anger to motivate herself instead of rejecting constructive ideas. I also intuited that Thom had a talent for nurturing the special gift of each of his vocal students and suggested she try things his way for a bit.

Should Jeanne have continued to insist that she was the only one with any creativity or a special, worthy approach, and hence listened to no one but herself, she would not have benefited from the creative way Thom teaches. Because she learned to honor his ideas and those of her equally creative publicist, Grant, she went on to thrill many an audience with her unique singing style.

Everyone involved, including Jeanne, benefited from everyone else's preferred approach. This does not mean that Jeanne never disagrees with her teacher or publicist. However, now when she views things differently from them, she sometimes bows to their expertise so that she has time to focus on her own realms of expertise. Other times she might tell them her thoughts then discuss with them the pros and cons of each person's preference. In doing this, they often come to a better solution than any of them had originally proposed. But this discussion can happen only because Jeanne acknowledges someone else's ideas are creative. Only through honoring each other's gifts does each of us get to do what we are best at; otherwise, we would all be trying to do everything ourselves.

If you have gone through, or are going through, hellish times or are a pagan who already went through a terribly difficult initiation, a vision of a world full of matchless individuals helps you know there is a community to support you. So if you have or have had problems you never heard of anyone else experiencing, please realize that I likely have heard folks with the same problems or related difficulties, *no matter how unusual your problems seem to you.* You are not alone.

Every Atom of the Cosmos Is Woven with Every Other Atom

The Goddess is in everything, every last person, place, rock, atom, and empty space, every shadow and darkness, every bonfire and cigarette lighter. She expresses Herself through weaving all these parts of Herself into a united dance and song of happiness. Somehow a cigarette lighter in Japan is relevant to a rock in a desert in Arizona, to a ballet dancer in New York City, to a hungry child in Appalachia, to a bonfire in Ireland.

In the same weaving, the Celtic shaman's quest for self-expression and self-fulfillment is one way that Faerie shamanic training will supplement and empower other (shamanic) trainings, spiritual paths, and mundane processes in which one might be involved. It will facilitate and deepen anything from Buddhist meditation to learning to drive a car to falling in love to strengthening a unique style of magic you have already created.

Linda, Nick, and I Get Happy by Being Part of the Cosmic Weave

Linda felt let down by her Christian practices, as if something important was missing. Devoted in her love of Jesus, she didn't want to change her religion, and, looking for solutions, this open-minded woman took a Shamanism 101 class with me to broaden her outlook. The practices of a shaman are holistic, a complex and thorough weave: the shamanic lifestyle encompasses all parts of oneself, since the shaman views all aspects of life as important and sacred; and each shamanic tool affects many parts of the practitioner's being and life. I will illustrate a few of the many ways Linda's Christian life was enhanced by shamanic lessons we did.

I taught Linda a ritual in this book, "Kissed by a Star: A Spiritual Cleansing." During the ritual you identify an inner block to your happiness and send it out to a special star that transforms the negative trait into whatever positive trait you need instead. Doing this exercise, Linda discovered her profound need to serve community in order to be fulfilled.

Another ritual in this book, "Ritual for Common Sense and Inspiration," which clears one's internal blocks to trusting one's own inner voice, taught her to honor her desire to express her profound religious feelings in a creative way. She also applied "Kissed by a Star" to her embarrassment over her singing and became filled with confidence in her musical ability. (She, like many of my clients, had been told at some point, "You can't sing!" Someday, I hope to find the person who has gone all over the world telling so many folks so convincingly that their voice is awful. I am going to throw that person in a magical cauldron and murmur ancient chants over them until they are so happy that any human voice raised in song seems a miracle and joy to them.)

All these rituals cleared the way for Linda to join her church choir. Singing in church gave her a sense of communion with her god, helped her feel like she was doing something for her community, and enhanced her religious devotion. Thus the Goddess offers a complex weaving that can really do the trick! (Mine is an interfaith Goddess. She is perfectly happy helping anyone regardless of their religious beliefs. She doesn't mind if She doesn't get credit for it. She just wants to help. I think She sets a good example for us.)

Another example of the intricate magic God weaves: When Nick studied with me he had lots of experience with magic. He was committed to the style of rituals he had created and to developing it further. As before, the endlessly intricate weave that Celtic shamanism recognizes influenced all parts of Nick—hence his own style of magic. A few examples of the many ways the weave worked for him will give you the picture. Several rituals increased his confidence in his own way of doing things. One of these was "Ritual for Common Sense and Inspiration," through which he cleansed himself of his fear that if he listened to his intuition people would laugh at him. As his confidence increased, he was able to let himself be more creative when writing his own spells. More creativity came when he used "Kissed by a Star: A Spiritual Cleansing." After he sent the star his belief that he did not deserve self-nurturance, he realized that he did not always give himself the time he needed to write his rituals because he didn't think he merited the happiness he felt when he did so.

I assured him that we can all hear God directly. He had always felt the Goddess talking to him, and though he acted on it a great deal, he didn't as much as he might have because some part of him was ashamed, wrongly believing himself arrogant to think he heard God. He used "Ritual for Common Sense and Inspiration" again; clearing that sense of shame further helped the situation. Now he listens even more to what God has to say and so can rely more on God's wonderful guidance when writing.

A last example: I wanted the independence that driving would give me, professionally and in my leisure time. I have an extreme learning disability that makes me slow to grasp—slow to the point of madness—spatial relations, including all those, well, um, technical thingamabobby-doohickies that one needs to understand in order to drive. Occasionally in the past when I was taught anything that touched on my disability, I became flustered, less because of my disability than from embarrassment at my difficulty in following the instructor. At that point, it's a lost cause; I can learn nothing.

I gave the Goddess my embarrassment. I asked Her to take it away from me. Being ashamed of one's deficits doesn't help anything. But that wasn't enough. I also needed to explain to my driving instructor my problem and what she could do to help me learn despite it. Being free from shame somewhat helped me do that. But the disability is so extreme that I don't have the understanding needed to even explain the problem without sometimes getting so confused that no explanation comes forth. So I prayed for two things: calm on my part and a recognition that my teacher deserved as much calmness from me as possible.

The latter item embodies a core principle for living that shamanism teaches: we do not treat ourselves well unless we are treating others well. Yet, when I am suffering from confusion, embarrassment, fear, anger at being betrayed, and so on—legitimate and expected feelings—it is easy to forget that any person in the room with me might be feeling equally vulnerable about his own confusion, embarrassment, fear, and so forth. (Okay, everyone who relates, raise your hand so I don't feel like a fool for being the only one here who is baring her soul.) I try to remember that others need just as much sensitivity, compassion, and care from me as I need from them because they are as capable of being hurt by me as I am of being hurt by them. Also, they have as many limits and human frailties as I do, so I can't expect them to be perfect just because I am having troubles. I don't want to be so lost within my own problems I forget others have theirs.

The Goddess granted me calm. And I was able to help Her do so: during my driving lessons, I told myself, "Francesca, you may be feeling frustrated, but remember, the person with you may also be feeling stressed today. And it takes lots of patience to teach someone to drive."

With the Goddess's rituals and care, I was able to ask my instructor for the help I needed and be the student *she* needed. Thus I learned to drive.

Every atom of the cosmos is woven with every other atom. The shaman does not live in a cold, mechanistic world but in a vast creation in which each thing weaves joyfully and lovingly with all others. When I whisper silly nothings in my lover's ear, a star in another galaxy smiles without knowing why. When a stone basks in sunlight, it enjoys the sunny warmth and sends out happiness that a fish in a nearby stream gathers to itself and relishes. Even if you don't choose it to be so or consciously intend it to do so, shamanism both draws from many arenas and also touches every part of your life. It is the Goddess's hand pulling skeins together in an odd mysterious weaving: a person's individuality mirrors the uniqueness of every other person; veneration—the celebration that God is great and good—does not negate our own beauty and grandeur but emphasizes it; my lessons teach you how to give yourself lessons. The shaman is not subject to a distant snobby god but enjoys a god who is lovingly busy in our daily lives, making us happy through every atom that touches our skin, and, every atom, being Her, blesses us with Her touch.

You can honor the cosmic weave by using this book to augment another training even if that training includes an initiation other than Third Road's. Or you can use this training to enrich your own eclectic spiritual path, which is not part of any tradition but with which you are perfectly happy. Or perhaps your main focus is spell casting; while you don't need an initiation to do magic or choose the Goddess as *your* god, this training will empower your magic further.

Or you can use this book to support your *mundane* studies, such as the acquisition of new business skills. The Third Road opens you up to life, to your own skills, to your intuition, and to enjoying the fruits of the Goddess's far-reaching hand at Her infinite loom. It helps you see that hand at work for the rest of your life so that you can always jump wholeheartedly into Her weave and take the fullest advantage of it. The Goddess of shamanism intertwines the strands of life into a whole, thus supporting your other trainings and processes long after you have finished the *Goddess Initiation* training.

Initiation as a word by itself is a dirty word. Initiation is part of a process. That process is your path, your spiritual path. That's what we're really talking about in this book: the shape of your spiritual and magical path, not only where it leads.

Part of that path is your so-called mundane life: your work life, your sex life, your family life, and so on. How happy you are in those arenas, how well you treat yourself and others there, whether you are moving toward your destiny each day or running away from it—these are all central to your spiritual journey. They are central not just in the sense of applying spiritual lessons there but in the sense that when you find a career that gives you job satisfaction or you allow yourself a great sex life or you create mundane happiness for yourself or others in any other way, that *is* spiritual work.

Your sex life is as holy as your meditations. So sexual satisfaction is not separate from your spiritual path. A shaman is concerned with self-fulfillment in the everyday.

Someone once said revolution is not the important event, that the work after it is the important thing. The same is true of initiation, except I would add that what's also important is the work *before*. Initiation is one rock in a river. The river is your life. No one rock is more important.

As a matter of fact, I was taught that there are times when it is best to not use the word *initiation* at all. So the first assignment is this:

Assignment: throughout the first month of training, avoid the word *initiation*. Don't be rigid about it, just do it as much as possible. If we find other words, as well as learn to hold silence, we might come to a greater understanding of four things:
- What an initiation actually is
- That the process is more important than one event or thing
- How the false ego (as opposed to the healthy ego, which takes reasonable pride in our accomplishments) and other inner blocks are obstacles to the real journey
- How the false ego offers an inflated sense of self, false sense of security, and other distractions from our true destiny and joy

You might find the assignment is impossible. Does that mean you've done it wrong? No. Perhaps I am giving you an impossible assignment. Half the fun of being a shaman is playing tricks on someone that help them be happy. The point is, whether you can avoid the word *initiation* or not, you will learn a lot about, uh, that thing there called, well, you know what I mean without my using the word, don't you? No? I mean *initiation*.

Reveling in the Goddess You Are

An initiation helps a Celtic shaman recognize the god(dess) that she or he is. This is accomplished, not in one moment in time, but in a process through which one finds deeper and deeper layers of one's inner god.

Georgia: Her God Within Showed Self-Love

When Georgia came to know herself to be a child of God, hence a god herself, she learned she was worthy of God's love. Later, when she more clearly knew herself a goddess, she started acting in ways that naturally and without ostentation commanded respect from the men in her life.

For example, she developed a smile on her face and a look in her eye that never implied an anxious "Am I beautiful enough to attract you?" but a content, buoyant "I am beautiful inside and out, and when a man is worthy, I will accept him."

Georgia expressed yet more of her inner deity when she learned that the Faerie gods are sexy gods. Sexy divinity suggested to her that sexuality is a blessing. Feeling freer to express her sensual nature, she took up tango dancing. The tango gave her a deeply creative, satisfying outlet.

Montgomery: His God Within Knew Passion to Be Sacred

When I told Montgomery that the fire of our male god is the same fire that burns in Montgomery's chest (and in the heart of all women as well), he was able to view his passions, whether for sex or for writing his novel or as expressed in his loving concern for his son's welfare, as sacred. This realization impelled him to fight racial discrimination that had kept him, a black man, from getting a grant he had applied for to fund the writing of his novel. I then taught him that pagan gods encourage us to be warriors who fight for our rights, our hopes, and our children's well-being. I had him imagine within himself the warrior god that is within all of us; he found strength and determination that helped him succeed at getting the grant.

Daniel: His God Within Was a Good Father

Because his own father had disciplined him in ways that were cruel and too strict, Daniel had avoided setting limits and disciplining his son, and his son suffered from this lack of parenting. I suggested Daniel meditate on our male god, whom I call "our good father whom we need not fear," by imagining what traits such a divinity would have. Daniel realized it was possible to be a strong father who set limits without doing so cruelly. By acting accordingly, he embodied the pagan god in himself. The benefits of experiencing one's inner deity are endless.

Any lesson Georgia gained, in the example above, a man could also, by finding the inner goddess within him. Or he might acquire the same lessons through recognizing his inner male god. It depends on his temperament and on which exact lesson or power would be conferred through recognizing inner goddess and which through recognizing inner god. We all have both the male and female god within us. Some Faerie shamans choose to recognize and experience both and find it an enormously powerful tool for personal growth.

For example, having pictured the male deity within myself and experienced His beauty as my own, I better love and enjoy the parts of myself that are viewed by some as male, such as my athletic stride and my love of cars. Loving those things in myself in turn increases my love and appreciation for the men in my life. What a shaman needs to grow healthy and powerful, feel happy, and be proud of who she is determines whether or not she needs to experience both gods within. As for Montgomery's and Daniel's god within, all their lessons are ones any woman could learn by feeling the male god within her. For example, Daniel's lesson about fatherhood could help a woman be a firm but fair parent. And a woman might find it useful to imagine within herself the male warrior god. There is definitely a warrior goddess, but men and women sometimes have different styles and strengths in battle, and at times the more male attributes might be more effective.

Francesca's Helpful Hints for Better Magic

Before going on to the ritual that accompanies the above section, here are some ideas to help you with that rite. Always read through a ritual—as well as any ritual instructions that precede or follow the rite—before you do it. Thus you've a chance to gather your tools and ingredients, and you have a general sense of the instructions and the exercise, all of which helps you focus on your magic when you actually do the rite.

You will see that the ritual below is divided into many small steps. As with all other rites in this book, do each step before moving on to the next. This intensifies the power of the rite a great deal by helping you get the best possible experience of each step, and all the steps then add up to real power. It also breaks the ritual down into bite-sized pieces. For example, if imagination is needed in many of the steps, it can be hard—even overwhelming or impossible—to visualize many things at once. If one visualizes aspects of the rite one step at a time, one can get a handle on each part of the visualization. One can then build a strong experience through incremental additions to the imagined experience.

For example, in imagining yourself to be a goddess, you might imagine yourself having a strong body, then a spirit that is unbowed, then a heart that holds the entire universe within, then a smile as wide as the sky above us, then the sun as a crown on your head, until all these images, each one clear and strong since it received your full focus, add up to your experiencing yourself as a goddess through and through in all your parts and feeling great!

This step-by-step approach to visualization and other magical techniques also builds skills. As always, if the rite is not done as given—in this case step-by-step—it might not be effective and may even cause problems.

Do the best you can with any rite. If you feel you've done a bad job of it, don't worry. Relax, no matter how badly you think you did. That includes, "Oh, but I didn't try hard enough" and "I couldn't get myself to really focus." The bottom line is doing the work, not how we do it! Spiritually speaking, all God asks is that we show up. She only wants us to try. (I believe we all do the best we can, and whatever we do is our best.) In terms of magical—again, if you prefer, call them psychic—skills, we improve our concentration and our other skills only by doing the rituals. That's why they call it *training*. By doing the work, bit by bit, however badly we start out doing it, we improve.

While "Francesca's Helpful Hints for Better Magic" provides a fun and easy way to develop magical expertise, the rest of the book also offers you many instructions for developing magical skills. In fact, every part of the training helps your magic. Anything we do that makes us stronger, happier, or more in touch with ourselves has a profound impact on the effectiveness and power of Faerie magic. A Faerie shaman is her or his own primary magical tool.

Many parts of *Goddess Initiation*'s training that are not overt magical instruction improve one's psychic skills, such as exercises that help one become more creative, hence more in tune with the universe's ever-present need to create itself anew, an urge often expressed through magical phenomenon.

RITUAL

Nourishing One's Spirit

This ritual is in fact two rituals. Please don't skip to the second one before doing the first.

RITUAL #1

Kissed by a Star: A Spiritual Cleansing

TOOLS AND INGREDIENTS

Optional: a star. Not as in a movie, but as in the sky. It can be a piece of jewelry, a Yule tree decoration, a picture of a star, a crystal window ornament, a pentacle—the five-pointed star some pagans wear as jewelry—or whatever other star you might have. If you are outdoors with a clear view on a clear night, you have many stars to choose from.

Feeding our souls is one step toward finding the god within. As we flourish in spirit, we naturally begin to feel our divinity more and more. For example, if you nourish your spirit then find yourself harshly criticizing yourself for getting to work late through no fault of your own, you are more likely to think, "Wait, I am a child of god, I shouldn't be mean to myself." As the spirit flourishes we gain confidence and trust in the universe. This, along with other tools in the book, will help godhood emerge, perhaps without our even seeing how it happens. Eventually, anyone can easily and readily think, "I am a goddess."

Though "Nourishing One's Spirit" is a step toward that proclamation, please do the ritual for its own sake. Do it simply because you deserve to have your spirit nurtured and given tender care.

Step 1. Place your star before you. Or if your star is in the sky, be in a place you can see it. If you have no star, that is fine; just skip this step.

Step 2. Get comfortable. Perhaps that means loosening your belt, settling back into your chair, or sitting on a soft pillow.

Step 3. Pick one thing—just one—inside yourself that keeps you from nurturing your soul. Something that you would like to cleanse away in this ritual. It might be a fear. For example, your spirit might long to express itself by opening a restaurant but you are afraid that if you try, you might fail and be ridiculed by your family. Or maybe your father expressed his power by being a tyrant in the home, thus leaving you with a fear that if you get strong spiritually you'll hurt others.

You might have a fear that makes you hedge about training, though this very training is a way to nourish the spirit. You may fear folks' mockery and judgment. Or you have a fear of magic that you *know* deep down is off base but that still lingers, making it hard for you to keep on with your shamanic studies.

Another type of inner block is the self-defeating belief. Maybe you think that you are not worthy of self-nurturance. Or you tell yourself, "I am not important in the scheme of things." Yes, you are! Who else is there in the scheme of things but each and every one of us, all of us both tiny and grand in the Goddess's eyes? Why would the Goddess make you if you are not important and worthy of nurture? After all, God is pretty important, so I doubt She wastes her time making anything She doesn't care about.

Other examples of unhealthy beliefs that may keep you from taking care of yourself are: "It's too much time just for my own selfish needs" and "I don't know what I need anyway."

You can use this purification ritual to stop beating yourself up with false humility. Real humility is knowing oneself, limits *as well as* strong points; it is *not* an absence of self-respect and pride in one's achievement and good traits. Nor is real humility the equivalent of self-denigration.

If you want to cleanse away false humility in this ritual, choose just one belief or fear or other inner attribute that contributes to your false humility. It might be telling yourself, "I am not worth all this fuss." Or not being proud of your accomplishments or being too afraid to tell others about them. The latter block keeps healthy pride from filling your soul with kindness; it also means that you have no inner recognition of past accomplishments to keep you going when times are hard. It is also false humility to believe that you are too unskilled or unusual or uncreative to have what it takes to get your needs met; this belief can be removed!

Then there are blocks that might seem irrelevant to feeding the spirit. Geraldine, as we saw, wanted a job, one of many steps toward a career goal that would nurture her spirit by helping her fulfill her destiny. Her inner block was her belief that no one would value her business skills.

And let's take the bull by the horns and deal with another problem discussed previously: the "I want to nurture myself by singing but am not a good singer" block. Or "I want to dance but can't" or "I want to write but can't."

When I was younger, I wanted to perform professionally and didn't know if I was good enough. A wise woman, Mavis De Wees, asked me if I had listened to what's out there. She said quality didn't matter regarding what one wanted to do with one's time. All that mattered was whether one wanted to do it or not. Yes!

In addition, I have many times heard someone say, "I can't sing," then a beautiful song would emerge from his mouth. Still, the person would be thoroughly convinced, beyond all dispute, that he sings flat or too softly or too harshly.

I am offering an informed opinion when I say most people can sing or at least can learn. I was playing major clubs before I left the music business for a contemplative life as a shaman. (When my music followed me into my shaman's cave, I discovered music was part of my spirituality. If you are interested in the musical album that resulted, see the "Supplementary Magical Resources" at this book's end.) I've seen some folks who really couldn't sing at first learn to sing quite well. The same is likely true about dance or archery or public speaking or . . .

Step 4. Close your eyes. (Just peek to read a step, then close your eyes to execute that step.)

Step 5. Imagine that far out in the sky is a star that God made just for you. Just to heal you. God loves you so much She created this star just to help *you.* Your own special and private healing star. Pretend such a star exists.

Even if you can't believe in this star, imagine it anyway as a way to get in touch with it. But you needn't believe in it. Just pretend it is real. It does exist.

One way to pretend or imagine this is to picture the star in your mind. Or after deciding how you would feel if such a star existed—perhaps you would feel more hopeful that you can change for the better—imagine you feel that way.

As always, don't worry how well you execute ritual instructions. Do what you can. For example, doing this step you may get only a faint inkling of such a star or only barely be able to imagine it, but even if you can do nothing with this step, continue on.

Step 6. While doing this step, try to retain the image (feeling, imagined scene, or whatever) that you had during step 5.

Get in touch with whatever inner block you have decided you want to be cleansed of. Feel it as much as possible.

Step 7. Send your inner block far, far out to your special healing star. Imagine the block traveling a long, long, long way to the star.

Step 8. Imagine the star kisses that block. This changes the block into a gift for you, but that is not part of the visualization. The gift is whatever internal attribute you need instead of the block, but you needn't know what the gift is or picture it. Let the Goddess decide what the gift is.

But so as not to confuse, and so that you are more open to your gift's arrival, here are some examples of this gift: If you sent the star a fear of being deserted by friends, your gift may be the knowledge that the Goddess will always take care of you or a hunch that your friends will stand by you. If you viewed your needs as unimportant, you may be given the gift of feeling how strongly God loves you and the assurance that She takes your needs as a top priority. A fear of coming to power may be replaced by joy and the cheerful thought "Success could feel mighty good!" Fear of magic might be replaced by an understanding of why God gave you your psychic abilities. If you felt defeated because you didn't know what you need to nurture yourself, maybe you will find out or realize that in time you will know all you need to know.

Step 9. Sit quietly for a minute or two. Be open to your gift coming to you. You may feel something. If you don't, that's good too; it can still be working. Don't worry about whether things are working or not. Worry is counterproductive and might even interfere with the magic. Just sit in as receptive a state as you can, perhaps by relaxing your body and, again, refraining from worry. If you end up writing a grocery list in your mind, well, that's as receptive as you are able to be at that moment and that's fine. Skills develop only by our trying to use them, and our first efforts are not always great.

As is often the case, the above ritual entails a lot of instructions but takes very little time to do. On to Ritual #2 of "Nourishing One's Spirit":

RITUAL # 2

In the Mother's Milk Is Your Soul

TOOLS AND INGREDIENTS

Optional: Any container into which you can pour milk: a bowl, coffee cup, lovely chalice, or mayonnaise jar, as long as you can drink from it.

Optional: Milk. If you are allergic to milk, soy milk is fine. If neither is an option, use water or grape juice. It may be tempting to use wine in this ritual; while you are always your own best authority, using wine will likely deplete this specific exercise of its power.

Step 1. Have your tools and ingredients in front of you. It is ideal to collect needed items before an exercise so that you don't lose power and focus by stopping the spell to get them. Since you can assume this is always the case, I will leave this step out of future exercises.

Step 2. Any prayer or recitation in this book can be made out loud or in silence unless otherwise noted.

You are a priestess just because you exist. To be priestess of this ritual takes no more than doing the rite. Priestess, please proclaim the following:

Pour a cup of milk. In the Cup is the Mother's milk.
What is in Her milk? Drink that from the Cup, drinking half the
   milk.
In the Mother's milk is your soul—drain the Cup.
Now tell yourself, proclaim: I will drink from Her daily;
while every breath we take is imperfect,
every breath we take is both good and divine.

The Mother opens my eyes to all truths I need see,
truths both harsh and sweet.
She heals the damage in my soul,
and gives me faith in the goodness of the days ahead.

This is truth I have spoken, and thus it is and will be.

During step 2, don't perform the actions you are describing in the recitation; you are describing them to get in the mood to do them *after* the recitation ends and you move on to step 3. In other words, step 2 involves proclamation *only;* step 3 and subsequent steps have you take *action.* For example, do not pour a cup of milk until the *entire* recitation is finished and you have moved on to step 3 and following steps in which you are then instructed to pour milk, drink it, and execute all the actions that you have already described during step 2.

Step 3. Pour a cup of milk. For this and subsequent steps, if you choose to do this spell without cup or beverage: mime each step, or close your eyes and picture yourself in action. You may want to close your eyes whenever possible in this ritual anyway; you might discover the ritual to be more fruitful and its experience richer.

Step 4. Think about what the Great Mother's milk would have in it; Her milk has what you need to nourish your spirit, a goal of this rite. Would Her milk contain nurturance? Abundance, beauty, inspiration? What things do you need to feed your soul; would Her milk offer you joy, confidence, faith in Her goodness? Would it give you common sense? Upon drinking Her milk would you receive Her love, compassion, peace? Pick from one to five items that you want to imbibe, things you think would be in Her milk. More than five might blur the ritual's effectiveness.

Step 5. Pick up your cup. Then imagine that in your vessel is the Mother's milk.

Step 6. Imagine that the desired items you chose in step 4 are in fact in that milk.

Step 7. Drink half the milk in Her cup. As you do, you might imagine those attributes you chose in step 4 filling you.

Step 8. Tell yourself, "In the Mother's milk is my soul."

Step 9. Drain the cup. You are taking your soul to yourself. Your soul has always been yours, of course; you are just deepening that.

Step 10. Announce: "This is truth I have said and done, and thus it is and will be."

RITUAL

Grounding

In this section I will differentiate between ritual—spells, exercises, and so on—and simple prayer, whether that prayer is a few spontaneous words or a formal address. If a prayer is not short and involves visualization or other more ritual-like activities, consider it a ritual for the purposes of this section.

After doing a Third Road ritual, one might be in an altered state without realizing it. If you then do something like drive, walk at night along a city street, or cook, you could possibly go through a red light, get mugged, or burn yourself, all because you were off in another world! Third Road shamans believe in being magical *and* safe. The grounding exercise below takes care of that. It also helps you have your head in the clouds and feet on the ground in another way: instead of your ritual life being irrelevant or even an obstacle to your "real" life—it is all real, but that is a way to get my point across—this exercise is one of the tools you will learn to take the fruits of whatever rite you've done into your mundane life in a practical, viable, and sensible way. So, after you finish any ritual, do the following steps.

Step 1. Stretch every part of your body. Stretch a wee bit everywhere instead of being hurried and perfunctory about it. It takes me less than two and a half minutes to do my whole body. Perhaps it will take some folks a minute or two longer.

Step 2. Gently slap yourself all over. Again, do it everywhere. When you get to your face and head, switch to using your fingertips to gently tap that more sensitive part of yourself.

The following is an example of a necessary adaptation to The Third Road training. Certain injuries keep one from stretching without further injury. So don't stretch. Simple. Try to find a substitute; if you can, perhaps gently run your hands over your entire body, which takes thirty to forty-five seconds. I don't like this substitute; being more relaxing than brisk, it almost entirely misses the mark. But it might be the best you can do, and as important as this step is, there is no point in getting mad at yourself or being a nervous wreck since there is nothing you can do about it. So it goes with necessary adaptations; I do not expect my students to follow my instructions perfectly anyway. Perfection is an important goal to *strive* toward, but you cannot possibly attain it.

Step 3. Spend at least fifteen seconds consciously focusing on the embodied, mundane plane by making your mind concentrate on physical objects. Look at the chair next to you, the floor, your hands.

Mundane items might look unusual at this time because you have just done a ritual. It might be fun to focus on that, but don't. Not when doing this exercise. To concentrate on that enticing phenomenon only brings you back into your ritual mind-set. Instead, give your attention to the physical realm by looking at it with the most mundane, everyday eyes you can. For example, after a ritual, a cup may be glinting beautifully in the sunlight, and because of your ritual frame of mind, the cup seems to glisten even more, and you can almost see Faeries drinking sunlight from the cup, and your imagination wanders off into Faerie tales you heard as a child. That's fabulous! But *during* a ritual! After a rite, focus on that cup being an inert densely physical object, made of ceramic, sitting solidly on a table. A cup that you can drink water from to take care of your dense physical body if you are thirsty after all your ritual work.

Step 4. Continue this focusing by looking both ways carefully when crossing streets or paying special, conscientious attention to kitchen safety or whatever focus is appropriate to the activity in which you become involved. Use this step until you are clearly in, and well focused on, not the otherworldly realms but the everyday, embodied plane.

You may feel very sharp and alert and so think there is no need to come back to this realm. Quick-witted and attentive as you are, you might nevertheless be alert only to the *spirit* plane! Taking the time to become alert to the physical realm by doing this exercise is the only way you might realize you weren't tuned in to it in the first place. Fact is, maybe most of the time you'll be in this realm when you finish a rite and have no need to "come back," but Third Road exercises are such that you can't know this until you finish the grounding.

Third Road rituals may be far simpler than ones both adepts and beginners are used to, and therein lies a danger: these rituals can shift your perception without your realizing it. They've done it to me, and I made the stuff up! So do this grounding.

Step 5. By now, the job should be done. But on the rare chance you still feel spacey or "out there," here are several things you can do:

- Eat something without sugar in it. You might focus on heavier foods such as nuts, cheese, whole-grain bread, beef, potatoes, carrots. Drinking milk can also be grounding, but immediately after the above rite the taste of milk is more likely to move you back toward an altered state.

- Engage in very physical but safe activities that will focus you onto your own body. For example, dance about the house or go for a walk.

Assignment: starting the second week of your training, do "Nourishing One's Spirit" once a week for three weeks. Ideally, each time you do both rituals—the cleansing and the milk exercise—do them in one sitting. In each cleansing, pick a different inner block you want to be free of.

While this book's rituals have immediate applications to the training, they can also be used in innumerable ways for as long as you want to apply them—lifelong applications that can empower you in all arenas of your daily life, always available when you want to improve your life, overcome a challenge, or successfully take advantage of a new opportunity. Whether it is about career advancement, overcoming confusion caused by a new relationship, getting rid of useless guilt, heading off your anger when it starts to get the better of you, or any of the other endless concerns we have from day to day, you will have effective tools to deal with them.

A Book of Shadows (A Magical Journal)

The sort of person who is drawn to my classes, and by extrapolation my writing, is the sort who should write their own bible. No, I am not being profane. I am not trivializing the sacredness of the Judeo-Christian Bible. Some spiritual traditions have sacred texts, and I use the word *bible* to mean a sacred text. It also makes a strong point: while much of religious practice is based on what believers feel is the transcribed word of God, shamans base their practice elsewhere. As a group, they do not have one basic written text, and they do not hold any one text or person above all other sources as the ultimate and indisputable authority. Instead, shamanism honors the direct experience one has and teaches that God talks clearly to each of us. (Shamans also gain guidance from their elders, but we will deal with that later.)

Asking you to write your own bible honors the sacredness of your own thoughts, revelations, insights, intuitions, experiences, even your doubts and failures. I am hoping your writing from this training will be the beginning of a notebook—call it a journal, Book of Shadows, or George—that you personally create as part of your spiritual and magical process. Please keep that in mind as you do the journaling assignments.

"But write a bible?" you might say. "Wow, what an undertaking!" Nope, it is not that hard, not if you understand what I am actually asking of you. Many children write their own bible entries every day and start them out with "Dear Diary." My personal bible, or Book of Shadows, as it is called by witches, is simply a journal that records my triumphs and discoveries, my bumbling attempts at self-improvement, my hopes and insights—even when they later prove to be wrong—my fears and thoughts about how I will never achieve my goals, and any other honest thoughts and feelings. Hmm, and dishonest ones, too!

Hearing the word *bible* might lead some to think their writing should be inflated in order to be important. A diary is important because it is about *your* life. So get the idea of your personal bible down to size.

On the other hand, no false humility. Your Book of Shadows shouldn't focus on making you sound less of a person than you really are. That is not spirituality, that is pretension. Displaying false humility is just as pompous as trying to appear better than you are.

If you find yourself constantly using your journal to beat yourself up by telling yourself you are stupid or weird or uncreative or anything else that makes you feel bad to write down, please stop hurting yourself that way. You should nurture yourself in a journal; this great application of the ritual "Nourishing One's Spirit," which can help you stop being mean to yourself.

I look at my childhood diary entries and, despite all their naïveté and overly dramatic outpourings, see the seeds of a young writer; I gain nourishment from my early memoirs. If you write poems, you may want to put them in your magical journal. (Did I hear you say they are not good enough? They are likely far better than you think. I've heard endless numbers of poems their authors thought were bad. They were usually good poetry. In any case, good or bad, they deserve to be in your bible if you want them there. They are part of you and your life and your divine nature.) Or include any other use of words. It can list your favorite recipes. After all, food is sacred! It can even be a place where you draw pictures as a way to express your thoughts. Whatever you want to put in the journal is great!

It can also be a venue for you to brag privately about things you accomplish. Leigh and Charlap's song "I've Got to Crow!" from the show *Peter Pan* expressed it well. It is healthy to be proud of and even record outstanding or useful things you've done. Outstanding needn't be defined by the obviously heroic or otherwise spectacular acts. It can take a lot of work to summon up the nerve to try a new recipe if one has no confidence in one's culinary skills. Things that are trivial to one person can be an accomplishment worthy of great praise when done by someone else. I consider it outstanding that I get out of bed in the morning. Take pride in getting your teeth brushed if you need to feel you've gotten something done on a given day and having practiced dental hygiene is the only thing that comes to mind.

It is healthy and furthers your spiritual growth to record ideas you have—or hear or read—that help you through the day. Everyone on this planet has profound thoughts, insights, and maybe even methods about how to make life better for themselves or others. If you want an example of journal writing about one's own methods, see the eleventh month's lesson: my journal excerpts in the section "How to Perform a Self-Initiation Ritual" are the seeds of rituals in the thirteenth month's lesson, in the section called "Gentle Heart, Palm Up: Self Love."

If a magical journal still sounds like more than you can accomplish, don't worry. Using a Book of Shadows is optional except when assigned, at which times, I will lead you step-by-step through the process. You'll only be required to do a bit of writing if that is all you want to do. Don't worry—you'll be able to do it. Of course, you *can* write in your journal as much as you want.

Assignment: to be done over three weeks' time. Start the last week of the first month. This will give you the time to finish the exercise in time for the first written assignment. Remember, while time parameters of assignments are to be followed as closely as possible, you can be flexible if needed. In fact, here are examples of not being rigid: if the only way you'll get a month's work done is to do the second assignment and then the first assignment, be realistic and do the second ritual first. Or if there are certain exercises you just can't get yourself to do, for whatever reason, don't worry. You get the picture: do your darndest without being so rigid you can't do *anything* for fear of making mistakes. Now:

Find a notebook for your Book of Shadows. Anything will do the trick, whether it's a spiral-bound notebook or beautifully hand-bound linen pages or loose sheets of paper that you hope someday to put in a three-ring binder. "What?" you ask. "That is too simple an assignment, too easy." Nope! It is a subtle ritual; perhaps it will even be a celebration for some of you. This is a religion of joy. We get to enjoy our path. And that is not meant metaphorically. Have you ever seen a person who says that her spirituality makes her happy, but her smile is false and strained, and you can tell that her stomach is so twisted in knots from repressing her true feelings that it is a wonder she can breathe? Well, in our journey, spiritual happiness means feeling good the way you feel after a good meal! A shaman embraces a joyful spirituality expressed through living life fully; he welcomes humor, self-love, and plain old fun.

One cannot understand this lesson of joyous spirituality solely through the intellect. One has to *experience* this lesson. This assignment is a small step toward that. I give you a whole three weeks to find the notebook not so that you take lots of time to sweat and worry about how to find the perfect object or beat yourself up for every thought you have about the notebook and every action you take—or don't take. I give you three weeks so you needn't worry about getting the assignment done on time, needn't rush, and maybe will just stumble over the right Book of Shadows.

You may not yet be able to actually enjoy the process of finding the notebook, but in the attempt to do so you might *experience* that God doesn't want us to have a hard time of things, doesn't want to make things hard for us. That is a big step toward understanding that God wants us to enjoy our spiritual path. Besides, the ends is the means. A goal of this training is to be happy and relaxed; how can you become that without being so in the process sometimes? And if all you find is a scrap of paper, paper napkin, or paper plate on which to write your first writing assignment, you've done your homework. Yes, this is another trick assignment. Playing tricks is a big part of my spirituality! I even let people know what tricks I am playing on them. Hee hee hee, the tricks can still work.

Table of Assignments

A table of assignments at the end of every month's lesson helps you be clear about when in that month each of its assignments is to be done and provides its page number. The table gives only a rough sketch of each assignment; see the lessons themselves to determine all an assignment's parts, everything it requires to be fulfilled, as well as its other parameters and explanations.

Do these assignments during the first month:

The first week:

- Avoid the word *initiation*. pg. 47

The second week:

- Enjoy the ritual "Nourishing One's Spirit" once. pg. 59
- Continue to avoid the word *initiation*. pg. 47

The third week:

- Perform the ritual "Nourishing One's Spirit" again. pg. 59
- Continue to avoid the word *initiation*. pg. 47

The fourth week:

- Use the ritual "Nourishing One's Spirit" again. pg. 59
- Start finding a notebook for your Book of Shadows. Give yourself three weeks to do this; this means the assignment bleeds a week or so into the second month's work. pg. 62
- Continue to avoid the word *initiation*. pg. 47

The Self as Magic Wand

The Third Road practitioner is her own magical cauldron, altar, and wand. I am not using *magic* as a metaphor for changing one's inner being, though that is part of magic. I'm talking about *old-fashioned* magic, as in Cinderella's Faerie Godmother miraculously creating ball-gowns and fabulous coaches. *This* is what is practiced by shamans.

And as is the magician, so goes the spell. As her own primary magical tool, the shaman must strive to cleanse herself of inner blocks to happiness, or they sabotage her spells. If you feel you are unworthy of love, your love spell might not work as intended, but draw a disrespectful lover. In the same vein, poor ethics can make a spell backfire. A Third Road magical technique or rite is often taught with corresponding personal work to net effective, safe, and ethical results.

This removal of inner blocks is the same work an ancient shaman would have done to overcome the initial trauma and gain his powers. Not through a psychological process but through a magical (or call it psychic) one, a Third Road shaman undertakes a journey into his deepest self. There is no exploration more wondrous and more fruitful because finally there is nothing but the self to face, embrace, cleanse, celebrate, and love, until one can also love and serve all things.

What *Is* a Priestess?

We all have dreams. One woman might want to marry and have children, another may want to write the great American novel, and yet another may want both. This society makes it hard to have dreams. We are taught to doubt ourselves, to trust so-called authorities instead of the conclusions we reach ourselves.

Jillian and Alex Learn to Honor What Is Different in Themselves

As a child, Jillian enthusiastically proffered her opinions on everything from what makes cats purr to the way to end world hunger. What she had to say was always naysayed. Her ideas about life received an indignant "I know better than you" from her mom. Her original, unusual ideas in school were met with a look of superior impatience or a condescending "Don't you think you should leave that to experts, dear?"

No one praised Jillian for her attempts to think things out for herself. When her childhood conclusions were erroneous, instead of correcting her gently and in a manner that encouraged her to use her fine mind, adults wrote her ideas off without much thought other than a stinging "That's just silly!"

Jillian's story demonstrates a few of the many factors in both society and in individual families that can cause people to develop traits and ideas that keep them from trusting, or even hearing, their own beliefs about life and their hopes for their personal future. For example, Jillian came to believe she should leave analysis to others and that she had no power to define or implement solutions to problems in our society. She also came to think that if she followed her heart in thought or deed, everyone would laugh at her. Thus, after the age of ten she wouldn't let herself even *know* what she thought or wanted to do with herself.

Jillian was a typical child in her eagerness to observe and analyze her surroundings. Had her attempts been met with enthusiasm and respect for her burgeoning intellect, she could have developed confidence in her brilliance, discernment, and ability to make a difference. She also would have realized her spirited interest in everything around her was a gift instead of something to be squelched for fear of mockery.

Jillian displayed common sense as a little girl. Her solution to end world hunger was: "If every person with extra money fed one hungry person, no one would be hungry." Her down-to-earth remarks often shrewdly hit the political nail on the head, embarrassing adults who didn't want to face their lackadaisical attitude toward community problems. Because of her upbringing, the adult Jillian viewed her common-sense ideas as silly and her earthy solutions as insufficiently informed.

Alex's fears and beliefs are another example of traits that develop through societal or parental pressure to give up one's own ideas and dreams. Alex feared that if he excelled in anything, people would attack him; any excellence he had showed as a child had been ridiculed by his parents, who mistakenly thought that their derision would save Alex from becoming egotistical. Alex never fully developed his remarkable athletic talents, though he deeply longed to be a long-distance runner. His parents' well-meaning but misplaced mockery instilled a belief in Alex that it is always best to just go along with the crowd instead of pursuing one's deepest desires.

RITUAL

Ritual for Common Sense and Inspiration

Jillian and Alex used this ritual as an important step toward gaining self-confidence in both how they view the world and their own unique way of doing things. And so can you.

Step 1. Find one thing in yourself that keeps you from trusting or maybe even hearing your inner voice, your own opinions, your observations that happen throughout the course of the day, your own hopes and dreams.

Comparing yourself to Jillian might help you see one such thing in yourself: Have you come to think others inevitably know better than you? Has fear of ridicule sometimes kept you from trying to think your own thoughts? Or maybe you can't even let yourself know what you think or want.

Perhaps, like Jillian, you've come to believe that an enthusiastic interest in life is embarrassing so you squelch any spark of interest you feel, no matter how tiny. Perhaps you can't even let yourself feel a preference for wheat toast over croissants. You might not think a breakfast menu is important in the scheme of things, but to Tandie it was the magic key.

Tandie was a client who had survived the trauma of incest. Like many trauma survivors, she couldn't feel even the smallest desires. When counseling, I ask the Goddess what my clients need, and then tell them what I hear in response. Part of why all my spiritual counseling can be called shamanic counseling, psychic readings, and psychic counseling is that I psychically listen to God's words. God told me that if Tandie could come to feel and act on such a small preference as what she wanted for breakfast, Tandie would open an inner gate to the larger preferences in her life, the desires that would help her choose her own fulfilling lifestyle and life's purpose. So I wrote "Ritual for Common Sense and Inspiration" and asked Tandie to use it to remove her lack of awareness about what she wanted for breakfast. Tandie wanted French toast with maple syrup! Over time she became comfortable with little choices, which helped her open up to her deepest desire, which was to become a journalist. She now writes for her local newspaper!

If you rarely know what you want for breakfast or can never pick a movie or can hardly decide which blouse you like best when shopping, you may want to apply this prayer the same way Tandie did. Again, focus on one thing—your lack of being able to choose breakfast *or* blouses *or* movies.

Another way one might not trust oneself would be to invalidate one's common sense, like Jillian did hers. You are doing this if you ignore what your plain old everyday observations and simple logic tell you: "He's not really being sexist; I must be misreading things."

Here are other examples of inner blocks to inspiration and common sense: fear of success; belief that you will be too lonely if you forsake the safe path that everyone else follows; fear that God will punish you if you trust yourself.

If you identify with a lot of the examples above, be patient with yourself; focus on only one inner block in this ritual. Growth must happen in stages. Over time you can focus on other blocks.

This rite helped Jillian rekindle the perceptiveness she had lost as a child and started her on a path of self-expression that culminated in her becoming a political activist whose savvy was always appreciated by her colleagues. Alex remembered his desire for excellence and with more training was able to act on it: he became a successful lawyer and a weekend basketball coach for his son's team.

Step 2. To be free of your block, recite the following:

PRAYER FOR SPIRITUAL CLEANSING, COMMON SENSE, WISDOM, AND INSPIRATION

Lady, cleanse me of this block.
Help me know through and through that:
the earth has wisdom, my body has wisdom,
a tree has wisdom, my heart has wisdom,
a bird has wisdom, my mind has wisdom.

Lady, cleanse me of this block.
Help me realize:
an ocean holds knowledge, just so does my mind;
a fox has wiles, just so am I wily;
a child knows God, and so do I.
Help me find my innate wisdom and knowledge.

Lady, cleanse me of this block.
Help me know these things:
common sense feeds the soul;
lyrical mysticism and visionary hope
belong in the everyday world;
I can grow and stretch a bit spiritually, every day.

Thank you, Goddess.

Assignment: starting the first week of this month, do "Ritual for Common Sense and Inspiration" once a week for three weeks. Each time you do this rite, focus on another inner block.

"I Hate My Wife!" and Original Sin

No matter *what* your inner blocks and faults are, don't belittle yourself. For example, your fear of success may be illogical, but shortcomings often don't make logical sense. When the natural health of one's psyche is awry, one's innate logic is gone.

Or perhaps you are blocked by an anger you are ashamed of. This can happen for many reasons. Maybe the religion of your youth made you ashamed of your perfectly human feelings so that you never realized that *everyone* gets unreasonably angry, jealous, or petty.

If you are responding to my last statement with "But I feel such extreme anger (jealousy, pettiness, whatever)": That's my point exactly! *Everyone* feels extreme feelings. How you choose to deal with them and whether you act on them or not is a different matter—and a vitally important one—but the point at hand is that everyone feels these things, and being ashamed doesn't help you change.

In saying everyone has faults I am not suggesting that you be proud of your shortcomings or that you needn't change them. But you can get so swamped in a quagmire of shame that you are immobilized, unable to change feelings or behavior. Not to mention that shame makes it hard—if not impossible—to admit one's shortcomings. However, you cannot change unless you admit, at least to yourself, what your problem is. Hiding from your extreme feelings—even hate—only makes you push those feelings down, down, down into a dark, frightened part of yourself. It makes you sit in judgment of others who feel the same.

It can be difficult facing my scarier feelings. Sometimes I need help to do it. If you need help confronting your frightening emotions, you will learn to secure the assistance you desire in next month's lesson, "Finding Your Good Faeries: Creating Support to Live Your Dreams."

When I'm training a group in which someone is "politically incorrect" or shows lack of moral fiber, I ask the others not to jump down that person's throat. Such a reaction doesn't heal. Nor does it create a safe environment in which people can talk freely and learn from their mistakes. And, again, how can anyone get help to improve if they can't voice their problems? Practice patience and compassion. Remember how valuable it might have been for you to reveal scary secrets about yourself to someone who didn't make you feel bad for it. Try to think when you might have done something you did not feel proud of, and decide what response you would have needed if you owned up to your misdeed. Then, when someone makes an embarrassing disclosure to you, act in the way you wish someone had acted for you. When you don't agree with what someone is saying, listen for what he *really means* instead of listening to just his words. If all else fails, place your tongue gently between your teeth to stop it from wagging.

We all do things that are wrong and sometimes cannot find out how to change a behavior unless we know we can trust someone to be kind if we tell him our secret.

Jake: If Someone Listens to a Man's Problems, He Can Overcome Them

The first thing that my new client, Jake, blurted out in his first appointment was that he hated his wife.

People have ways of revealing themselves, even revealing themselves *to* themselves, that are not always straightforward; they don't always say or even know what's really on their minds. What I heard Jake *really* saying, whether he knew it or not, was, "My wife hurt my feelings really badly, but I am going to tell you that in an obnoxious way. I want to make sure, before I say one more thing, that I can say whatever I need to and I will be heard with compassion and an open mind. I might accidentally say something I don't really mean, because I'm fumbling to find and express my thoughts and feelings; if I think I'll get jumped on for doing so, I'll be so nervous that I won't be able to even *try* to express myself."

My response to "I hate my wife" was, "Yeah, I don't think marriage is possible without feeling that way sometimes. But other times hate feels like something to worry about. Are you worried about it?"

Finding acceptance for what he figured was the worst thing he could say, he tried to explain his situation. He stumbled and bumbled but kept on talking, knowing that no attempt at expressing himself, however poorly, would bring down rains of censure.

Being allowed to think out loud, he figured out why he was so upset with his wife and could express himself more and more clearly. In sometimes misleading bits and pieces, he explained that she had had so little time for him recently that he thought she was perhaps cheating on him. He loved her so dearly that the thought of infidelity caused him tremendous pain.

Once he found that another woman—me—was willing to listen to him without jumping to conclusions, he trusted his wife might do the same. He talked to her about her recent distractedness and found out that she loved him as much as always but was absorbed by worries about her sister who had entered into a bad relationship. Realizing that her absentmindedness had nothing to do with him, Jake was no longer hurt by it. He was able to express his loving traits to her in her time of need. A far cry from hating his wife.

If you have done things that you think are too awful to admit, disclosing them might be necessary in order to change. But that change may be possible only if the confession is met with compassion and love. Whatever one has done—*whatever*—can be transformed if one encounters loving, healing support instead of condemnation, verbal assault, denouncement, belittling, or insult. None of these will help change a thing.

I am not letting anyone off the hook, mind you: we are accountable for each and every way we have hurt anyone. And part of being accountable is to try to refrain from repeating past wrongs, which can't always be accomplished all on our own.

As a child, Bernadette was beaten by her mother. She became afraid, often even terrified, that if she got close to anyone they would hurt her. As an adult she rarely dated, and the few brief relationships she did have painfully filled her with alternating hope and dread. In one of her longer relationships, with Chris, her absolute terror kept her from noticing when she seriously hurt Chris's feelings. Chris, a person just as frightened as Bernadette, was so wounded by her he could not ask anyone else out for years.

Bernadette is not a monster. In fact, she's typical in that her authentic pain blinded her to the pain she might cause others. Bernadette is only one example of how normal, caring people, who wouldn't hurt a fly and would usually be sensitive to other people's needs, can hurt others badly.

When I hear, perhaps from a client or on the news, a wrongdoing that appalls me, I try to remind myself that we all have done awful things in our lives. When examining my own behavior, I try not to run from the idea that I might have hurt someone. Be clear: I am not taking a lazy attitude and saying that it is acceptable to seriously hurt others. But the pretense that outlandish wrongs are done only by an exceptional few, only by those who are somehow "different" or "greatly worse" than the rest of the human race, does terrible harm to us all. It makes us hide from any great wrong we might have done so that we do not have to think of ourselves as monsters who might be shunned by "better" people, our loved ones, who are so central to our lives. By hiding in this way, we only repeat our mistakes or let them eat away at us. Hiding leaves us without the spiritual resources necessary to change ourselves for the better.

I try to think, "I can't know what drove that person to do what they did. Would I inevitably have done the same with his lack of resources or the beating life gave him?" The Goddess is happy to love all of us and heal us of the things that make us hurt ourselves and others.

Sometimes a person thinks she has done something awful that is, in fact, not that bad at all. Perhaps her actions did not measure up to her perfectionism. For example, a mother snaps at her toddler and then thinks herself a monster. Occasionally snapping at one's child doesn't cause deep wounds and is inevitable if, as is often the case with mothers of young children, the mother is isolated, overworked, and lacking support.

Sometimes a person thinks she has done something awful that is actually good. A person who does too much for others instead of ever taking care of herself might be filled with remorse when she finally says, "No, just this one night I need to relax in front of the TV and get a good night's sleep." Her guilt can gnaw away at her.

Sometimes a person lives in tremendous pain, blaming herself for the wrongdoing of others. An incest survivor may blame herself for the perpetrator's actions. In fact, no child *under any circumstances* is responsible for abuse committed by an adult against her. Never.

Whether it is misjudging one's actions as worse than they are, misperceiving a proper course of action as a mistake, or blaming oneself for someone else's deed: if one can trust someone to listen to one's self-doubt without judgment, one can risk telling the deepest of secrets, the so-called "awful wrong." Disclosure may be the only way one can get the feedback needed to discover the truth of one's actions and be freed from unnecessary guilt.

While everyone deserves healing, compassion, and decent treatment, not everyone might be capable of hearing what you have say. For example, a married woman having an affair may feel it is wrong and want support from her friends to end the situation. But what if another woman in that group is suffering because of her own husband's infidelity? Even if she intellectually understands that no one is perfect and that we all make mistakes, infidelity can cause enormous pain, and hearing her friend's tale might remind her of more pain than she can tolerate. Or the betrayed wife may be so upset upon hearing the details of her friend's woes that, to avoid anguish, she retreats into a pained silence that seems like an indictment. Thus, no one is helped. In this situation the woman having the affair may want to talk with only part of her group. Situations like this might also play out when a group is working its way though this book together. (By the way, a *coven* is a group who works together ritually. Another name for a group of witches is a *circle*. A witch who works alone is called a *solitary*.)

Here is another example concerning appropriate people with whom to risk disclosures. Due to circumstances over which she had little control, Megan lost custody of her young daughter, Joyce. Years later, Megan was able to tell some of her friends that not getting to raise her own child was one of the greatest sorrows of her life. She never had a chance to say this to her child in a way her daughter could understand. But Megan's friends knew that, year after year throughout Joyce's childhood, Megan would make her monthly phone call to Joyce, then float uselessly in dazed pain for days after. The brief, yearly visits between mother and daughter combined heaven and hell for Megan; it was joyous to hug her daughter and cook meals for her and heartbreaking to see her beloved child right there in the same room since they were to be separated again so soon.

The only way Joyce could make peace with her feelings of loss and rejection was to view her mother as uncaring, as if Megan didn't have the human feelings of a "real" mother. Joyce's pain was so great there was not room to come to grips with it *and* her mom's. I do not fault Joyce for this; humans have limits.

Loving her daughter, Megan struggled to respect the way Joyce had come to grips with an enormous challenge. Megan realized it was inappropriate to share her own pain with her daughter, who showed a justifiable sense of self-preservation in her inability to see that the situation was a tragedy for *everyone* involved—a catastrophe over which everyone was powerless and in which everyone suffered. Megan healed by sharing her pain elsewhere.

An inability to listen caringly to a certain person's problems can happen even in the therapeutic community. For example, a rape survivor who becomes a therapist might choose not to counsel rapists because she knows that she has unresolved issues that would make her unable to extend the compassion that such a client needs in order to change. That particular therapist might be unable to offer effective therapeutic treatment when a rapist needs to talk about his feelings of shame at having violated someone.

Next month's lesson will point out how to create a support network and find resources related to the issues touched upon in this section. There is a place on God's immense lap for all Her children.

While we're on the topic of shortcomings, let's touch on another aspect of it. Most pagans do not believe in original sin, since it is often understood by society as follows: you are bad for wanting sex, you are bad for wanting self-fulfillment, and you are just plain old bad no matter what you do simply because you exist and breathe. You should live in shame without self-respect, groveling in front of a god and priests who represent that god. No wonder no one wants to believe in original sin!

Sex is holy, the Goddess wants us to be fulfilled, and She, like any good mom, wants us to strive to be our best but thinks we are swell just the way we are. She does not want us to grovel but to enjoy Her presence, to dance in the moonlight with Her blessing. She anoints us all as her priests who stand proudly with Her approval.

But I often see folks who, in rightly rejecting the shame and horror of original sin, feel that they cannot or need not admit to any faults. For example, since they recognize that sex is holy, they do not see themselves as accountable for any harm they cause by having irresponsible sex. So without meaning to be cruel, they hurt others.

I propose an alternative between the two extremes: I believe in original sin, but I have another interpretation of those two words that will not make people feel worthless and ashamed of their sexual desires, their lust for living, and their every and most-sacred breath. My hope is that people will be freed from the unholy guilt that the prevailing views of original sin perpetuate.

To me, original sin means that I was created a human, to be human, and I am just that—only human, in all my glory and all my imperfections. It is not my job to be perfect. I am freed of that burden and the guilt that goes with it. It is my job to strive to be the best person I can conceive of, *and* to know that the ideals I work toward cannot be reached. God made me in such a way that I *can never* meet those absolute measures, so I don't have to hate myself for not achieving a level of perfection. And I can admit my faults and thus be in a position to change the ways in which I hurt myself and others; knowing I am imperfect does not imply that I am bad or that I should suffer the disdain of others. Admitting to an imperfection does not mean I am a contemptible fool who is only worthy of being a doormat that everyone, including God, can walk on. Original sin can be a wonderful concept if it is free of the taint of self-hate and does not belittle us for our inevitable mistakes, both the large and the many, small daily errors we make.

A fresh perspective on original sin says instead, "God didn't intend me to be perfect; She only intended me to try my best. I know that She loves me just for who I am. God is my mother. And like all good mothers,

She worships the ground Her children walk on. She thinks I'm wonderful, beautiful, and knows I do my best. No matter how badly I am doing, it is the best I can do. No matter *how* badly."

Recognizing inner flaws does not necessitate self-denigration. We can love ourselves in our imperfections. You can honor every breath you take as sacred yet be relieved from the burden of having to be perfect. Recognizing your own imperfection does not imply you don't care about, and strive toward, being a good person, a person with the highest ethics.

Naomi's tale exemplifies a completely different reason why some people dread their imperfections.

Naomi: A Perfectionist Learns She Can Survive Her Mistakes

People who are about to marry sometimes agonize over their decision. Naomi's terror was so monumental she felt physically nauseated for an entire week. Four days before her wedding, she came to class and shared her problem.

Intuiting the core issue, I told her I was going to ask her a trick question: "Yes, Naomi, maybe your choice of mate is wrong. What if that is true and you marry him?"

Naomi said, "Everything will be ruined. I will never survive it."

"That's what I thought: I know you were raised to fear a punishing god who taught you all your moral lessons by inflicting pain on you. I know that in becoming a pagan you escaped that god. You have a new god. What will She do if you are mistaken about your marriage?"

Naomi bit her lip, looked down, and after a moment's consideration lifted her chin. Looking me straight in the eye, she responded, "Nothing! What does this have to do with Her? The Goddess doesn't try to run the show by pulling on puppet strings attached to us like my parents' God does. That's why I like Her."

Continuing to listen to the words Goddess gave me, I gave them to Naomi: "She doesn't boss us around. She *does* runs the show, only in the sense it is a show She created to benefit us and in that She wants to keep it in good working condition. She created this garden of earthly delight, and you can think of Her as the garden keeper. She wants us to be happy in Her garden. She wants us to enjoy the bounty of the garden She planted for us.

"And like all good and loving mothers, when we, Her children, make mistakes that cause us to fall down, She catches us in Her arms to keep us from harm. She doesn't desert us."

I intuited that Roseanne, my teaching apprentice and Naomi's close friend, had a few thoughts on this, so I asked her if she wanted to chime in. She added, "I've known you since we were kids, Naomi. You try to be perfect in everything you do. Your clothing, your makeup, your school-work, the ethics of your actions, your checkbook balance, and now your marriage—everything has to be flawless down to the last inch. You are trying to do the impossible. Because you think that if you make a mistake, no one will be there to catch you. As you said, you think you will be ruined if you marry the wrong guy."

Naomi's eyebrows raised hopefully, but she was just about holding her breath. Roseanne looked expectantly at me. I moved to Naomi, put my arms around her, and tried to keep letting Goddess talk through me: "Let Goddess love you as much as She wants. I know how much you want the full love of your divine parent. Receive it *now:* by knowing it is not your job to be perfect, it is Hers. You do the best you can and start trusting that Goddess will, for want of a better term, pick up the slack."

Naomi interjected, "But I don't want to be lazy and avoid my re-sponsibilities." But her breathing had become more relaxed, and her gaze searched my eyes as if she hoped to find an answer there.

"Naomi, your sense of responsibility and high standards are great, just don't go overboard. You panic over every detail in life because you think it is all up to you. You try to make sure every atom of the universe is in its right place; I think you do this to ensure no disasters can possi-bly overtake you. But Goddess is already putting all those atoms in place for you because She knows it is beyond your power to do that, to control *everything*. She wants you to stop running yourself ragged trying to avoid disaster. Perfection is not your job, it is Hers, and She *will* do it for you."

And it just so happens Naomi made the right choice in her man. But you know what? I don't believe Naomi made that choice all on her own. I suspect Goddess went out and found that guy for Naomi in the first place!

Every breath I take is sacred. Every breath I take is imperfect. In the same vein, my wisdom is incomplete, my knowledge unsound, and that is as it should be. But I will try to act according to my best judgment with reasonable trust in my own abilities to succeed at my daily goals. And I will strive to know that You, Goddess, are there to be the perfect counterpart to my imperfect attempts. Though all my attempts and every breath I take are imperfect, God is breathing for me. In, out, each breath She takes perfectly sustains all my efforts, all my breaths, all my days in perfect fulfillment of everything I need and of my deepest desires.

More About: What *Is* a Priestess?

This month's lesson started with the question "What is a priestess?" I referred to how different each person's dream is, whether it is to be a movie star, a nursery school teacher, the scientist who discovers the cure for cancer, or a hermit who meditates on world peace. From there we discussed blocks to those dreams, how to face one's shortcomings, and a new take on original sin. It was all part of getting to the question: What *is* a priestess?

Most Wiccan priests are lay ministers because the Wiccan religion is first and foremost hearth centered. Generally, one's service or Wiccan priesthood is for one's family, whether the family involved is biological, chosen, coven, or the larger family called community—a community that can range from humankind to animal kin to land to cosmos. So, one's priesthood can consist of getting married and raising children, being a nurse, midwife, movie star, or lawyer, offering psychic readings, or facilitating public rituals. Those dreams mentioned earlier, those deepest longings, when fulfilled, are what a priestess does as her own ministry. Each person is a priestess in a very different way.

All witches are priests: captains of their own souls; every person worthy of serving Gods, community, and planet. The Third Road initiation brings one further into this responsibility and joy through ordination into priesthood, lay or otherwise.

But you can be a priest without initiation. Wicca is not about a hierarchy enforced by some so-called initiation, after which one is permitted to be a priest. When I write "All witches are priests" I am not saying, "If you study witchcraft and learn it well, then you are a priest." You are a priest the moment you choose to say you are! You can do the work of a priest yet never have to call yourself one if you don't want to. The Third Road initiation is about helping you do what you long to do *anyway* or deepen what you are already doing.

Note: Hierarchy has forms other than the dysfunctional imposition of the will of one person or group over another person or group. For example, a mother who grabs her toddler out of the road and onto the sidewalk because a car is coming is imposing her will. It is her duty. To do other *would* be dysfunctional, and responsible mothers many times every week must fulfill their hierarchically structured obligations. However, the term *hierarchy,* as used in this text, does not refer to healthy hierarchical structures, only those that are unhealthy.

Assignment: to be done the third week. This is the first assigned use of your magical journal: write down your own definitions of priesthood. While it may be helpful to include abstract or general items such as "To serve God" or "to help others," the assignment is to list the concrete, specific things you want to do with your own life, such as "I want to be president (be an acupuncturist, open a big-city health-food store where customers and workers enjoy an actual community, find a man who worships the ground I walk on and run a farm with him, manage a shelter for battered women)."

The best way to do this assignment might be to forget the word *priest* and instead ask yourself, "What do I want to do before I die?" because priesthood is basically *your life's work,* whether or not it is how you earn money.

Apply the spirit of the following guidelines for this assignment to all your training, from writing assignments to reading the lessons:

In doing this assignment you may not be able to answer the question. You may have no idea what you want to do with your life. Many students don't at the beginning of their study. That changes! The "Ritual for Common Sense and Inspiration" provides one of the many powerful steps in your shamanic journey toward self-knowledge.

In finding what we love to do, what fulfills us, we end up doing the very things that will most help others. I will not have my students thinking they always have to choose between themselves and others. The things you need to do to be happy are also what guide you toward your life's work. God gave us desires and inclinations so that we would follow them toward our destiny. Of course, it is unhealthy to do every last thing we want or lean toward. But organized religion has a history of swinging to the other extreme. A true spiritual path is defined not just by what you can do for others but also by what you long to do for yourself. If that seems selfish, it is a healthy selfishness that makes it possible to be of service to your family, friends, and community.

You can write as little or as much as you want. One sentence, one item, written down *truly* can fulfill this assignment. Any attempt is good. Any start, however small or irrelevant, means you can eventually go further. If you can write nothing, the attempt to write moves you forward so that the time will come when you know what your priesthood is.

Brainstorming necessitates you be open to "bad" ideas. I say *bad ideas* for two reasons:

1. Bad ideas often set the stage for good ideas. "A new idea is delicate. It can be killed by a sneer or a yawn; it can be stabbed to death by a quip."* Write down any ideas that pop into your head, even if they seem silly, unrealistic, ungrounded, counterproductive, irrelevant, and so on. Though the idea in and of itself might be useless, it might be your subconscious mind moving you toward an "Aha!" If all you can write down is one thing you like to do that seems irrelevant to any big life choices—like reading science fiction—that's great. Your

---

*Says Charles H. Brower, according to *Random House Webster's Quotationary*

priesthood may turn out to be happily editing science fiction! Which brings me to the next item:

2. People often discount their wonderful ideas. When I teach a lesson on creating rituals, I ask, "What has to be done to make a rite effective?" Students often sit silent. So I ask them to share *whatever* they have been refraining from saying, even if they consider their thoughts irrelevant or dumb. Usually what comes out of each student's mouth is a fabulous, relevant concept or the exciting germ of one.

I suggest you do an experiment when you fulfill this assignment: instead of condemning whatever thoughts come into your head, write them down first and evaluate them later. When you do make your assessment, don't simply say of an idea, "It's good," or "It's bad." Play with an idea, write a stream of consciousness on it, read it to a friend, try to remember if it relates to anything that's important to you. In other words, test the soundness of your ideas by working with them in any way you can think of, instead of by sitting a million miles away from them, analyzing them without involvement. The latter mode doesn't necessarily give you a chance to see the value in what you've written.

If you have no ideas, write about that. Sometimes we cannot determine our goals until we have done other work. For example, writing about a lack of ideas may help you discover other inner blocks to hearing and trusting your hopes and dreams. Apply "Ritual for Common Sense and Inspiration" to become open to your soul's wisdom.

One need only spend a little time writing. Don't be overwhelmed or intimidated; five minutes is plenty of writing time. The writing assignments, and the answers to questions I sometimes ask when giving them, cannot be finished in the year of your training. It takes a lifetime to write your own bible; some issues and questions should be explored one's whole life. And don't become overwhelmed now that I've said this is a lifelong process; so is breathing. Use the understanding that this is an entire life's journey to let yourself just write a bit, be proud of doing that much, and be free of worry since you know you can always write more later.

The Mother's Cloak: A Circle of Protection and Love (optional)

Recite the following circle casting:

The Mother wraps Her cloak around us. Thus we are protected.

The Mother takes the girdle from Her waist,
and wraps it around us.
Thus we are held within Her passion for Her consort.
Thus we are held within Her passion for us.
Thus we are held within Her passion for Herself.

Around us the Mother lets down Her hair—
blond like beach sand,
dark like earth and the empty far reaches of space.
She lets Her hair down around us,
that we may nestle within it like children
playing, hidden within the bowers of a weeping willow.

Her arms encircle us in Her love.

She pulls from Her body Joyfire,
Joyfire whose name is God, Our Father,
and She wraps this circle of joy around us.

Around us are the elements of life that are Herself in truth—
by these we are protected, calmed,
given peace and joy.

Within this circle we share space with the animal people,
with the land, and the land of spirits,
within the weaving of all the Cosmos.

This circle casting can be used before a ritual when you want protection, to create sacred space, to gain power and blessings, and/or to help participants focus. The same benefits are gained by casting the circle before a nonritual event, which could be anything from childbirth to your weekly class with me to a walk on the beach. This ritual is not quite right for regular, mundane events like a day at the office (though you could surely use "The Mother's Cloak" at your job if you wanted to steal a few minutes for meditation). Even a moment's rest at work would be a good reason to use this ritual. "The Mother's Cloak" can also be done for its own sweet sake, and like all the book's rites, it can be used on your own or with other people.

While reciting the above liturgy you might want to point your finger at the floor, describing a circle in a clockwise direction around the space in which your subsequent rite or event will occur. You can delineate this circle once during the recitation or continually as you speak. Instead of your finger, you can also point a knife, staff, or even a small stick the size of, yes, the magic wand you see in Disney cartoons about Faerie Godmothers and witches. This helps you focus. So would pointing a pencil, flute, or soup ladle. (Yes, I'm joking, but it's also true and perfectly legitimate magic. A shaman uses what's on hand. Though using the soup ladle might make you laugh so hard you *lose* focus.)

When the event is over, recite the following circle opening, and, if you want, describe the same circle counterclockwise:

We have been protected by the Mother's cloak.
Though She now withdraws it, we are always in Her protection.

We have been wrapped within the Mother's passion.
Though She leaves us now,
Her passion is always there for us if we move toward it.

We have been hidden in the Goddess's tresses,
that we might play unnoticed.
Now we return to the mundane world,
its responsibilities and pleasures.

Though we leave this *circle of love,*
we are always held by Her love and care.

.   .   .

Though we leave this circle of joy,
our Good Father's joy is always within us.

Though the elements of life spin back into their everyday order,
these same elements are always there, to be Her hands holding us.

We have shared space with the animal people,
with the land, and the land of spirits,
within the weaving of all the Cosmos.

Let me share my process in creating "The Mother's Cloak." In 1988 I attended a ritual. The priestess officiating asked me to cast a circle by placing the Goddess's girdle about us. I was not instructed to use the girdle as a symbol of passion. I don't know if envisioning the girdle as a circle casting was an original or traditional idea. If original, it was likely done in ancient times; the original mind is all minds. Since that priestess asked to remain anonymous as a witch, I will not use her name, but acknowledgment—and respect—of all sources is part of both ancestor worship and tending to the earth, so I acknowledge her namelessly. We are not powerful in anything we create, including our writing of rituals, unless we honor and name our sources. We must honor ourselves when we're the source.

After the 1988 rite, I wrote "The Mother's Cloak," a piece of liturgy I often change to suit the rite I am leading. As early as 1990 I wrapped my celebrations within the Lady's hair, Her passion, and the joy that is God and decided to consciously share that circle, as the liturgy says, with the animal people. The above version, written around 1995, is similar to many I wrote prior to that time and is suitable to this training.

I share this history for several reasons. I want you to acknowledge your sources. Since we have been raised in a society that acknowledges only written sources, we are still learning how to acknowledge information drawn from *oral* tradition. This history provides a template.

Oral tradition is the passing on of information through word of mouth. Acknowledging oral sources when chatting with a pal or teaching a class is difficult but no less important than acknowledging written sources when writing. Perhaps it is even more important, since oral transmission is sometimes closer to the original source. Which is, no surprise, often uncredited because it is "just a woman" (or housekeeper, cab driver, or other person—often part of a disenfranchised group—who is not taken as an authority because he or she does not have a degree). My above history of the circle liturgy is detailed because I tried to demonstrate an ideal. Yet attribution is sometimes impossible, or must be minimal.

The above history also provides a template for respecting and acknowledging yourself as a source when you create a ritual, a meal, or an approach to living.

I also share the history because I want you to see that if you perceive a truth, the fact that it is "ancient" or "everyday" does not invalidate your deserving recognition for your discovery. That which is obvious is often obvious only once someone has stated it. A sociologist who recognizes a class dynamic that has existed for centuries is acknowledged for identifying it. Honor your findings as the result of your genius! I want every reader of this book to know how smart they are. As I wrote earlier, the belief is prevalent that there are few geniuses. *No!* We are all capable of drawing important conclusions and creating this world's future.

RITUAL

Protection Bubble (optional)

If, when performing "The Mother's Cloak," you feel you need added protection, do the following when you recite the first line of the rite, "The Mother wraps Her cloak around us. Thus we are protected": imagine a sphere surrounding the area you want made safe. Imagine this "bubble" protects you and that area from all evil yet allows in all that is good and loving. This simple act can also be used as a rite on its own, without any part of "The Mother's Cloak," to provide quick, easy, and effective protection from negativity of all sorts.

Once you have done this rite, the sphere will stay up of its own unless you choose to take it down. I let mine stay up providing protection until they dissolve, which is anywhere from a day to a few months. But if you choose otherwise, simply imagine that you are breathing the bubble into yourself, after which you might feel a lovely tingling of power.

You might wonder, "If the Goddess is all-powerful, why would I need the added protection of a bubble?" I pray, "Goddess, keep me safe," but I still lock my door at night. In the same vein, I construct psychic barriers to unpleasant events. If you are ever the least bit worried about safety concerning a rite you are about to do, or you start to worry in the middle of a ritual, simply create a protective sphere. It takes only a minute or two!

The Bloodline Initiation: The Mysteries of Your Blood, Bone, and Ancestors

What are the mysteries and secrets unique to you, the mysteries of your blood, bone, and ancestors? Come find out. Find out if the heart of your fire is the magic of dragons or trees, of water or bees. Or of . . . ? Is your truest magic that of the wind or the sea, of sewing needles flashing as they embroider, or of moonlight? Or is your magic that of unicorns and whispers, or of guitars and song? Of flowers and garden hoes? Is your magic a combination of many seemingly disparate things that you know are part of your DNA, or does your DNA emanate a powerful singular style of magic to which you give all your focus?

One focus of this book will be the bloodline initiation. As you work toward it you will discover, or more fully draw on, the magic of your deepest being, the magic that is especially yours, and thus especially powerful, and through which your mystical and creative aspects find self-expression.

The Third Road curriculum, oddly enough, teaches both a way of doing magic and how to do magic your own way, your own style. If you do magic your own way, you *are* doing Third Road magic. This is a tradition that doesn't trap you into following the leader in every last thing she does. Though I tell you not to adapt the training or rituals, the training and rituals draw out your own unique power in two ways: there will be a sometimes indefinable difference in the manner you do a Third Road rite, even though you follow its instructions to the letter, and if you choose to write your own rituals, you are in better shape to do so having studied Third Road.

It is somewhat like studying music: one learns scales and music theory then writes one's own songs. Or one sings other people's songs exactly as written but with one's own unique singing voice, making the songs one's own. Of course, many people without previous training in music write exquisite distinctive songs or sing in a wonderfully unusual manner. People attracted to Third Road often already have their own style of magic (and life) with or without magical training. For them, The Third Road enhances their already existing style. It will not always be apparent how the curriculum accomplishes all this—all things weave with one another seamlessly and miraculously—but the lessons that move you toward the bloodline initiation are part of how this is done.

The bloodline initiation is a process that happens over the training; it is not just the rite at training's end. Throughout this process the steps of bloodline initiation will be laid out for you. It is best not to cover them all in one month's lessons. All the different parts of initiation— again, initiation is not only a moment in time but a process to be enjoyed throughout the year's training—need to simmer between one step and the next. Also, they all need to weave with each other in their subtle (sometimes invisible) ways as the journey moves forward.

In the ritual below, you will learn the mysteries of your blood, bone, and ancestors. Blood? You might have Fey blood or human blood— well, we all have both, but more on that later—or be green blooded or orange blooded or tree blooded or have the blood of a rock or . . . on and on and on.

In the ancient prototypical shamanic European village that we all like to imagine existed, everyone was a witch. There was also a particular "village witch" who engaged in specific and advanced magic. While everyone in this imaginary village did magic to benefit people other than themselves, the village witch was different. She did overtly magical service for the community full-time and spent a lifetime of focus on magical studies not possible to those who also had to tend crops, raise children, and earn a living. (The village witch might also raise a garden and children, but she—or he—couldn't take on all the typical mundane responsibilities and still have time for her studies and community work. Her living was made by her community service.)

Whether you're a village witch or a regular witch, and whether you're doing advanced or early work, the magic you do is of your blood, even if you don't realize it: a person with Fey blood does Fey magic, a person with turtle blood does turtle magic, and so on. Thus village witches could have been Fey mages (*mage* is a term for magical practitioner) or human-blooded mages or green blooded or any of the other endless multitude of possibilities. The village witch did different, not better, work than the others. Everybody's own unique magic was needed in the community.

Some people think their magic is not important or powerful, especially if they are down-to-earth, which in fact is as powerful a magic as exists. I am very Fey. Some of my students have thought themselves inauthentic or less powerful because they were not just like their teacher. The magic of the Fey Folk is not better than human or orange or turtle-blood magic.

Faerie Tradition is simply a style of craft (*craft* is synonymous with *witchcraft*) touched to some extent by Fey magic. But it is first and foremost a human magic. Third Road was created for the human-blooded mage who loves the Fey. (I am as Fey as one can be, so my personal style of magic is very Fey, but I am still a *human* who loves the Fey. And, like all Third Road shamans, no matter how many nonhuman magics run in my veins, I must follow the magical urges of my human blood. I must do this to the same degree that I follow the longings of my Fey aspects, or I am in big trouble. We must be true to who we are, *all* parts of ourselves.)

The extent that the Faerie energy empowers each Third Roader's magic depends on one's blood. We all have a bit of Fey blood, and all need to be touched at least a bit by the Fey Folk, especially in this mechanized day and age. So, to some extent, all Third Road practitioners do Faerie magic. But sooner or later on the shamanic journey, one must find one's own blood and not chase after other people's destinies.

This society so consistently categorizes people within narrow definitions that it's hard to realize that the possibilities of what one's blood might be are endless. Human, Faerie, moon blood, blueberry blood. If we ignore our blood, whatever it is, in pursuit of dreams not our own, whether Faerie dreams, moon dreams, tree dreams, blueberry dreams, or money dreams, there will be heavy penalties to pay.

Christopher is a small man with a bushy beard, wild hair halfway down his back, and a propensity for gardening, dancing, wearing large floppy hats, and listening to the Grateful Dead. He came to me for a psychic reading and asked if he was Fey. I told him, "No, but I perceive that you are *something* otherworldly, and you need to figure that out and find your bloodline so you can do that kind of magic. Maybe you are a unicorn. You'll find out whatever you are."

I explained that many people prefer magic that is not otherworldly but is more of this realm. They find immense power and as strong results as one can imagine. I told Christopher, "I read that you will likely come to embrace two styles, one of the other realm and one of this earthy realm. Though that is true of all of us, in that we are all a bit Fey and all human, often the otherworldly part of one's true power is quite small. You, I suspect, will practice a lot of *some* power from one of the lands beyond the veil, as well as a great deal of something very earthy, like mud magic."

I added, only half in jest, "Maybe dirt runs in your blood." After all, Christopher seems to always have garden dirt under his nails and an earthy idea under his hat!

RITUAL

Blood, Bone, and Ancestors

In this exercise you will meditate on your skin, muscles, bones, and blood. You'll discover that your blood runs not only in your veins, but also flows back in time to its ancestral source. Thus you can find or better determine your spiritual and magical roots, the exploration of which will be part of your own unique brand of shamanic training and initiation.

You may have surprising ancestral sources. You might uncover Celtic roots or discover Faerie roots or imagine yourself to be the child of a dragon. Fanciful forms of identification have traditionally helped shamans in Celtic and other cultures inspire themselves to greater achievement and achieve a sense of wonder about the world they live in.

Sometimes, within a given step of a ritual, three dots (. . .) appear between phrases or sentences. This means that within the step are additional steps. Always follow the directions that precede three dots before pursuing any additional instructions that come after the dots.

Step 1. Peek ahead to "The Magic Formula" in the third month's lesson, and do its first step, the breathwork.

Step 2. If your eyes are not already closed, close them, then feel your skin, and focus on it. This might be hard to do. Shamanic techniques take a lot of time to perfect, and narrowing focus onto one's skin can be very difficult for some people. Don't worry; do what you can, no matter how little. An awareness of your clothing against your skin in a few places is fine, as is the vaguest picture in your mind of your *having* skin.

Step 3. Acknowledge that it is through your skin that you interact with all things. Do this however you choose. Here are some examples: Read the first sentence of this step several times; declare, "It is through my skin that I interact with all things"; visualize that sentence to be so.

Step 4. Acknowledge that it is your skin that keeps you separate from all things . . . Feel yourself a being who is thus separate from all things . . . Feel how quiet you are, contained within yourself. Again, you can feel this quiet self-containment any way you want, such as imagining it to be so, stating it to be so, or remembering a time when you felt happily self-contained. If you choose the latter, you might then imagine you feel that way right now; you could imagine your body relaxed, your mind serenely confident, or your spirit free from intrusion and fear.

Step 5. Feel your muscles and bones. One way to do this is to visualize them under your skin. Or you might move your body—the smallest possible amount, so that you are less likely to lose focus—as you picture your bones solid, dense, and providing a frame, which, in your imagination, your muscles maneuver, vividly filled with vitality.

Step 6. Feel your blood. One way to do this is to imagine it running in your veins.

Step 7. What does your blood tell you? Anything? Be open: see if you hear anything or if a thought pops into your mind or you get a sense of some feeling stirring in your body or idea peeking at you in your thoughts.

Step 8. Say:

> *My blood is of a river,*
> *my blood flows through the dark void of time and space,*
> *back to its source.*
> *What is its source?*
> *Where did it come from?*
> *What did my blood do at that time,*
> *in that place?*

Step 9. Again, visualize the blood running in your veins . . . Imagine it flows past you like a stream or brook, not in the sense it would if you were injured but in a miraculous, mystical pilgrimage . . . Imagine your blood flowing through a safe, comforting darkness.

Step 10. Imagine your blood arrives at its source. Perhaps you will suddenly get a picture of, or sense, an ancient people. Note what you can about them: their dress, actions, language, thoughts. Or maybe you will see a pool of water and get a sense of it being a mermaid lair and know yourself to be a mermaid at heart. The possibilities of what happens in this step are endless. You might encounter anything from a star in the sky to a specific race of people or species of animals to a plant to a mythical beast. You might not *see* anything. You might instead hear, smell, or simply get a sense of your ancestral source; modes of psychic perceptions are endless, and no one is better than another. An idea, word, or phrase that comes to mind might be your psychic perception, even if it makes no sense yet.

As always, in any step of a ritual, if you find that nothing happens or you don't understand how to apply the step's instructions, that is okay.

Having tried is all that counts, and that effort will move you toward your goal whether you see how that is so or not.

Step 11. Note what is happening at that far-off time and place: Are you doing anything? Are your ancestors? Are there words or sounds? Do you have any feelings or impressions?

Step 12. Are you given any gifts?

Step 13. Say to your ancestors, even if you experience nothing in this voyage, "I thank you for this visit."

Step 14. Imagine, picture, somehow be aware of your blood traveling a long distance back through time and space . . . After you have been aware of this a tiny bit, add the following to the picture, sensibility, or other awareness you have thus far created in this step: imagine that the space you're traveling to is dark, safe, and comfortable . . . Without letting go of whatever "picture" or experience you have thus far created in this step, imagine your blood flows through this space carrying any gifts you gained in step 12 . . . Be aware your blood flows all the way back to you, arriving with its new gifts.

Step 15. Feel your blood flow through you, replete with its new gifts and power.

Step 16. Feel your skin . . . Feel how it interacts with your clothes . . . Feel how it interacts with the seat under you . . . Feel how it interacts with the air.

Don't forget to follow up this exercise with the grounding ritual from last month. The grounding can be found easily: at the front of this book is a table of rituals, right after the table of contents.

Assignment: during week 4, do the ritual "Blood, Bone, and Ancestors," then immediately write down what you learn, what gifts you receive, and anything else you want.

Francesca's Helpful Hints for Better Magic

Focus is a ritual technique that one builds over time. At first, it is to be expected that during ritual the mind constantly wanders. All of one's life there will be times when this is true. Perfect focus is a goal, not a reality. We work hard to achieve it and never do.

As our focus strengthens, so does our magic. Our day-to-day life improves: tasks get done more quickly, we savor a moment's pleasure better, and—less distracted by worries about work and errands—we can focus on our bodies when making love.

What is true about focus is true of other magical skills. For example, if I ask you to imagine something and you can't, the very effort of trying will help you to be better able to do so next time, until bit by bit you excel at the use of imagination in ritual.

Many rituals in this book are to be done with closed eyes. As noted previously, you have to peek to read each step, but after you read a step, please shut your eyes again to execute the step you have just read. Unfortunately, opening and shutting your eyes might make it difficult to focus, but doing your best to not be distracted each time you open your eyes is, in the long run, a practice that builds up an exceptionally strong focus for ritual work.

When doing a ritual that requires physical actions—picking up a magic wand, lighting incense—whether with a group or alone, it helps to build focus if one does not talk about or engage in irrelevant issues at that time, and perhaps even holds silence. If Theresa, mid-rite, is lighting incense, and Roger and Nina chat, they may weaken Theresa's magic by distracting her—and thus weaken the magic of the group as a whole. They'll also lose focus for their own next step. In addition, ritual silence is an exercise in and of itself for building focus. If you choose to drink mother's milk again, think of this when you are pouring milk, then drinking it, then taking your next step, and so on.

Table of Assignments

Do these assignments during the second month:

The first week:
- Perform "Ritual for Common Sense and Inspiration" once. pg. 69

The second week:
- Enjoy "Ritual for Common Sense and Inspiration" again. pg. 69

The third week:
- Use "Ritual for Common Sense and Inspiration" once more. pg. 69
- Write down your own definitions of priesthood. pg. 80

The fourth week:
- Perform the ritual "Blood, Bone, and Ancestors," then write about that experience. pg. 93

The Magic Formula

Now that you have made a good start, the following exercise provides basics needed to do effective, safe rituals and to avoid some of the pitfalls found along any spiritual path. This information has not been needed up to now, though from now on it should be used with any ritual previously taught in this book.

RITUAL

The Magic Formula

"The Magic Formula" is a series of simple spells that, when put together, create effectiveness in all your spell work. It should be used before doing any shamanic ritual except a short, simple prayer, whether that prayer is a spontaneous chat with God during the course of your day or a formal address. Longer prayers accompanied by visualization or other "ritual" activities should be preceded by "The Magic Formula." (Teaching the ritual "Grounding" in the first month's lesson, I made the same differentiation, when discussing what types of prayer must be followed by grounding.) You may want to try "The Magic Formula" before a mundane event—such as a business meeting, the writing of a difficult letter, or even an activity done just for pleasure such as a party or a hike in the woods—to create peace of mind, success, enjoyment, and inner wisdom during that undertaking.

Step 1. Breathing Exercise:

step 1a. Close your eyes, then take four deep breaths. You needn't study yoga to do this step or hold a specific posture or anything else. Just four normal breaths. You would be taking them anyway! The difference is that you notice. Don't make a big deal out of noticing, either; these are really just a few deep natural breaths. Though more contrived manners of breathing have real value in certain situations—swimming competitions, certain types of Third Road magic—the point in this exercise is that our breath is one of our closest links to nature and one of the primary ways we take in the world. When our breaths are relaxed and natural, we become closer to nature and God.

step 1b. With four more deep breaths, relax your belly and throat. It is easy to have a full, deep, natural breath if we get out of our own way—simply by relaxing. It is better to avoid focusing on *creating* a relaxed breath, and instead focus on relaxing, which lets your body take over. Your body already knows how to breathe pleasantly.

step 1c. Optional: Singers have been known to run around the block to get their breath natural, normal, and ready for performance. It also relieves you of mental preoccupations, which will relax your breath and make for better ritual. Alternatives consist of brief: stretching; jumping jacks; shimmying of your body; yawning; or any combination of the options in this step. While you do this step, try to turn over your breathing to the body by continuing to relax the throat and belly, and breathe in sets of four.

You can prolong any of the breathwork steps. This might help when you are upset, particularly distracted, or preparing for a major or intimidating ritual. Or maybe you just enjoy doing breathwork.

Step 2. Pre-ritual Cleansing: Do a cleansing of anything inside yourself that might make you less than you could be during the upcoming ritual or event:

step 2a. Get comfortable and close your eyes, if you haven't done so already.

step 2b. Look for any and all inner blocks that might interfere with things like focus, pleasure, spirituality, effectiveness, power, a relaxed state of being, and being reasonable. Are you distracted by family or work worries? Are you so angry about what happened on your bus ride home that you can't focus or might be unable to feel joy in a rite or at a party to which you are applying "The Magic Formula"? Is fear or nervousness about an upcoming date preoccupying you before a ritual? (You could even use "The Magic Formula" before the date!) Do you think you have no chance of success in ritual work because you come from an alcoholic, poor family that failed at everything it tried? These examples—worry, anger, fear, nervousness, unsureness about one's abilities or chance of success—are some of the internal attributes that can interfere with a ritual or event. Find any such inner barriers, then pray:

step 2c. Recite, "Mother, if you deem it best, remove these blocks to love, joy, protection, power, and serving others."

Step 3. Invocation: *Invocation* means to invite God to be with you. Ask the Goddess and God, "Please be with me/us, and help, guide, and watch over me/us."

Step 4. Enjoy the ritual or event.

Step 5. Devocation: The important second half of invocation is *devocation,* which means saying good-bye to God: "Sweet, powerful Mother and good, mighty Father, I/we thank you for your help and say good-bye." The Gods are always with us, but we say good-bye because we are leaving both an aspect of them and a certain way of dealing with them.

Step 6. Do the ritual "Grounding" taught in the first month's lesson.

These simple steps do not involve tools like wands or chalices, yet they create effectiveness and joy in our magic and lives. You can prove this by using them; you'll watch your life improve. "The Magic Formula" takes lots of words to explain but can be done quickly.

Although "The Magic Formula" appeared in my previous book, *Be a Goddess!,* I have tailored it differently here to suit this specific training. If you have trained in *Be a Goddess!,* please use this book's "Magic Formula" during this training and see how it goes. You who did not work *Be a Goddess!* may find it fun to move on to that book when you're done with *Goddess Initiation.* The more one pursues a system of personal growth, the more one grows; and the more one grows, the more one enjoys life. One can reap the benefits of doing both trainings and of both magic formulas!

Assignment: to be done the first week. As of now, use "The Magic Formula" at the times described above. You can always find it quickly by referring to the table of rituals, which is at the front of this book. Each of the rites that make up "The Magic Formula" is listed on its own in the table of rituals.

Finding Your Good Faeries: Creating Support to Live Your Dreams

It can be hard to get oneself started on a spiritual journey. It *is* hard to continue it unaided. One should not have to get anything of value done without help. Usually one can't, no matter what you see in the movies. While there are exceptions, please don't think you are one. Please don't think this book is one. There are too many problems, pitfalls, hardships, and times of discouragement when you go it alone. And you *can have* a support system for, and feedback on, your work with this book. You can have the support you need to be happy and to join other spiritual seekers and priests in a network of inspiring fellowship and uplifting community!

Your support network—your Good Faeries—needn't be pagan or even religious and can consist of anything from a professional psychic to your mom.

A person needn't have a college degree or other official acknowledgment of expertise regarding life, spirituality, religion, psychology, magic, or anything else in order to be one of your Good Faeries. A Good Faerie *can* be someone who is officially recognized as an expert, and as such she or he may be exactly what you need, but it isn't required. It depends on the person and your needs. Sometimes one needs experts, other times one doesn't. You will need different types of help at different times in your life. And when you need support from someone with expertise, often the real experts are not those with titles but those who watch life with fresh eyes and are willing to do some hard thinking.

Resist thinking that no one wants to support you. People get a lot out of helping others, and there are endless reasons a person might do it. Perhaps she enjoys nurturing friends or finds you interesting and stimulating to talk to. Maybe she wants to establish mutual support and community just as much as you do. Mutual support is true community.

If you are working with a group, you can of course be Good Faeries for one another, but you may want more. The more the merrier.

The following is all it takes to give you the support you need. Here's what to look for in a Good Faerie:

A good heart. There is no greater wisdom.

The desire to be in touch with independent thinkers. A Good Faerie accepts people who think differently than they do. They do not try to force their own views or solutions on anyone. God's many faces are revealed in the faces of her human children. We are all magnificently unusual, and the Fey Folk have always supported humans to be themselves. God also shows herself in many forms in the types of religion or spirituality people practice (one can be spiritual without being religious) and how they practice it (one can be devout without attending church). God's wonderfully diverse nature is even reflected in a person who doesn't pursue spirituality. So your Good Faerie needs to feel reasonably okay about your being you.

The ability to provide some degree of safety when you talk to them. No one is perfect, but you have to feel *some* amount of assurance when sharing your Third Road journey. For example, you know there are at least some things that you can discuss with one of your Good Faeries without his being preachy, pushy, or dictating. Or even if you can't tell a certain Good Faerie all the details of a particular problem, you may be able to discuss it in general terms and explain to her that you feel overwhelmed and hopeless without her judging you as weak for your feelings. And she may then be able to give you solace and nurturing (much-needed support when one is striving for excellence).

There will never be a perfectly and completely safe person to whom you can tell your problems, triumphs, thoughts, and feelings. That would make them a perfect being.

As much as I love myself, and as many inner blocks to self-love as I have removed, I cannot always be compassionate and fair to myself. Sometimes I am so self-critical that I'm just plain old mean to myself, though I don't intend it as such. I may not even notice what I am doing. I might tell myself I should have done better when there was no way I could have and in fact should be giving myself a pat on the back for doing as well as I did under fire.

When I look at how far away I am from my ideal of how I want to treat myself, I have a realistic measure regarding how others treat me: I can see that we are *all* only human, hence *no one* is perfectly safe. I need to cut others the same slack I cut myself. Even a friend who deeply loves me and is truly aware and supportive will not measure up to unfair expectations. I remind myself, "How can I expect others to be so much better than me? Not that I am some high and mighty exceptional being for others to measure themselves against, but it is unfair of me to expect others to provide the impossible; I must measure them within the realm of human possibility."

It might be necessary to determine what sort of disclosures you feel comfortable making with a given Good Faerie. Maybe you cannot discuss certain topics with your mom but she is great with other subjects. You might need to be aware of *when* to share with a specific person: perhaps your best friend has an alcoholic sister, and, whenever they visit, your friend becomes too upset to be much help to anyone. Also, decide to what degree you can share with someone: maybe your roommate is good with feedback on sexual dilemmas as long as you don't tell her graphic details, which tend to shock her and leave her tongue-tied.

Mind you, all this talk about the limits of humankind might sound discouraging when you want help. Remember, what people do offer is outstanding; I want to make sure you get it, and you can if you leave behind unfair expectations. When you are open to it, you'll find that people will hold your hand when you face difficult inner blocks, listen to your problems almost endlessly, stay up all night with you if needed, cry with you over your tragedies, bear with you when you make absurd remarks while puzzling things out, and give so many types of support that I am convinced the world is filled with amazing individuals.

Assignment: to be done the first week. There is one last trait or set of traits to be looked for when you are picking your support team: Good Faeries should fulfill whatever you as an individual need in a supportive person. Now, write in your journal about what *you* need for support.

Some of you may need only a few minutes to do this assignment. Others may have special needs that demand an extensive list of traits necessary in their Good Faeries. But it might be best, even for them, if the list is short. If you list a few traits, you are more likely to find someone who has them or several people who, between them, have all the traits you write down. In this way, you'll have support in your life even if it isn't everything you want yet.

Writing a lengthy ideal portrait of who you want can go several ways. The list may keep you from settling for less than you deserve so that you find a fabulous friend. You may finally realize that your nearest and dearest don't give you *any* support and thus become motivated to change that. On the other hand, you may have such a high standard that no one can qualify! While waiting for the ideal friend to come along, you might refuse what is available. Don't accept all or nothing. You can always improve on things later. I suggest you get Good Faeries in your life *now,* and a brief list can be the first step. But, as always, you are the best judge of your situation. So complete this assignment as you think best.

And if you get *some* love in your life now, it can be a stepping-stone to getting more later. Some folks have to learn, bit by bit, to get support.

An essential part of creating and maintaining community, as well as living your dream life, is knowing that no one person can meet all our needs; and if we delay participation in life until we get the exact support we want from the perfect people we picture, there is no progress or community ever, and we stand unfulfilled and lonely.

Accepting too little or expecting too much are only two types of inner blocks that can keep one from cultivating community and support. Others will be addressed later.

When writing in your journal, keep in mind that it helps some people if one or more of their support team shares their economic background (or lifestyle choice or race, and so forth). If you grew up poor and start feeling a failure because the home you just bought isn't as grand as your boss's, a Good Faerie from your old neighborhood might be more likely to remind you to measure yourself not by your boss's standards but according to what you have accomplished with what you were given. If you are a person of color and you run up against prejudice among your co-workers, another person of color might be less likely to tell you it is all a figment of your imagination.

While you may not have a support system in place yet, I'd like to share with you the advantages of doing so. With this information, you'll be better equipped to choose your support team:

Good Faeries provide inspiration, motivation, and encouragement that keep you on your path. Writing *Be a Goddess!* and getting it published was one of the hopes and challenges of my shamanic journey. Though I believed in my bones it was something God wanted me to do, it was hard going. For example, there were ten long years between writing the book and selling it, and the manuscript received twenty rejections. That is typical enough for a first book, but it was still difficult to go through. A friend who believed in the project kept telling me the manuscript would be bought. That friend's kind words kept me doing the things I needed to do to see the book in print.

My friend and former professor, Kush, is one of my Good Faeries. Because he is a lunatic—in the best sense of the word. And he has made a place for himself in this world, a place in which he is respected, is of immense use to those around him, and is able to follow his dream. Because of his example, I was able to forsake my seemingly reasonable plan to become a college professor and instead teach the way I really wanted: I gave my full commitment to establishing a shamanic institute. At this time, this was unheard-of lunacy, especially the way I did it, which was with a mystical and poetic base instead of an academic foundation. Kush's example continues to inspire me to do what I believe in.

If you want similar support and don't know how to get it, here's an easy means. Phone, e-mail, or visit a Good Faerie and ask something along the lines of, "I want inspiration, motivation, and encouragement to keep on my path. Can you say a few encouraging words? It would mean a lot to me." Use what words you will. I had a friend tell me exactly what words she wanted to hear from me when she was about to face a challenging day!

Good Faeries provide you with feedback. This culture makes it hard to trust your inner voice. One of my dearest hopes as a teacher is that there will come a time when everyone hears their own inner wisdom and all people respect other people's rights to their own views. I work hard with clients and students to help them gain access to their own authority. *But* it is easy to swing to the other extreme. There was a man who trusted his inner voice and nothing else: Hitler. He thought God told him to kill anyone who didn't conform to his "master race." While Hitler is an extreme example, I offer it to show that thinking one's inner voice infallible is as dangerous as having no trust in it at all.

It is a bit of a predicament. For some people it is a long struggle to trust their feelings as accurate perceptions. And there is a certain internal "something" that happens when you are absolutely right. Nevertheless, that certain "something" can be wrong, wrong, wrong. There is no means, ever, to ensure infallibility.

People often ask me, "How do I know when my intuition is right (what God is telling me, if I am hearing God)?" I then teach them ways to strengthen the accuracy of their intuition (hear God more clearly) and to test whether their perceptions are wrong or right. I add that it is important to make as strong as possible their ability to hear God and their intuition, because these two skills are means to both personal authority and knowledge of what is right for themselves.

But I always add that in the end there is no way to ensure complete accuracy. I know God talks to me when I counsel my clients. But I listen with human ears, and human ears can't comprehend everything God is saying. As a psychic, I am as accurate as you can get. Nevertheless, I know *I make a lot of mistakes during every session, because that is the nature of human perception, whether psychic, visual, or intellectual.*

So embodied feedback—input from a person still on this plane as opposed to from a spirit—is necessary as a check and balance to inner guidance, providing groundedness, ethics, and safety. Anything intuitive, including guidance from a spirit, can be misunderstood. Even masters of any form, whether spiritual, psychic, or academic, need the basic discipline of asking for and receiving feedback.

I've made it a priority to have people in my life who'll tell me if they see me fooling myself. Please have such people in *your* life. Maybe even tell one or a few of your Good Faeries you want this. Remember, this feedback is not the same thing as attacking or shaming you for your shortcomings. This is compassionate support given with the understanding that we all make mistakes and need to help each other if we are to refrain from repeating those errors.

If you can't find anyone who is so forthright, don't worry. Ask the Goddess to provide the best support team for you. And if it is not all you want yet, it will be eventually!

I ask for ideas from people without knowing if they might have the answers I need. Who knows what might happen? I like it when people give bad answers or silly suggestions. After hearing them I might suddenly hear the relevant answer in my own mind.

Good Faeries help out when things are scary, confusing, or difficult. Sometimes emotions run high. Maybe doing this work unearths pain or anger about a betrayal that happened in your childhood, and the feelings are so intense you feel overwhelmed. Venting or talking it out with a friend or therapist can relieve your sense of being at the mercy of your feelings and may help you grow from the experience and heal from your childhood. A therapist might be part of your support group.

Or maybe one has a psychic experience that is frightening or bewildering or that needs to be better understood. A witchy friend or professional psychic might provide you with what you need.

Or in sincerely striving toward inner growth or outer achievements, one can be trying and trying and getting nowhere. Friends, therapists, spiritual counselors, and psychics can help. (With regard to the counseling I do, I use the terms *spiritual counselor* and *psychic* synonymously. However, I want to differentiate between the two here so that you know that not all spiritual counselors are psychics, and vice versa. Thus in looking for support you know you have both options at your disposal!)

The "Supplementary Magical Resources" at the end of this book might help you find Good Faeries. The section suggests ways to find pagans in your area, provides an on-line list of people exploring The Third Road, and lists contact information about my services as a spiritual counselor, whether for one appointment or for ongoing support.

Paulo, Patricia, and Karl Do What It Takes

Paulo told his therapist that no matter what he tried he could not finish the book he was writing about volunteers in American community centers. The therapist showed Paulo how he was sabotaging himself: Paulo felt, on an unconscious level, that his opinions weren't worth reading. So he would delay writing—straightening up his desk, running errands, reading other people's books—until it was time to go to his job as a taxi driver. The therapist helped Paulo realize how absurd it was to have a low opinion of his own ideas: he had an excellent track record when it came to useful opinions. As a volunteer at his local community center, he had organized a successful after-school program for latchkey kids. He himself decided how to do effective outreach, the best ways to fund the program, and what the program would offer young attendees. Once the therapist had helped Paulo see how strong his community leadership had been, he was able to stop procrastinating and finish his book; his writing problem was solved. A therapist can often help you make that crucial breakthrough when all else fails.

Patricia dealt with her block to finishing writing a book by going to the same therapist. Whenever Patricia sat down to write, she became too upset to proceed, without knowing the cause. With the therapist she was able to see that writing always brought up feelings of grief: her mother had died when Patricia was a child, and because the act of writing always brought her in touch with her deepest parts, the grief inevitably surfaced. Not recognizing this sorrow as such, Patricia simply got too confused and overwhelmed to write. Once the therapist helped Patricia name and face her feelings, she was able to make headway in the manuscript. But it was insufficient progress. She was able to write for only very brief stints.

Patricia asked if I might help. Sometimes a spiritual counselor can help when a psychologist can't. As explained earlier, the ancient shaman went through immense personal healing through a spiritually and psychically based process, not a psychologically based one. While not a substitute for therapy, sometimes spiritual or psychic counseling can address a problem that is spiritual or psychic rather than psychological.

I told Patricia, "I intuit that you feel it sinful to move past your grief completely, that you think to do so would make you a bad daughter. This shame is happening on an unconscious level." Patricia responded with "My god, you're right!" I then taught her how to use "Kissed by a Star" to be free of her shame. Thus the realization she gained with me did not lie fallow; she moved past her deep sorrow. In the case of Patricia's writing block, she found that using both a therapist and a spiritual counselor did the trick. Use all the tools you can.

I had a Christian client, Karl, who had done years of therapy but still couldn't hold a job. When counseling Karl, I read (by *read* I mean psychically perceived or heard God tell me) the following: Karl's Christian religious upbringing had been shame based, restrictive, and punishing; yet Karl had an authentic need to have Jesus as part of his life. I also read that Karl, hoping to find a more genuine relationship with God, had gone to the other extreme: he decided that all structured institutions and events, whether a church service, baseball game, or business, were reflections of that cruel, tyrannical religious upbringing. Once he heard all that I had read, I was able, bit by bit, to help him differentiate between healthy and unhealthy forms of structure. We did rites to help him stop rejecting the healthy ones. He not only found and kept a job he loved but also joined a Christian congregation in which Jesus' true message of love, kindness, and tolerance was expressed.

If you are working through a trauma that occurred in your life, it may be of great value to you to find a related support group. A rape survivor can find validation, comfort, and wisdom with others who have gone through the same thing. A member of the armed forces who has suffered the horrors of war may need to find a veterans' support group. Perhaps you were a soldier who had to kill someone in the line of duty. Few who did not go through that would understand that *you* were a victim of sorts: in your extreme youth and low economic bracket you saw no other choice than to join the military; once in battle you realized it was kill or be killed; and now you need healing from that awful experience.

Most people—and I include the finest, best, kindest, and most compassionate people imaginable—do not have the tools needed to help their loved ones through life's true horrors. Read that sentence three times, please, to really get its point. When a person has suffered rape, incest, the trauma of war, or other comparable horrors, family or close friends will usually not be there for them, especially if the event is recent. Perfectly wonderful, compassionate people fail in this regard. It is not that they are bad. Again, I am talking about the best of people, many of whom, for various reasons, are ill equipped to handle crisis in this context; they may say or do the wrong things, even things that are horribly damaging, without intending to do so.

This is more the case if the traumatizing event is recent as opposed to in the far past. The fresher it is, the harder it can be for friends and family to hear without responding inappropriately. In such cases, a support group of others with similar issues or the professional help of a therapist might be in order. Of course, you might discover one or two of your friends are exceptions to the above. That's great. Remember, I said *many* people, not *all*—but don't fault your friends if they aren't exceptions!

While the material on Good Faeries may not seem relevant to you right now, you have gained a lot of knowledge about getting and using crucial support. You can use this information at any point throughout your entire lifetime's journey toward being happy, whole, and a god.

Assignment: to be done over weeks 2, 3, and 4. Find your Good Faeries. This process varies from person to person. You may already know who you want on your team. Or you may have good support in place but want to add a person or two for specific things. Or you may feel isolated. Here are some ideas:

After you do the earlier assignment about what type of support you want, look through your address book. I often forget the skilled folks I have access to until I go through my address book or database. (I have a computer in my shaman's hut. I also have two cats, one of whom, Mud, thinks *she* is the real shaman. But I don't compete with her. I think she's right! Well, actually I think the other cat who lives here, Teenie, is far wiser than Mud, but they both outstrip me. While I am writing this book, trying to convey what bits of wisdom I have eked out of the earth over my lifetime, they are smart enough to spend the greater part of their days sleeping, and thus are far better teachers than me!)

There are exceptions to the list I gave of qualities that make up a Good Faerie. For example, someone who is set in their ways and doesn't understand independent thinkers can be just what you need at a certain moment or for certain things. For example, someone who thinks that anyone who practices anything other than Christianity is immoral may not be an appropriate person to whom to disclose your pagan spirituality. But he or she might love to cheer you on as you strive toward the outer manifestations of your spirituality, such as finding a better job, leaving a bad marriage, or returning to college. These can be intimidating or otherwise difficult things to accomplish, and some sympathetic bolstering from a relative or friend can be vital. So don't stick to the list rigidly.

Here are a few more suggestions about Good Faeries.

You may only find one Good Faerie. That is great!

Though books are no substitute for personal contact, I find I am better able to walk my desired path, and am more inspired, consoled, and confident, after reading certain authors. The reading list at the back of this book might be some support for you.

How to approach someone you want as a Good Faerie depends on both them and your personal style. You needn't tell a Good Faerie that you are exploring paganism if she is not pagan and your announcement might confuse her too much. Just ask for help with a specific problem when you need it. You needn't even tell a pagan friend that he is your Good Faerie. Again, just ask for help when you need it. Usually with pagans, it can be fun and powerful to let them in on the whole story; some people will feel honored and enjoy their new title.

Getting support will become easier with time. Once we do something, it becomes easier and easier to integrate that practice into our lives.

You may not need to draw on your Good Faeries yet. Maybe all you need at this point is to select your team. That way, they will be in place for you when you need them. Just knowing this may give you incredible power to keep going.

While I will continue to point out the ways Good Faeries can help you, I strongly urge you to take the initiative throughout this training and ask your Good Faeries for any support that might come to mind and for all the support you want!

I suggest you don't delay this assignment just because you have three weeks. Three weeks may give you a leisurely pace. And what with other assignments, they might all pile up if you delay.

I am Absolutely Safe in the Goddess's Care

No matter how hard we try, we cannot always have a Good Faerie in our lives. There are moments or even long periods when circumstances isolate us. Perhaps not one of our friends picks up the phone no matter how many people we dial. Or you are a stay-at-home mother of two preschool children, with just enough time to do this training but little opportunity to talk to an adult about it. Or perhaps you are a merchant marine working on ships at sea for many weeks, without a close friend on board. But God is *always* available. And She will give us everything we need.

Assignment: as of the third week, make the following prayer to the Goddess each morning.

MORNING PRAYER TO THE MOTHER

Please protect me in my magic and life, guide my thoughts and deeds, and give me the power to live life according to Your generous wisdom.

A short prayer is easy to do each morning. It takes seven seconds to say, and if you don't want to take the time to put this book by your bed each night before you go to sleep, it take two minutes to find a scrap of paper, write the prayer on it, and put it by your bed. (I've made this prayer take about an hour by using fifty-nine minutes thinking about how hard it might be to do it, how I am so tired I should not expend the energy, etc.) The prayer's brief simplicity means than after a week or so you will have it memorized without even trying.

This prayer, though not performed at the same moment as "The Magic Formula," is in fact part of it. In other words, doing this prayer each morning adds crucial elements to "The Magic Formula." You were introduced to "The Magic Formula" during the first week so that you could get used to it before adding this newer element to it.

This prayer is a strong part of your path in and of itself. With God walking next to us, at our backs defending us, in our hearts guiding us, there is nothing we cannot achieve, nothing that can stop us, nothing that is too much for us. With God in our life in the specific ways requested in "Morning Prayer to the Mother," we can find wholeness instead of falling into such pitfalls as spiritual arrogance. Among the many forms of this arrogance is one in which a person thinks harshly of others who have not done as much spiritual work as he has. That is dangerous!

Don't be surprised if this prayer has unexpected results. Shortly after using this prayer for the first time you may get a call from a good friend asking you to dinner. Or you may bump into an old buddy who walks with you for a while as you are on your way to work. Or your pet cat who loathes being petted may become very cuddly and sit in your lap all day, keeping you good company. You have asked the Lady to be with you and to walk with you and to sit with you. She has any number of interesting ways to answer requests—anything from a cat acting for Her to something as subtle as a sense of well-being that you gain after your request, either immediately or in time. Perhaps you see a way to break a bad habit. Or an idea that's long eluded you suddenly pops into your head. (Whether the needed idea relates to motherhood, art, or marketing, She can send it! I give marketing solutions to clients all the time!)

The simple things asked for in this prayer provide some of the greatest powers; all parts of our lives are radically improved by this prayer. One such way this prayer might manifest God in your daily life is that you might notice how you are getting in your own way—banging your head against a brick wall instead of looking for the door. God is very smart, there is none smarter, so She can point out when we are not choosing the easier ways to live our lives.

Removing Blocks to Self-Healing, Prosperity, and Great Sex

JOURNAL EXCERPT

Ten months ago I made prayer to understand sacrifice. I've been saying what a dumb prayer that was, because I got what I prayed for. And I've had to learn this lesson not in just an abstract meta-physical way but through a grueling ten months of life events. It's been hell week for ten months. But I'm getting the lesson: I need to learn to love myself better.

You can remove just about any inner block that keeps you from success and happiness, for example: low self-esteem, self-doubts, paralyzing fear, self-sabotage, self-destructive beliefs.

Sometimes it hurts to grow, and we have to give up something precious and important, such as a dear friend or a rare business opportunity. On the other hand, *sacrifice* comes from the Latin word for "to make sacred." Sometimes the true sacrifice is giving up the blocks that *keep us from having* what is precious and important, giving up something that keeps us from being happy and healthy.

The ritual in this section can be used on inner blocks to receiving anything from a thrilling romance to wealth—if thrilling romance and wealth are truly what will make you happy and whole. We can offer up our inner blocks, our "impurities," *sacrifice* them so that they be made hale and whole, "made sacred," once again. We can sacrifice the outer blocks to happiness—a low-paying job, an abusive relationship—so that they, whether person, object, or situation, can be made sacred by taking their right place in the universe. This ritual can be used on the inner blocks, after which one can have the power to walk away from—or battle—the outer impediments.

You can also apply this ritual to inner blocks discussed in the first lesson: fear of personal growth, including the growth that a shamanic journey demands; and characteristics that might drive you to create unnecessary problems in your life and shamanic training. Here are examples of such traits. Let's start with some self-defeating beliefs:

- "Suffering or martyrdom is the only way to grow."
- "You must be miserable in order to be spiritual."
- "Drama is change."

Sometimes a person creates a lot of hubbub in the mistaken belief that big sparks flying about, causing disruption and misery in everyone's life, are the equivalent of real change. Joe had an affair because he was sick of "not feeling alive." The affair in the long run only fed his pattern of unsatisfying sex. The real solution was to face the lack of communication in his marriage; it was not his wife but his inability to talk with her that caused a lack of lively, fulfilling sex. The affair with its ensuing problems—sleepless nights, tears and shouting, longings and misgivings—made it seem like something was really going on, a real change was in the works. Joe left his wife to live with his new mistress. Of course, nothing changed. Soon he was as sexually bored as ever. Such events are commonly called *drama*.

Drama can be an attempt to avoid real change without the person in question having any awareness of this subconscious motivation. This is one place where feedback from another person is invaluable!

- "I'm so different I can't . . . (finish the lessons, overcome obstacles, 'make it,' follow my dreams, be happy, go back to school)."

I beg you, if you have read this belief and thought, "But I really am too different," please use this ritual on what you just thought! Trust me on this, I have gone through it!

- "To change by doing this training (following my star, improving my confidence) means loss of all company."

Another example of a belief that makes personal growth harder than it has to be is having a hyperheroic sense of what a challenge actually is. This makes one prone to taking on bigger challenges than one can possibly conquer, such as trying to grow too fast or making a job change during both a divorce and child custody battle when the career move isn't necessary or can be deferred.

We often don't see our need for inner cleansing. For example, though we might believe on an intellectual level that sexual desires are healthy and normal, another part of us may believe or feel otherwise. Intellectual realizations are not enough. Self-defeating beliefs, fears, and other feelings that contradict our reasonable thoughts can drive us ruthlessly. This includes the healthiest of us.

Legitimate fears—as well as anger and guilt—are healthy and sometimes protect us, but when they rule us, we need to get rid of them or at least not be controlled by them.

Even when we cleanse away blocks, sometimes they reemerge years later. This does not necessarily mean our earlier work failed, although *it often will feel exactly like that.* Perhaps a block is deeply ingrained; even though work on it nets great results, or at least improves things, eventually another layer or aspect of the problem might come forth to be healed. Don't be quick to say, "Oh, I know better than to be afraid of a punishing God," or, "I got over thinking 'It is not okay to take good care of myself' years ago. I am too sophisticated to worry about such things anymore."

Intellectual beliefs that one has fought hard to gain are important blessings. Let's say your parents were rigid in their religious beliefs and you had to fight the good fight to come to your own outlook. And that left you with the hard-won, valuable intensity that can accompany a belief one has struggled to gain. But your intensity, like many valuable traits, is a two-edged sword. It helps you stand up to those who try to control you, but it can also be used to resist a layer of healing needed before you can embody, or better embody, those precious beliefs in your actions and reap their benefits. If you believe that sex is sacred but you aren't sexually fulfilled, never ask anyone out on a date, or have intimacy issues, try not to use the wonderful intensity of your intellectual belief to resist questioning whether you have fears or other blocks that need to be cleansed before you can act according to how you think.

You can apply this ritual to any inner block that keeps you from allowing others to give you support. When discussing Good Faeries, I talked about accepting too little from people. You can cleanse away that

self-defeating behavior. Other traits that interfere with community include: not thinking you deserve support, a fear of intimacy that is so
great that you let no one help you ever, shame that you need help.

You already know the ritual I have been describing and needn't learn
a new one. All you need to do is to make a minor adaptation to step 3 of
the ritual "Kissed by a Star: A Spiritual Cleansing," in the first month's
lesson. (My favorite magical tool is a paper clip. It is a little bit of God:
with a paper clip I never lose my place. Before reading farther, you may
want to put a paper clip on this page and the page with "Kissed by a
Star." In fact, each month you can paper-clip all the pages with assignments to quickly find your homework.)

Adaptation of step 3: The focus is no longer on those things inside
yourself that keep you from nurturing your soul. Though, of course, you
can continue to apply the rite to such things whenever you want, in this
newer version the focal point is *anything* inside yourself that is giving
you trouble with *any part of your life*. This new version gives you a far
wider usage of the ritual.

So you can use this ritual on any fear that stands in your way, such as
fear of success, power, mockery, saying no to your sister when she asks
for favors and you are too busy to help, telling your sweetheart you want
to try something new in bed, never feeling happy again.

It often helps to cleanse a specific, rather than a general, fear. To
be rid of your fear of speaking in public you might begin by cleansing
your fear of giving a toast at an upcoming wedding. Should the fear
return the next time you are about to speak publicly, you can apply the
rite again to that situation. One might think it is always more powerful
to cleanse the general, but when we focus on something specific and of
immediate or upcoming relevance, it becomes more pressing and thus
the fear is more present. In this way, we can touch the heart of the problem, and—ta da!—the rite might cleanse away the general, underlying
fear.

This rite can cleanse away any self-defeating belief that one may
have: I am not pretty enough to get a date; nice guys like me never get
the girl; I have no special talents or skills; it is selfish to want a room of
my own; my penis (or bust) is too small; there's no point in trying, I'll

only fail; who am I to think I can rule the world—okay, I had to slip that in.

This all-purpose cleansing can rid one of other negative traits and bad habits, such as procrastination, shame, lack of self-acceptance, confusion, guilt, anger, inability to feel emotions, lack of serenity, indecisiveness.

Whenever you do the rite, cleanse only one block, not all the blocks you can think of regarding a specific event or issue in your life. Just one block regarding that specific issue or event or one block that causes you problems in many ways.

Here are examples of the gift that might come to you during step 8. If you let go of a fear of public speaking, you might be filled with confidence in your charisma and wit. If you cleanse a belief that you are not pretty enough (not thin enough, not "well-endowed" enough), you might see how absolutely attractive, special, and desirable you are!

Assignment: use this ritual once a week during weeks 2, 3, and 4.

Table of Assignments

Do these assignments during the third month, except where otherwise specified:

The first week:
- Starting now, and henceforth, apply "The Magic Formula" according to the instructions in the third month's lesson. pg. 99
- Write in your journal about what you, as a unique individual, need in a person to whom you turn for support. pg. 102

The second week:
- Start finding your Good Faeries. pg. 108
- Perform the ritual "Kissed by a Star: A Spiritual Cleansing" once. pg. 116

The third week:
- Continue finding your Good Faeries. pg. 108
- Perform the ritual "Kissed by a Star: A Spiritual Cleansing" again. pg. 116
- As of now, recite "Morning Prayer to the Mother" every morning. pg. 110

The fourth week:
- Finish (so to speak) finding your Good Faeries. pg. 108
- Perform the ritual "Kissed by a Star: A Spiritual Cleansing" again. pg. 116

A Search for the Goddess Within and Without

The Goddess is a sensual god. She is the far-reaching night sky embracing us. She is the wind blowing away our sorrow and fatigue. The earth is the Goddess Herself. We can live close to, and as, God in all life's daily ways—cooking, lovemaking, sleeping. When you feed your own body healthy food, you feed the god you are. When you refuse to accept treatment that is disrespectful, you respect the god you are. If you run from yourself, you cannot find the god within or without.

The Goddess is in everything. Our life in the world with its mundane responsibilities and joys is the true spiritual quest, as opposed to so-called shamanic journeys that take us away from those same challenges and satisfactions.

In loving or hurting anyone or anything—friend, ozone layer, mother, or minority—we love or hurt the Gods. Even a city is Her, its bright lights the embroidery on Her sleeves as She beckons, "Let me dance for you. Please keep me company. Don't pass me by and neglect me." In recognizing the sacredness of our duty to our mate, children, parents, and community, we meet God in all Her beauty and receive Her bounty.

Assignment: to be done the first week. Read the following instructions—"The Goddess's Face"—three times. Reading them is a ritual. Don't worry about whether you understand what you're supposed to accomplish by reading it. Don't force a realization. Don't worry about whether the material makes sense. Just read it. Even if you read this to yourself silently, do so in a self-loving voice. When an assignment is to be done several times in one week, don't crowd it all into one sitting or day. It is ideal to spread it out over the week.

THE GODDESS'S FACE

Look into God's face: do not sketch or paint a picture of the tree you behold. Look at the tree. Can you still have any worry, think your problems are problems?

Look into God's face: see the expanse of a green field; you can entrust yourself to God's plans.

Look into God's face: watch the birds—rustling in fallen leaves as they gather food, scurrying on the ground chirping—and smile at your foolish worries.

Look into God's face: watch the middle-aged woman hurrying on her way to work—you can know you are of a communion of souls who are in pain, who struggle, who move the world toward an eventual state of holiness.

Look into God's face.

The Path of Power

As was stated earlier, initiation is only one step on the path of power. The path itself is a means for you to learn how to:

1. Live fully; act in a responsible, moral manner; be happy; and serve others
2. Do those things in accordance with your own definition of *fully, moral, happy, serve,* and so on.

The sort of selfhood embodied by both items 1 and 2 is vital to any quest and is the essence of these lessons.

Assignment: during week 2, write a bit about your own definitions of *fully, moral, happy, serve,* and so forth. If nothing comes to mind about every item, that is fine. Instead of writing down definitions, you may find yourself writing about your lack of personal definitions. Great!

You may want to reread the assignment in the second month's lesson on writing in your journal about your definitions of priesthood; it has instructions for writing assignments in general. (A brief review: write as little or as much as you want, even one phrase is good; you can always write more later. You've got your whole life to fulfill these writing assignments, so feel good about writing only a bit for now. If you sit down and nothing comes to you, that is good, too.)

Don't criticize your writing style. The point is not whether you are a "real writer" (whatever that awful phrase means) or not. Your mandate is simply to do the assignment. Besides, you may be a writing genius and not know it yet! Many a writer has thought their own words profoundly poor, only to be later acclaimed as exceptional, innovative, and critical.

Our Journey to Ourselves

We live in times that demand we forsake outdated modes of power, teaching, and leadership.

Though less widespread than it used to be, a common leadership, teaching, and ministerial mode is "I will teach you the right way to do things. You know nothing." While I do teach ethics, magical techniques, and the like, in a sense all I do is teach you what you already know. All a shamanic teacher does is draw out your own unique wisdom. I might show you how to better and more joyously do what you already do, but it is still your essential self I am coaching rather than trying to eradicate.

For both student and teacher, real power is gained not from lording it over students but from helping them come to God and their own true nature. Ultimately, no one can train you for self-initiation. I strive for ethical integrity as a teacher by trying to empower your *own* process, both by being a guide through it and supplementing it. In the final analysis, there are times when it is up to you, times when you stand with only God as your guide.

If you have not already learned to take responsibility for yourself, you can do so bit by bit. This book teaches you how, in ways that might often seem to have nothing to do with that goal. Use your common sense, and think for yourself, and you'll be on your way.

Our good Father, whom we need not fear, can help us on our journey to ourselves.

Many people grow up without the support of a healthy father figure. They carry that void with them into adult life and may be unable to "father" themselves internally or rely on a *supportive* God.

One way this void manifests relates to receiving support to succeed in the world. When a child falls down, an ideal mother might be quick to say, "Oh, well. I love you anyway. Come home with me, and I'll kiss the boo-boo, and if you want you can stay home with me as long as you want." She provides a much-needed comfort, haven, and unconditional love. A healthy father might offer a very different kind of devotion. When a child falls down, the ideal father refrains from the all-too-typical "For crying out loud, can't you do anything right? You are a jerk!" Instead, he says with unconditional love, "Let me help you up. And you know what? I *know* you can do it right this time. I'll even show you how if you need me to. Go for it, kiddo!"

With this sort of father in mind, I wrote the following prayer for my student Cam, who had been pushed by the harsher aspects of this society until she had fallen down.

I offer it to you in the hope that if you fall down this prayer might help you find the Celtic male deity, a loving Father who will support you. In many ways we can be toppled, whether momentarily or for a long time. For example, we might face discouragement, tremendous weariness of spirit, immobilizing sadness, unshakable cynicism, or loss of trust in everything and everybody. In the course of life one might face things like job loss, prejudice, slander, or emotional abuse.

You can even use this prayer when you are just feeling low. My loving Father wants to be used when I have caved in even for a moment or even *feel* as if I had fallen down.

PRAYER TO THE LOVING FATHER

I have been knocked down and ridiculed.
Lift me up back onto my feet.

People have tried to shame me.
Walk with me so that I can be proud.

They have tried to stop me from being healthy.
Stand by me while I make myself whole.

They have tried to keep me from my power.
Show me my power,
which is inside me already, reflecting yours.

Blessings on you, Father.

Assignment: during the second week, use this prayer once whether you think you need it or not. Having discovered its power, you will be able to use it if you wish, as you wish, whenever you wish, throughout your life. The more you use it, the more its powers will reveal themselves to you.

Though you can say the prayer without any inner or outer problem in mind, it's also helpful to apply it to a very specific feeling or event. For example, I spoke earlier of the need to heal after being at an initiatory gate where one's chance to be powerful was stolen. Being robbed of an important chance to come to power can devastate someone. That gate can be a ritual—or an important moment along any spiritual or religious path—that a dominating teacher or priest mishandles. The gate can also be a life event, such as delivering one's baby with a doctor who is disempowering. You can say the prayer with such healing in mind.

Initiation as a Priestess; a Shaman Is a Servant

JOURNAL EXCERPTS

Last night I realized that there will always be the shadow of
death. But you need to keep being of some help to those around
you. You need to act like an adult. You need to keep doing your

work. Do you accept that hum of death and continue on despite it? Yes.

Death makes me present. That alone justifies sacrifice.

The shamanic initiation—remember, initiation includes the work that precedes and follows the moment usually recognized as the initiation—makes you a new person or deepens your existing positive aspects. Initiation helps you find the god that you are. It also makes one a priest or deepens one's priesthood.

In our nonhierarchical religion, titles and pomp do not make priests; priesthood is a function. A priest is someone who, committed to service, gets work done. A shaman is a *servant*.

I advise you not to focus on the title of "priestess" but instead to *be* a true priestess, actually ministering by, for example, patiently listening to a friend's litany of complaints about his new job, collecting clothes for the homeless, making documentaries that inspire social change, or cooking wholesome meals for your children. Or telling jokes that make people laugh. Laughter is sacred. The Celts understood that pleasure is sacred in and of itself; pleasure needn't have meaning, or a goal other than pleasure, to be holy. Any fun that doesn't hurt anyone is sacred. The point is, if you want to be a priest, minister to the world around you. (With an exception: perhaps you cannot help others until you do a lot of work on yourself. In which case, your main focus—and your priesthood—briefly or even for several years, will be self-healing.)

Some people spend their entire lives gaining titles, degrees, and prestigious positions and actually *accomplish* little. Don't use them as models or feel inferior. Do your work instead. Some profound community servants have religious titles, some do not; Laura Nyro, the remarkable songwriter, did not read sheet music.

Service fulfills one truly, deeply, and in ways sex never can. I am blessed in that, when I make love, I enjoy a sustained pitch of ecstasy, bring the spiritual depths of my being into play, and am left profoundly satisfied in body and soul. So my comparison of sex and service means something. And service surely fulfills in ways that money, possessions, romance, and prestige never can.

Serving others keeps me sane and happy. Being able to give to others is one of the most profound gifts my God has given me, and it is a main focus of my life because it makes me thoroughly joyous.

Assignment: during week 3, say the following prayer three times. This prayer is a step toward reaping the joy, spiritual depth, and self-healing that come only from serving others. Everything from our self-esteem to our romantic life is improved when we serve others. Honest! In the following meditation, we pray for others and in doing so pray for ourselves:

PRAYER TO FIND AND CELEBRATE THE
SELF THROUGH SELFLESSNESS

*In seeing you, who are planet, animal, friend, stranger,
rock or tree, I see myself.*

*In pleasing you, who are planet, animal, friend, stranger,
rock or tree, I please myself.*

*In loving you, who are planet, animal, friend, stranger,
rock or tree, I love myself.*

*There is no point at which I stop being you.
There is no time in which your fate is not mine.
There is no hope that can exist unshared.*

*There is no sacrifice made
that does not return wonders and bounty to me many times over.*

*God, grant me the powers to serve myself by serving others.
Grant me the powers to join in the dance of life.*

Titles and Pomp Do Not a Priestess Make

JOURNAL EXCERPTS

*The Goddess has all things in Her. God is an aspect of Her,
though in no way inferior to Her. She beheld Him and lusted for*

Him. However, She has no need of Him in the sense of needing Him to complete Herself. She does however need love. But She will have it, there is no doubt of that. Therefore, there is no giving needed except what we need to give just for the sake of giving, for the love of giving. Love and sacrifice need each other. That is the real *need.*

*We need (*need, *as in have a* need *inside ourselves that must be fulfilled) to heal each other. Therein lies passion, whether for sex, writing, or saving the world.*

By embracing opposites, The Third Road teaches that contradictions of the above "Prayer to Find and Celebrate the Self Through Selflessness" are equally valid. For example, there are unhealthy sacrifices, and there are times to withdraw and focus only on one's own needs or even one's pleasures. Sometimes we have to ignore what others want or need and please only ourselves; sometimes, no matter how painful it might be or how much we might want to help, we have to leave others to their own fate. And yet when we do these very things, we are still serving others! For one thing, without this self-care, we lack the stamina and calm to help people. For another, as long as a person's pursuit of health is not based in a lifestyle or mind-set geared only toward self-seeking, the health one attains causes the health of all others. The entire human race and all other parts of this planet are woven together in what you might view as a larger organism; if any part of that larger body is ailing, the rest of the body suffers illness.

One must avoid unhealthy ways of giving.

Marlina: Learning When Sacrifice Is Healthy and When to Say No

Marlina was filled with uncertainty and self-doubt. Her boyfriend of many years, Albert, would not marry her. She wanted to move on from the relationship but felt it cruel, hurtful, and selfish to do so when Albert explained that he couldn't give himself fully to Marlina because his work as a doctor was so demanding.

Marlina called me for phone counseling from a small backwoods town in Europe where Albert tended to people too poor to otherwise receive medical care. Marlina told me, "Albert's clinic takes all his time. He's devoted to the project, and if he doesn't give it his constant attention the clinic will close. I hinted at a breakup. He said that my support gave him the strength to continue his valuable work. I don't work at the clinic; he wants me by his side at home.

"All my life I've dreamed of marriage and having children. That is one of the few directions that has ever made any sense to me. That and continuing my work as a midwife. I want to spend a lifetime with Mr. Right. But I feel I should support Albert's commitment to his clinic; his work is so important.

"When he said that we can't let things develop into marriage it upset me badly. Maybe I'm too clingy, too concerned with whether we end up married. But I think I was put on this earth to be a wife, mother, and midwife."

I responded, "There are many commitments: to marry and to build a family; to make the coffee every week for an Alcoholics Anonymous meeting; to be in a lifelong nonmarried relationship; to be celibate. One can commit to sacrifice a personal life for community service or to go to school. Albert has a commitment to stay unmarried. You respect that.

"But that's not where your health is. He's splendid—but you are, too, and you need to take care of yourself."

Saying no to sacrifices that are not ours to make, whether for strangers or loved ones, can be hard. Even when said with a loving intent, and with health in mind, the person to whom we say no may not want to listen or be able to understand. It may estrange him. But maybe he would become estranged anyway if you kept giving him more than you should, or in ways other than you should.

I told Marlina, "I believe in engaging in life, participating in the heart of existence. In my case, a commitment to monogamy is part of that. For someone else, their idea of being engaged in life might mean celibacy or a nonmonogamous marriage. Or ice hockey! God wants people to follow their passion, whether it's passion for sex, art, architecture, law, or whatever. That is part of how people follow their destiny. For you, commitment—engaging in life, following your passion—means marriage."

Many contradictions. As said previously, one can't always have one's own way; sacrifice is often part of the spiritual path. Sometimes we have to sacrifice things we hold so dear that we can hardly bear to be without them. Sacrifice and love need each other. Therein lies passion. Even if at times it *seems* we are being robbed of any chance to follow our passions. At such times, we must trust that God forces no one into a life that will always be as dry and as meaningless as the dust under our beds; life always turns around and provides abundance of the spirit and of the senses.

And sometimes we need to delay getting what we want. After dating someone briefly, I couldn't commit to a marriage, but I could be open to developing that relationship, with commitment perhaps happening later. If pressured to commit too soon, I would stop keeping company with that person. The right type of discipline doesn't stifle passion but fosters it. Delaying an inappropriate marital commitment (the delay constitutes a healthy discipline) means I have fun dating and thoroughly enjoy a marriage when it is right (both of which pleasures embody passion). Passion demands sacrifice.

It can be a dilemma to know which side of the argument—sacrifice or no—is the healthy one in a given situation. This is where feedback is invaluable. To keep using marriage as an example: one client might tell me she doesn't want to wait to marry though her boyfriend promises he will eventually make the commitment. I might psychically read that she talks to him so much about matrimony and expects marriage so soon that she is pushing him away. Another woman might tell me the exact same story, and I might intuit that the man's not really in love with her and she may have to break up with him.

In Marlina's case, I said, "I want you to honor your healthy need and respect yourself enough to tell Albert, 'I love you. I know you love me and want me, and it's in a way that may make another woman ecstatic, but is not right for me. I want to date someone who might want me the way I want to be wanted. I'm worth that desire.' "

If another woman came to me with the exact same story as Marlina's (not much chance of that, I know), I might have intuited that she was fooling herself if she left Albert to get married. Let's say this other woman deep down really wanted to work as a midwife at Albert's clinic and was misled in thinking she had an intrinsic interest in marriage. Let's say she'd had it deeply ingrained in her by her mother that all women belong only in the kitchen and nursery. In acting on what seemed a true desire to get married, that woman would be miserable the rest of her life.

A person can take only so much sacrifice, struggle, and pain. But a person may need to accept far more sacrifice, struggle, and pain than they think possible, appropriate, or right. When faced with the dilemma of whether or not to sacrifice, one might need input. Here is a place a Good Faerie can help. You shouldn't mindlessly follow what any Good Faerie tells you, but, remember, two heads are better than one.

Another reminder: God's advice, the voice inside, the words of a spirit, can easily be misinterpreted no matter how advanced one gets. Have a check and balance by asking a Good Faerie what he thinks.

What I have said about sacrifice and feedback applies to many of the contradictory statements of The Third Road. It is frequently hard to know which side of a contradiction to live at any given moment. And it's often crucial to make the right choice, for reasons of ethics, magical safety, and personal fulfillment. And the choice that seems the least likely way to fulfill one may, in fact, be the very option one needs to pursue for one's self-fulfillment. Get help deciding.

The longer one walks the shamanic path, the more crucial it becomes to get such input. I cannot stress that enough. As we advance, the dangers become greater. The more magic we control, the greater the consequence of an accident or wrong decision. Just as important, *anything* that gives us power, and that includes spirituality, can be used wrongly: there is never a time when we are so spiritually advanced that we do not need input from embodied, physical beings (as opposed to spirits or deities). When we think we have reached such a time, our arrogance puts us in grave danger. I am not referring solely to moral danger but to the loss of the things we hold most dear and the risk of terrible unhappiness.

No matter how long she tries, a spiritually advanced person will never be perfect and so will inevitably make mistakes. Nevertheless, we can strive for excellence. Here is guidance for minimizing self-deception.

Let's start with a list of traits that, though divinely given, are not to be followed in all situations: a sense of authority, compelling arguments, charisma, majesty, a sense of righteousness or righteous indignation, a history of sound ethics, an internal driving force. A longtime seeker is more likely to use these traits to blind himself to his errors, but a novice can easily do the same. For example, *history of sound ethics* made my client Patrick believe he was incapable of unconsciously sabotaging his friend Angelo's success. Patrick's *sense of authority* was hard-won and hence was another reason he was hesitant to question whether perception of his own motives was accurate. *Majesty:* to honor himself as precious and absolutely magnificent was quite a spiritual accomplishment for Patrick, as it is for anyone; his leftover doubts about his self-worth made him fear relinquishing that sense of majesty for the few moments it would take to acknowledge his mistreatment of Angelo. *Compelling arguments:* having been around the spiritual block quite a few times, Patrick was able to use perfectly rendered spiritual oratory to justify his actions toward Angelo, thus burying the truth even further.

Ethical decisions cannot be reasoned through the intellect alone but also demand the reasoning of a pure heart. Hence a need for working through those inner blocks that break the heart and blur the mind. When faced with a tough or confusing moral choice, you can do a cleansing ritual. It is easy to think that attributes like hate, bigotry, selfishness, jealousy, and intolerance are the only inner blocks to sound ethical positions. But fear, low self-esteem, unwarranted guilt, or shame drive a basically good person to cause untold harm without the person who is doing the damage even realizing they are hurting anyone. Sometimes the force with which the spiritual injuries we have suffered drive us to hurt others causes a tragedy:

Lily was an incest survivor. When she divorced her husband, Robin, she was revisited by her childhood fear that there is no safe haven on this planet for any child. When negotiating custody of her and Robin's son, James, her fear so overpowered her that she wrongly assumed that Robin would be irresponsible as a father when he visited alone with James. Her lawyer was able to severely limit James's times with his father. Lily thought she was truly acting in the best interests of her son. Had she repeatedly done cleansing rites over the period of the divorce settlement to rid herself of that fear and other soul wounds that took away her clear head, she might have spared herself, Robin, and James great sorrow.

When confronting a demanding or puzzling moral choice, do at least one cleansing ritual. If needed, delay the decision as long as possible so that you can, cleansing by cleansing, eliminate all that stands in the way of sound judgment. In this way, you avoid pain for yourself and others.

Assignment: during week 4, say the following prayer three times. Many people grew up learning to give to others in ways that are unhealthy; there are endless types of self-destructive giving. Duty can be misinterpreted as a reason one should ceaselessly forsake one's own needs; guilt can convince one it is selfish to want anything for oneself so that one becomes ill or seriously depressed from spending too much time, energy, and focus on others; one might justify working in a job that makes one unhappy because the job implements a worthy project.

This assignment aside, you can use the following prayer whenever needed throughout your life to help you give to others without unhealthy martyrdom.

The ancients understood that the earth is a goddess. Gaia, a word used in this prayer, is the name for this god.

PRAYER FOR SERENE GENEROSITY

Help me serve.

Help me know when it is right to serve. And how.
So that I serve from the heart, not from fear.
So that I serve not out of shame but out of love.
So that I serve not out of panic,
but from knowing that in serving others I serve myself.

Help me know my correct service:
whether it is to be at large in the public eye,
or to quietly help my family,
or to pray for others without acknowledgment,
or to fight injustice in a courtroom,

or to educate in the classroom or by example at the Laundromat,
or to take bubble baths
just for the pleasure of watching the bubbles!
Help me know that
I add to the health of all humankind and heal Gaia
just by being happy: I am of profound service
by enjoying the pleasures I choose,
and by following my star.
Sometimes my pleasure is the very service,
and the only service, God wants me to achieve.

Thank you, God.

Table of Assignments

Do these assignments during the fourth month:

The first week:
- Read the brief piece "The Goddess's Face" three times. pg. 117

The second week:
- Write about your own definitions of *fully, moral, happy, serve,* etc. pg. 119
- Recite "Prayer to the Loving Father" once. pg. 121

The third week:
- Enjoy "Prayer to Find and Celebrate the Self Through Selflessness" three times. pg. 123

The fourth week:
- Say the "Prayer for Serene Generosity" three times. pg. 129

If You Walk the Path, the Initiation Will Happen of Its Own

Assignment: during week 1, read the following two sentences once a day for six days. *Initiation has a life of its own. If you walk the path, to a certain extent the initiation will happen on its own.* It is an important truth. It is also the framework for the rest of this section, though you of course needn't do the assignment before reading further.

I cannot emphasize enough that shamanic training is far more about self-directed living than about a specific initiation ritual that happens one day. The path is the real thing. I've said this already, but it bears repeating.

Your training here is about becoming self-defined. For the many people drawn to my work because they were walking a unique path well before coming to The Third Road, the training gives them fresh means to create their own unique ways better than ever and to find a truer, more powerful self to propel self-directed life choices.

Don't be overwhelmed if you do not feel self-determined. Maybe your personal choice is to do things "by the book." That's a valid self-directed choice. The point I am making, right now, is that The Third Road is about doing things your own way: *follow your star and it will lead you along The Third Road. Following your passion and destiny is the path; the Celtic initiation happens as a result.* Following your star is more important than a title (for example, "Great Exalted Wiccan High Priestess Who Must Be Obeyed by All That She Surveys"). Even if it seems you are wandering, *if you are truly seeking power, happiness, and to serve others, you are following the shaman's route, and you are in training; hence your initiation will happen of itself.*

This is not a tradition of herd mentality. You needn't leave this tradition to be completely individual. Nor need you do all your work in groups. A great deal of the highly individualized work my postgraduates do is in one-on-one training.

At this point, you may not need such individualized work. Nor may you ever need it. You can do things "by the book" if you want. But some of my school's postgraduate students show how individualized a shaman's path can be at any stage:

Self-directed living is even more central a part, in fact the larger part, of a postgraduate's training. More individualized than ever, their work is to a great extent of their own choosing: the student (or class) picks his own topics and projects, the latter usually being *his actual work in the world.* He also chooses how often the class meets, if there should be homework, and the teaching methods I employ. Should I teach through lecture, have them involved in my community work, give lectures plus rituals, no lecture but only hands-on work? A novice might pursue knowledge in any of the same manners my postgraduates employ.

Part of self-directed living is researching one's choices, whether that includes a religious path or a career possibility. Research in libraries and field research done according to strict academic parameters are great methodologies, but common sense, intuition, subjective experiences, and a measure of compassion are just as valid methods for finding truth.

You might ask, "Who has time for research?" Research for me does not always imply clinically detached observation made during time set aside specially for that. What I simply observe during the course of my day may be far more valid "research." During my day I am involved in life, able to determine things firsthand. If I were trying to learn without being involved in a crucial, deeply personal way, I might miss much that is central to the issues at hand. I research every minute of the day.

Mind you, it is valid research only if I am willing to diligently analyze what I observe, then get thorough feedback from others. If we are to refute religious or other so-called authorities when they tell us what is right, we must take on that chore ourselves with the diligence and hard work it demands. We needn't do it all today, though; that would be unrealistic and self-abusive.

No matter how advanced or self-defined one is, or how much one becomes an authority on oneself, feedback from an elder is vital. It is easy when feeling oppressed by bullying, hierarchical structures to swing to the other extreme and listen to no one. But if one is to be one's own authority, listening to elders is part of the hard work entailed. In fact, the more advanced and an authority on oneself, the more one needs this feedback.

An elder is a person with more experience than you regarding whatever you need to discuss or learn. An elder can be younger in years but more experienced than you about magic, holding a corporate job, staying sober, or flying an airplane. Though age may not always bring wisdom, some people do grow wiser from their years on this planet; there are reasons we traditionally esteem the wisdom of an elder in age. We must be open to lessons passed down by those who have lived longer than us, lessons learned only through long years of trial and error, given us by people who have had spiritual rough edges worn down by living. There are wisdoms about magic or any other topic that only time reveals, and it is critical to draw on that sound judgment, just as it is vital to draw on the wisdom offered by the young: those fresh insights that youthful eyes see.

Listening to an elder is not a way of giving up one's power but a way of finding it, no matter how advanced one is. Virginia opened to her innate mysticism by studying with me. Until then she had been stuck, living entirely according to logic: she had a natural gift for magic, which she ignored because it "didn't make sense." If she was going to practice magic, she needed to understand that some truths make no logical sense. You understand shamanism with the part of yourself that knows or at least wishes Faeries to be real. I told Virginia to just pretend magic was real: imagination can open us up to shamanic truths. Pretending it would benefit her, she applied herself to her psychic exercises, until one day she was on the way to work and got a hunch to call her mother right then and there. She did so. Her mother told her that Virginia's best friend from childhood was in town for only a few hours, a friend Virginia had longed to see for years.

Virginia not only turned the car around to go enjoy a delightful visit but also learned that in drawing on the nonlogical parts of life—in this case, both her hunch and the exercises that opened her to having hunches—life is enhanced. Virginia was not a particularly wounded or terribly sad person. She didn't seek me out because she felt she was less than me. She liked her life. But she could gain more of *her own innate power* by listening to my input.

I arrived at the doorstep of my teacher, Victor Anderson, with different needs than Virginia's. I was already a mystic, poet, and advanced psychic practitioner. Years as a poet and musician had taught me to integrate my left (logical) brain with my right (creative) brain. I was already professionally teaching, counseling, and creating rituals. So what I received from Victor was what *I* needed for greater power.

At least half my training with Victor involved receiving his feedback about The Third Road material I was developing. We are well indoctrinated with the belief that leading is synonymous with controlling and that teaching is the equivalent of filling a student's head with information. So it can be difficult to see that you can get something much better from a teacher or to recognize why elders are consistently needed, even along one's advanced path. Or to read my story about Victor and misunderstand "receiving his feedback about The Third Road material I was developing" to mean that he spoon-fed me rituals and theories instead of supporting me as I developed my own.

A third example to add to Virginia's story and mine: if someone is combining several religious traditions in a spiritual amalgam—an eclectic blending—in order to make a suitable path for herself, it is my job to teach in a way that supports that.

So:

- Use your Good Faeries for feedback.
- Talk to elders and thereby learn the benefits of doing so in ways all my lectures on the topic could never reveal.
- Though this training does not offer my direct feedback, it does embody some of the principles of the teaching modes I am discussing.

When you get psychically advanced, you need feedback all the more. And spiritually speaking, the higher you get, the easier and farther it is to fall. A high IQ shouldn't make you feel as if you're too smart to listen to spiritual feedback. It shouldn't blind you to psychic errors you might make or, if you are a mentor for shamans, even teach!

A series of statements, some of which seem contradictory:

- Sound spiritual training is ultimately aimed at students taking on as much responsibility for themselves as possible.
- This does not imply being responsible without support, but that if one refuses to bow to an authority, one must be fully ready to be responsible for as many magical and moral details as one can.
- It *can* be responsible to accept someone else's details as yours, if they are a perfect match.
- One thing most true authorities can rightfully claim is putting in hard work, even if it's not the sort recognized by the mainstream as useful. It is not enough to think through details alone; one must do the hard work of seeking and listening to people with more experience, to learn what details one might have missed at any given moment, because no one is ever perfect. For example, it is easy when working alone to forget that everything has a crucial spiritual element and to discover what it is.

If you are now asking how to focus on self-directed living so that you don't lose the *real* prize—a path that, when walked, is a joyful and empowering experience—here is your answer. Simply do the exercises; don't worry about the initiation; and remember what I wrote earlier: following your passion is the path. Though it may seem you are wandering, when you are seeking power, happiness, and to serve others, you are following the shaman's route; you are in training.

Bardic Brats

The true power of the Faerie Faith is that each of us is a poet. Through poetry the Goddess talks to us. Each of us has our own style of poetry. One's poems can be anything from words on the page to rap music to fashion design to marketing ideas to an approach to parenting. One's poetry might be scientific language or math, so beautiful in its precise expression that it reveals God and love. Someone else's poetry might be their work in physics or biology. One form of my poetry is healing others through counseling, teaching, and music.

The Faerie star has seven points. It symbolizes the secrets unique to you, the star you follow, a special star that is yours alone. The Faerie star reflects the secret mysteries that only you know. They can be found only in your own heart and deep within the cells of your body. Odd as it may sound, others may realize the exact same truths, but only if they discover these truths inside themselves.

A while back, students gifted me with a pendant, a sterling silver Faerie star on a chain. That symbol had never interested me, but I suddenly felt it had power for me. I thanked the students profusely then joked, "Since I don't know the meaning of the Faerie star, I'll have to make one up." Half in jest I spouted a meaning of the star—basically the kernel of the above paragraph—and realized I had unconsciously arrived at my private, most personal interpretation of the Faerie star. This story embodies my symbolism for the Faerie star—finding one's own personal truth—and strikes me now as a wonderful cosmic joke, though I didn't realize it at the time. But I suspect those students saw the joke right then and there; they laughed hard.

I feel blessed in being open to whenever and however I find my truths; I trusted that my jesting interpretation of a symbol had authentic meaning. My unconscious mind was playing a terrific trick on me!

We all have such power to create meaning. Meaning in our lives.

Meaning out of our tragedies. Meaning for our children, friends, family, co-workers, clients, students, community, earth. We can create meaning if we only trust in our own type of poetry. We might also call it art or whatever is our own special way of bringing human dignity, creativity, and importance to what we do, whether it is cleaning house, supervising people on the job, or teaching math. When I say this, people often respond, "But I am not creative." Creativity is not exclusive to endeavors such as dance, painting, literature. A great idea in science, a means of juggling the family daily schedule so that everyone's needs get met, a style of dress, a cogent way to get a moral idea across to one's children or kindergarten students—these are all creative, they are all art, all poetry in which we need to trust. Poetry is picking up a rock you think is pretty or that reminds you of a truth of deep concern to you and putting that beauty or truth in your pocket.

It can take a lot of work to purify oneself of the blocks to one's poetry. It may take a lifetime; it has for me, maybe because I have such deep wounds that new layers of blocks keep surfacing. Also, once I finish one climb, I am on to the next mountain, so I have to constantly reaffirm, draw more deeply on, and reinvent my own version of poetry. (When *Be a Goddess!* was about to be released, I went into the studio to produce my first album of music. After facing the inner demons that needed to be cleansed before I could write that book, I faced more in the recording studio.) You have been doing that purification, and other relevant work, so don't worry; you are up to speed. The exercises in this book—even many of the exercises that seem unrelated to one's poetry—help you fend off those demons and live creatively.

I once called a friend for support because I had faced a lot of challenges. It had been a hard day, and I was feeling overwhelmed. She reminded me that I had once told her that I made a prayer, "Please give me the growth needed each day to face whatever challenges the day brings." She added that she had followed my example, and it was a gratifying solution to her problems. I responded, "Goodness, I must have been crazy to make that prayer!" She suggested I try that prayer again. I did, with good result. Therefore:

Optional assignment: Use the above prayer when it might be relevant. (I call it "The 'I-Must-Have-Been-Crazy-to-Make-That-Prayer' Prayer.")

Assignment: during week 1, write in your journal about how this section relates to you. Since this assignment is about your own sort of creativity, maybe you want to be creative in how you execute the assignment. For instance, you can use something other than words. If your styles of poetry include drawing and the way you work with children, perhaps draw a picture of how you work with children. Or do the assignment in an applied way by creating a new recipe, if creativity expresses itself in you through cooking. Or plan a party if your creativity is the way you entertain guests.

If you do choose to write, don't judge the way you write as good or bad. People often have their own way of using words, their own language. It is part of their power, of how they uncover and express important truths to themselves and others.

Finding my own language has been important to me. It has helped me know who I am. Also, a lot of my poetry (in this case I use *poetry* literally) expresses itself in my prose; I write in rhythms usually used only in poetry because those rhythms can touch a reader's heart and help her grasp truths.

My language has also been created by trying to construct imagery, rhythm, and beautiful sounds to convey the theories I developed. I dubbed the set of spells that I teach for psychic and spiritual power and safety "The Magic Formula." Some may think I was mocking my readers. No! Everyone wants "The Magic Formula," and I sincerely want to give it to them. Real magical power is not gained from looking outside oneself, but from taking responsibility and care with one's shamanic endeavors, which is what "The Magic Formula" does. I hope that the phrase "The Magic Formula" will help people see where true power lies.

My intuition and experience/research suggest that in a far-off hazy past, something like this set of spells was called "The Magic Formula." I write *experience/research* to reemphasize again: experience is a form of research. Your own modes of perception, analysis, and research are part of *your* poetry. Demonstrate respect for them: when you tell someone that your beliefs are "the results of your *experience,*" don't let others assume that said results were sloppily made or gleaned from other people's research.

I am a bard: a poet who teaches shamanism through her poems, music, and storytelling. A bard also creates tradition, as I created The Third Road. Though The Third Road, *being* my creation, consists of copyrighted material, anyone can be a Third Road bard because, in a sense, The Third Road tradition and its community are things we all create together by creating our own lives, our own way of living and of loving God, our own magic.

I confess, I'm what I call a "bardic brat," as I often make my point by making mischief. God's poets needn't be pompous. My wish for you: May you *create* great joy in your life in whatever your poetry is, whether it is the way you tell jokes, write poems on the page, work as a stripper, rule as a judge, or raise orchids. If you want, take the Faerie star as your bard's symbol.

Assignment: during week 2, do the following simple spell, which explores issues of self-fulfillment, sexual and otherwise. Perform the spell again in week 4.

RITUAL

The Goddess's Garden of Earthly Delights

Step 1. Choose a way to be nice to yourself, such as hugging yourself, brushing your hair, gently stroking your own face, making love to yourself, eating a fabulous dessert, taking yourself out for a special meal on your lunch break, enjoying a lazy morning in bed watching TV.

Step 2. Gather whatever you need to do the activity you have chosen (hairbrush, dessert, and so on).

Step 3. Execute your chosen act of self-love while affirming silently or out loud,

> *I deserve this. We are the children of Goddess,*
> *permitted, in fact welcomed,*
> *to live in Her Garden of Earthly Delight,*
> *blessed to receive Her love*
> *through our own hearts and hands,*
> *blessed to receive Her love*
> *through the hearts and hands of loved ones,*
> *blessed to receive Her love*
> *through the hearts and hands of the earth and sky.*
> *So be it!*

You have other work to do this month, so don't bite off more than you can chew. If you decide this ritual must entail an ambitious action—a day trip to the beach instead of just sitting down to a cup of your favorite tea—you may never get around to it. Or if you do pull it off, you may not have time for your other assignments. Choose a ritual-action of self-love that fits into your schedule. That is a realistic approach not just to the assignment but to avoiding self-sabotage of self-love: we are more able to treat ourselves well on a consistent basis if our plans to do so work within the scope of our daily lives.

You can even adapt the rite and use a mini-chant: "I deserve this, we are the children of Goddess living in Her Garden of Earthly Delight."

On the other hand, you might find it great fun to get quite elaborate in your preparations, and that may motivate you to do the rest of your assignments. Perhaps before brushing your hair you want to take a long scented bath; or before making love to yourself, put fresh perfumed sheets on the bed, light candles and incense, and decorate your bedroom with colorful scarves and huge swatches of velvet. You may want to play music while you pamper yourself.

Assignment: starting week 2, once a week for three weeks, determine an inner block to your happiness, and purify yourself of it simply by praying, "Mother, please take this from me if it is your will." *If it is your will:* because

She might know something you don't. You needn't do "The Magic Formula" (its page number is easily found by looking at the table of rituals) unless you feel it might lend focus and power. But if in doubt, use it; you might learn as from an experiment.

We Are All of Mythic Proportion

I am frustrated and angered by a media star system that tells us only a few individuals shine. We are all unique, each of us a shining star in the sky. Don't get me wrong, I love movies, rent home videos constantly, and as far as I am concerned, Marilyn Monroe is mythic. But we are all of mythic proportion. Becoming a shaman, and finding the subtle magic of one's own bones and cells and DNA, means finding one's *personal mythology.*

Personal mythology can be defined as follows. Some people have a film star they identify with. Or a Greek myth. Or a character in a Faerie tale or fantasy novel. Others might read a lot about wolves because they identify with the wild integrity of that animal. Or perhaps they have a nickname that says a lot about them. My student Joanne is often called Juju, which is a term for magic. Her friends think her warm buoyant personality is a magic of sorts because everyone blossoms around her.

One's myth might encompass all things that are watery—mermaids, shells, and the dark ocean bed—because they call to one with power and truth. Or one's myth might embrace all that is green: one's garden, the spirits that play in it, and the Green God, He whose emerald blood runs through all plants.

Both our Mother and Father, having many aspects, appear to us in various guises. So when I refer to the Green God or to this goddess or that goddess, I am speaking of one of our Divine Parents in one of their many guises, or "aspects."

One might identify with a certain aspect of the God or Goddess: perhaps, one counsels others about death and dying and identifies with the Crone, the elder aspect of the Goddess, She who is wise in years, serves as a guide, and embodies death, comfort, and transformation.

One needn't be limited in one's personal mythology. It can have many aspects. Your myth might even entail several Faerie tales (film stars, animals, images, . . .) woven together in a way that describes only you, affirming a core part of your soul.

I identify with several mythical creatures, including dragons and Pegasus. I also identify with the sacred fool, trickster, and Wounded Healer, and various others. Being a poet is part of my personal mythology.

There are many ways a personal mythology can manifest, so don't feel limited to the parameters implied in my examples. Some people might have personal myths they do not even recognize or may have many personal myths or one very simple myth; some people have built very complicated myths about themselves.

These identifications help us rise above our limits to achieve great things for ourselves and others. And they are another step in the bloodline initiation by bringing us closer to our truest, happiest selves.

Optional assignment: week 2 onward. Once started, this can be done anytime, as little or as much as you want, at any rate you want. As you prepare for your initiation, you may want to create a process that builds your mythos. Here are ways to do that, but do not limit yourself to my suggestions.

Look through your video collection, bookshelves, clothing, furniture, and so on, for ways you identify yourself. Write in your journal about this.

Hunt in libraries for books on mythology or Faerie tales to see if something catches your fancy. Write in your journal about it. It is perfectly valid and can be tremendously powerful to use something that is not a long-standing part of you as a piece of your personal myth. When developing your myth, you needn't worry if a legend, deity, animal, or anything else that draws you is truly yours or not; play with it, see whether you get anything from it or not, and time will tell the rest.

Make a mask of a character in a story, a character that appeals to you. Or create a mask of a part of you that no one ever gets to see. You needn't even wear it; just making it is a rite of sorts that can transform you.

Do a ritual in the mask, a rite you make up, or one in this book. Cook a meal in the mask! Or dance in it.

Write a story about yourself. The story can range from writing yourself into a myth you know to a record of what happened to you on the way to work yesterday to a stream-of-consciousness account that starts from whatever pops into your head and wanders whither it might. Write in the language of a folktale or in any other style of prose or poetry, such as a limerick or even the way you speak every day.

Don't worry if the story is "good" or is even longer than a sentence. You may want to just write the first thing that pops into your head. The goal is not the story but what the act of writing gives to you. If you find what you write irrelevant, you might want to set it aside for a week or so, then decide. Or tell the story to a Good Faerie to see if there are helpful truths in it that you are missing. Don't judge the tale while writing it. However good or bad the tale might be by some people's standards, this writing can reveal truths about you that you might not see until long after the story is written.

Draw a picture of yourself. It can be elaborate or a stick figure; it doesn't matter. Pictures can range from a drawing of you as a mythical beast to you at your office desk. Either one might reveal a new aspect of your myth to you, not even thought of until after the picture is drawn. If you try it, you might be surprised.

You can build your myth in simple, easy ways. It can take only three minutes of stream-of-consciousness writing to produce a tiny story. Don't think that bigger is always better! Or you may want extensive time in which to build your myth. It is a matter of preference.

Your Totem Animal

One way to build your mythos is to find and explore your power animal, also called your totem animal. A totem animal is a being you identify with, whose powers become yours, and whose wisdoms you possess as your own or need to learn. A turtle is slow and steady; you may plod along, really helping people without ever making any spectacular moves. Getting to know turtle might teach you ways to cherish your slowness and take fullest advantage of it. Or maybe you are a bear: you may be very motherly, with lots of children and adults constantly showing up at your door to talk about their problems and be nurtured. And you are always drawn to scientific books about bears. The bear is an ancient mother figure. Bear is an archetypal mom.

Here are some methods to find your totem, if you want to draw on the power of a totem animal.

I suggest you refrain for now from researching power animals in metaphysical books on the topic. I want you to try another approach first. If you already have found your totem by studying the literature on the subject, use or adapt the following material if it seems useful.

I suggest leaving the library because a more direct, personal experience offers something that books don't. A book may tell you that you are an eagle and that eagles have great compassion. But if you learn both those lessons firsthand, before any book tells you, you may own that wisdom at a deeper level. Also, *learning a shamanic truth intellectually first can make it difficult to learn the deepest layers of that shamanic truth. The logical mind gets in the way by being the initial access to that truth. If, however, the logical mind is given that truth after one has learned the truth experientially, logic adds to, rather than detracts from, wisdom.* As much as I love theory (despite my rants decrying it, I truly love it and will wax theoretical for hours if you happen to catch me off guard), I try to avoid it because I want instead to lead you to experiences. In the same vein, when I must share theory, I prefer to use simple, everyday language and poetry. They can convey deeper layers of wisdom than academic language and actually provide an experience in themselves! Regular, routine language is a poetry to me; through it I can express the truths, both simple and complex, that I have gleaned from years of studying not books but my own heart and that of the earth.

Pray for your totem to be revealed to you. Who knows how you might discover it?

Most of us do not live in nature, so your animal might come to you in the civilized world. You may happen upon it in a movie or book when all you were doing was enjoying a film or book that has nothing to do with totems. You may see a T-shirt with a picture of an animal on it and think, "Aha!" If a given animal keeps appearing in your life, or appears once in a way that feels significant, it might be your totem.

You might find your totem in one of the following activities: Take a walk in the woods. Go to the zoo. Pray for a vision of your totem in a dream. You can think of these as power quests.

Don't be impatient or worry. Your totem will appear when it is supposed to, often in places or ways you never expected to find it. Having a totem does not a shaman make. What makes a shaman is service.

After picking an animal whose vigor, serenity, or other attributes you admire and want to have as your own, emulate its powers, make them your own. One way to do this is to study that animal. Simply pursuing an interest in a given animal through learning one fact about it can be very powerful; you will see! If you cannot view it firsthand in the wild or at a farm or zoo, look for documentary films, special exhibits in schools or museums, and books. Research your animal not in metaphysical books but in the science section of a library. One enticing fact about an animal that strikes your fancy can act as a role model for you on a given day or throughout your life.

You needn't know if the animal that appeals to you is in fact your totem. I am drawn toward and have researched owl magic, yet it's clear to me I am not owl. But owl is part of my personal myth. I finally realized that there are animals who walk next to a person but who are not that person. I discovered that many of my human friends have owl as their totem. I learn much from owl, both the bird itself and my human friends who are owl. Owl lessons I gain from those human friends may not be consciously attributed as owl by anyone.

You can have a temporary totem, even for an hour. Recently in a circle (reminder: *circle* is a word for a gathering of shamans) one member randomly picked an animal for each attendee to take on as a momentary totem during a ritual similar to "Animal Wisdom," an exercise below. I was given ocelot—a small, wild cat—which surprised me because (1) I had no attraction to the animal and (2) unknown to the person who assigned me ocelot, I was actually going the very next day to a place where ocelots are raised, a startling synchronicity. (*Synchronicity:* a "coincidence" that seems intended by God to make us sit up and take note, help us learn, bless us with "a stroke of luck," or indicate a direction we should take.)

In the ritual, I experienced myself as a high-strung ocelot who was pacing nervously. I thought, "Ugh. I've worked so hard for so long to stop being nervous and high-strung, why would God want me to feel it as an ocelot, what wisdom is *this?*" Then I had a realization that brought me happy tears. Though I have improved remarkably regarding my painful tendencies to be jittery and jumpy, I still am far more that way than I would like to be. The cat's personality taught me that in my case, being on edge and tense is the other half of my passion and intensity, and that these latter two traits are gifts for myself and to those around me.

I cried as my perfectionist sense of failure about not getting completely over my anxious nature left me, and a new, tearful pride in my intensity took its place. I suddenly saw myself as a whole being, precious just the way I am. I continue to work hard not to be too nervous, but now I have an invaluable reminder that no one is perfect and that I am great even without improvement. By the way, when the rite was over I shared my experience with someone who exclaimed that ocelots are, in truth, nervous, high-strung, and edgy!

Here are more ways to draw on an animal whose power, serenity, or other attributes you admire: if a given animal keeps appearing in your life, or appears once in a way that feels significant, or you are simply drawn to it, pray for insight about why that animal is relevant, what lessons it has to teach you, how you might best use it as an example. And/or: write in your journal about it; imitate its virtues; apply its wisdoms. And/or do the following ritual. (Two reminders: use "The Magic Formula"; and anytime you feel the need for extra protection, employ the "Protection Bubble." An ideal time to construct the sphere is right before you invoke the Goddess.) An animal needn't be your power animal to teach you much in the following rite.

RITUAL

Animal Wisdom

Step 1. After choosing one animal to focus on, decide what that animal experiences. For instance, what do its muscles feel like when it lies down, what goes through its head, how does it feel physically and in spirit as it moves? What are its motivation and desires?

You may look at this step's instructions and say, "I cannot *really* know what it is like to be an animal," or, "I have no idea how an animal experiences life." Being accurate is not the point here. If you want, think of this exercise more as an exploration or fantasy.

Step 2. Closing your eyes, focus on the darkness that is there naturally when one's eyes are closed.

Step 3. Imagine yourself to be that animal any way you can.

Step 4. Continue to imagine yourself as that animal: pick one thing you discovered in step 1, and fancy yourself being that way. For example, if you chose a gorilla and decided in step 1 that a gorilla feels proud and unhampered when walking, see yourself walking that way in your mind's eye, imagine that you walk with freedom and pride. Or if you chose an alligator, and in step 1 you decided an alligator lies in quiet serenity, then imagine, picture, visualize yourself lying quietly with an alligator's scaly skin, with not a care in the world.

Step 5. Focus on another attribute that you determined in step 1, and use step 4's instructions on it.

Step 6. Repeat step 5 on as many attributes as you want.

After step 4, as you focus on additional attributes, you may want to do so without letting attributes imagined earlier in the ritual slip from your mind. In other words, if you fantasize a sense of serenity, then a sense of pride, try to hold both in your imagination. If you then want to, in addition, pretend your animal self is relaxed, add that visualized or otherwise imagined sense of relaxation to the imagined serenity and pride. This is difficult but is also an incredible way to build magical skills of focus and imagination. Of course, if at first your animal self is running, then walking, then sleeping, it is silly to picture those all at once. Only try to hold sequential details that add up to a complete picture. And don't worry if you do this accumulation of details poorly; it is a lot to try at once, and just the doing helps to increase your skills.

Step 7. If you want, write down what powers you felt or wisdom you gained. You may think you will remember forever, but that may not be the case. Often, I am so happy I wrote something down. I often see it just when I need it.

A Personal Magic

The following is another part of the bloodline initiation: a *personal magic* (also called a *personal heritage*). A personal magic might be your mundane ability as a gardener or your ability to talk to plants to help them to thrive. A personal magic might be an ability to read tarot cards, calm upset friends with kind words, throw fabulous parties, tell inspiring stories, make jokes that shake friends out of their self-pity, or find lost objects through hunches and/or common sense.

A *personal heritage* is from and beyond the scope of your bloodline but can be won as you move toward your blood heritage and is part of finding your uniquely personal path and vision. (And if you explore it, you may come to find it *is* your bloodline!) You may ask, "Then why a different category?" These categories help you to find information. As soon as the categories become stifling or otherwise restrictive, they are no longer a means of perception but a means of defeat. Don't use these categories rigidly; let them overlap with each other. As these categories actually exist in you, they often *do* overlap! It is only in the modern Western mind that everything supposedly fits into neat boxes, with no more blending than happens when two fearful souls have sex.

Your personal magic(s) might be the same as your major life goals as a priest. Or it might be the ways, large and small, that you implement those life goals and priestly visions. For example, if someone's aim in life is to educate others that life on the physical plane was given to us so that we might celebrate it, he might do it through a personal magic of jokes or dance, by being an events planner who creates marvelous parties for a living, or by writing celebratory rituals that help people trust the sacredness of pleasure. If someone's life goal is to be a healer, her personal magic might be her extraordinarily sensitive hands when performing surgery. The same life goal—healing others—could manifest instead in a friend's ability to listen attentively and caringly, a social worker's psychic ability to put clients at ease, or, well, my psychic ability to note the roadblocks to my clients' happiness.

Assignment: to be done during week 4. What are your personal magics? List them even if they lurk so quietly you can barely feel them and they need to "come into being"; or if you have developed them only a bit; or if they operate well but you want to develop them fully and/or use them more. It can be hard to validate our strengths, let alone think of them as powerful magic. If because of this you cannot do the assignment, you can overcome that block by asking a Good Faerie or the Goddess to tell you your personal magic. Or ask either of them what inside you keeps you from acknowledging your strengths. You may already know what inner trait blocks self-esteem. Use "Kissed by a Star" to cleanse the block away. If you have time, you may want to share the list with a Good Faerie to get feedback and support.

Francesca's Helpful Hints for Better Magic

When I focus on spirituality and personal happiness, you may think you are missing out on learning magic. But spiritual blocks and unhappiness impede psychic and magical powers. I heard of a group that strove for spiritual development and found psychic abilities; this relates to what I said earlier: we are each our own cauldron.

In the same vein, every bit of work on self-expression makes you more magical because it is part of your true self to just *be* psychic. When you express yourself better in other ways, your magical powers automatically improve.

In many other subtle ways the program as a whole improves your magic. If you so desire, enjoy a fun, intellectual exercise: look through the book, and try to discover one or more tidbits that are seemingly unrelated to magic but enhance psychic prowess.

Table of Assignments

Do these assignments during the fifth month:

The first week:

- Read the following two sentences once a day for six days: Initiation has a life of its own. If you walk the path, to a certain extent the initiation will happen on its own. pg. 131
- Optional assignment: Use "The 'I-Must-Have-Been-Crazy-to-Make-That-Prayer' Prayer" when it seems relevant, this week or ever. pg. 138
- Write in your journal about the section "Bardic Brats." pg. 138

The second week:

- Perform the spell "The Goddess's Garden of Earthly Delights." pg. 139
- Determine an inner block to your happiness, and pray, "Mother, please take this from me if it is your will." pg. 140
- Create a process that builds your mythos. This assignment is optional, to be done week two onward. Since it is optional, you may of course choose to do it later. pg. 142

The third week:

- Determine another inner block to your happiness, and pray, "Mother, please take this from me if it is your will." pg. 140

The fourth week:

- Determine another inner block to your happiness, and pray, "Mother, please take this from me if it is your will." pg. 140
- List your personal magics. pg. 149
- Enjoy the spell "The Goddess's Garden of Earthly Delights." pg. 139

Priesthood Is a Function

As earlier lessons said, priesthood is a function. So we can't define priesthood without defining a priestess's job. What does a pagan priest do? The answer might seem self-evident, and you have surely answered what *you* as a priestess hope or want to do in the future. But at this point it is good to explore the question at a deeper level, to help you better meet, and create, your self-identification. *Initiation* means beginning. It begins, among other things, your priesthood or a new level of it. With better definitions of priesthood, you can better perform the proper rituals to live as a priest.

Assignment: during week 1, write in your journal your answer to this question: What does a pagan priest do? Then make a list of all the ways you can think of that society tells us both that we can't be priests and that we must relinquish control of our spiritual direction to someone else. Then list the ways we are told that someone else should take responsibility for the planet, community, family, so that we shouldn't and needn't serve. By recognizing the societal elements that challenge your priesthood, you are more able to surmount such barriers.

It's Really Up to You—Go Walk in the Forest

Some witches train themselves by ferreting endlessly through metaphysical shops to find books, walking in the woods learning the wisdom of nature, doing the hard work of thinking for themselves. Other witches train with an embodied human. This book asks you to do neither alone but something in between. This can be confusing. I am sitting here as a teacher yet dropping you into the void and saying, "It's really up to you—go walk in the forest." That's not done in this culture. Yet that is my job as a shamanic teacher! I must help you face this specific challenge of shamanism.

I hope to teach you that, even though you're learning to depend on your own unique insights and strengths, you will not be deserted in the process. I and your other Good Faeries will continue to guide you; most important, so will the Goddess. This book offers specific ways you can be an individual in your own right and enhance your sense of self without having to feel isolated.

Even when it seems we are not working directly on it, The Third Road training increases our intuition. Often when I teach something pertaining to intuition, someone feels the lesson will not be applicable to her because she doesn't have intuitions. Do you instead have hunches, clairvoyance, or any other means of psychically gaining information or hearing God? If I refer to intuition (or any of these) and it doesn't seem relevant, you can perhaps substitute one of the other powers.

Another reason people feel such a lesson might not be relevant is that they do not validate whatever otherworldly mode(s) of perception they have. One woman told me she had no such methods. When pressed, she told me she resorts to tarot cards quite a bit. Tarot is a deck of cards traditionally used as a divination tool. Though the cards are a way this woman receives a great deal of useful information and guidance, she doesn't validate this method because she is self-taught and wrongly believes that one's tarot work (or any kind of work) is inconsequential unless one has received formal instruction in it. Whatever style of vision, hunches, premonition, odd impression, clairvoyance, clairsentience, or other type of otherworldly info you get, validate it. If it is weak, you can improve it if you acknowledge it. *Clairvoyance* means *clear seeing; clairsentience* means *clear knowing.* I am clairsentient; what my clients need appears in my mind as information rather than as images.

Intuition and the like can be a powerful, constant means to hear God's guidance. For me, it is an important tool. Again, do not take this process of "hearing" too literally. Some people hear words, others get an impression, others get a gut feeling of the right thing to do, and so on.

There are many otherworldly ways to perceive God's guidance. Do note that although intuition can be a means to hear God, it can also be a way to hear Her incorrectly.

Also, let's say that with my mundane senses I see my cat run into my home office and play with a pen that fell on the floor. It is merely an observance, just that and no more. Nor is it meant to be more. Another time I may see my cat playing and, still only with my mundane senses of seeing and intellect, know the cat's activities are God's way of telling me to take a break from work and go play. In the same way, I can observe things with my psychic sensibilities, whether intuition, clairvoyance, whatever, and it can simply be an observance. Other times, it will be a perception of God's guidance. What I just wrote was *not* to demonstrate that the intuition and the perception of the cat and the pen are always God's guidance if I am only open to it. I am instead saying that intuition is a psychic mode of perception and can be used for anything from hearing God's guidance to watching a ball game from miles away, but it is not in and of itself *always* God's guidance.

Our intuition and instinct can guide us through the day. The following assignment will help you strengthen your intuition, which you might be tapping in to more at this point in your training without always seeing it as such. You can view your intuition as your inner Good Faerie, that part of yourself that supports your dreams.

Assignment: during week 2, strengthen your inner Good Faerie in the following way. For one week pay special attention to your "hits": a word(s), idea(s), sensibility(s), picture(s), song(s), and the like that pop into your brain.

And if a hit seems silly, some silly hits are right on the money. When first working professionally as a counselor, I did a psychic reading for a woman who was totally new to that sort of thing. She wanted to try it.

I was told by the spirits that she needed a bath that would be a lengthy, spiritual purification ritual. I explained how to take such a bath. Then I psychically perceived she should end the bath by singing "Don't Rain on My Parade!"—a loud, raucous song from a musical. I was mortified. My intuition told me that it would help her tremendously to do this. But how could I tell this novice to the psychic world to sit sopping wet in her bathtub singing a rabble-rousing rendition of a Barbra Streisand tune? She certainly wasn't going to think that was much of a meditation! I thought, "I just can't tell her this. She will think I am a fraud."

After much inner debate and turmoil, I decided to trust the psychic gifts the Gods had given me. I gave her that part of the ritual instructions, feeling somewhat embarrassed. She broke out in delighted laughter, saying, "Do you know, that song's been in my head for days, and I've been dying to sing it!" She told me later that doing that silly part of the ritual uplifted and cheered her. A lesson to trust my abilities more!

Other things to do this week: you may find that if you explore and/or develop a hit, it could lead you to guidance that's powerful and important. One way to do this is by writing or speaking in stream of consciousness about your hit. Or by logically thinking out what the hit might mean. Or by sharing what's popped into your mind with a Good Faerie (thus developing yourself without having to do it alone!). Sometimes exploring hits playfully frees up the mind so wonderful insights occur. Many times in class, a student's joke about a hit has revealed its true meaning.

Every last thing that pops into your head is not gold. I don't want you to *know* how much nonsense comes into my mind all day long! But one cannot know the difference until one explores. And I cannot state strongly enough how many people I have seen completely ignore all the psychic perceptions they had. This assignment really helps with that.

Often, in developing intuition, it doesn't always come clearly at first. As a matter of fact, sometimes it comes in these very same puzzling or weak ways when you're a master. Also, you might find that in exploring a silly hit or any hit, it might go nowhere, but in pursuing it, you are nevertheless learning and strengthening the intuitive process. Part of the intuitive process is sifting through your data.

If a Good Faerie is available, discuss the results of this assignment with her or him. You need support to trust your inner Good Faerie. You also need people who'll help you not get lost in any so-called infallibility.

Intuition is one of many ways to hear God. She speaks to us in innumerable ways throughout the day. She guides us via a song that we happen to hear on the radio, the chance words of a colleague, the concerned question of a friend, the guidance of a therapist. When you ask for guidance, be open to the innumerable ways it might come.

Assignment: to be done during week 2. The Goddess tries to guide us and give us other help through our friends and community in ways one might reject from a sense of unworthiness, low self-esteem, the desire not to impose, unhealthy independence, self-defeating pride, and so on. When a concerned parent, wife, pal, or acquaintance takes us aside to say they're worried we're drinking too much, it is easy to think they are not speaking for God. And in fact, they might not be. But it is too easy to dismiss God when She appears as a human being. It is easy to ask God for financial help then reject a loan one's parents offer. While the loan might be inappropriate, one shouldn't ignore it out of hand. You may not want to take money from your parents, because they are as irritating as anyone could be, but this still might be God's hands reaching out to help. Three times this week pray:

PRAYER FOR DIVINE HELP

Goddess, help me receive your care by being open to care from my family, friends, and community. Cleanse my blocks that keep me from being helped by others. Thank you for the care you offer me.

More About: What Is an Initiation Ritual?

Though we have been working toward an initiation and defining one throughout these lessons, it is time to look more directly at the question "What is initiation?" It was necessary to start the initiation process instead of defining it because, as said earlier, a vital, gut-deep knowledge of certain things can be obscured if our first experience with that topic is theoretical. The analytical approach to shamanism is more useful once one has had firsthand experience.

I will briefly touch on some aspects or steps of a shamanic initiation ritual. I will explain them more fully later in the year, so don't worry if you are not completely clear about them. Initiation is:

A recognition of spiritual, magical, and mundane power gained, proven, or shown: this includes power of the heart such as humility and compassion. All things that are part of spiritual power must be considered so that, if appropriate, they are included in this step.

A conferring of greater power: both general and specific powers are included in this step.

A gifting of lineage and its power: whether that implies family, animal, specific religious tradition, rock, plant, or star. Someone might ask, "How can a rock, plant, or star be one's lineage?" One's lineage can be *anything.* Don't limit yourself; finding your true nature means being open to the widest range of possibilities.

A taking on of ministerial responsibilities: this can, but need not, be a commitment to a specific responsibility. One can take this step with a vague sense of the specific service one wants to perform, or one can simply make a commitment to take on a responsibility once one knows, and/or is able to take on, whatever service one is meant to do for others. Remember that service can mean anything from raising one's family or earning the money to put one's kids through college to saving the redwoods to praying for world peace to offering psychic readings commercially or to friends to a focus on healing oneself until one is in shape to help others.

There are other parts to the rite, but for now that is enough food for thought. And that much can help you contemplate the following step of the rite and its pertinent assignment.

Assignment: to be done during week 3. Is there some special result you would like to see your initiation produce, maybe something that you believe only you have ever thought of? Do you think there is something additional an initiation ritual achieves or that yours should? Write about it so you can create a rite to fulfill that personal definition or apply the book's rite to that goal.

It is fine if what you write in this assignment duplicates the initiation rite material you read above or will read later in this training or repeats other parts of this book. Coming up with it yourself is powerful. If you did already read it in this book, perhaps your unconscious mind has had a chance to digest it; then when you write about it in your own words, that act may help you better understand my lesson or arrive at additional truths that are not in my text. Besides, when we approach a subject from several different angles, more is realized.

Of course, over the year as you move toward your initiation, you can, and may need to, lengthen any list or other written assignment. Do as you see fit. Preparing for that ritual is a process; you can't know everything about the ritual until you've gone through the process, the path leading up to the rite. By that process and path I mean not only planning the ritual but living the daily path up to the point of the initiation. And since, as you will soon learn, initiation never stops, you have your whole life to make those lists and finish your journal assignments. Whatever doesn't get done this year can be done later.

An Accepting Goddess Who Is Devoted to Her Children

In the fifth month's ritual, "Animal Wisdom," I taught how to build an imagined picture or experience in steps by adding imaginary details one at a time without letting go of details already imagined. The following ritual might work better for you if you do your best to apply that approach. The steps themselves embody that approach: sometimes a sentence starts in one step, and once you have imagined that part of the sentence, you can move on to the next step, where the sentence continues.

RITUAL

In the Mother's Embrace

Step 1. Imagine yourself in the presence of a loving, nonjudgmental Goddess,

Step 2. who is not harsh or condemning

Step 3. but instead is everything an ideal parent would be

Step 4. but raised to the power of divinity.

Step 5. Show this deity a sexual hope, need, or desire you have. Pick one thing. Examples: the hope to find the person of your dreams; the desire for an orgasm if you've never had one; the wish for better orgasms; the wish for mind-boggling orgasms; the need to feel closer to your partner when you make love; the need to overcome the pain of a sexual trauma or disappointment; the hope to conquer sexual shyness; the desire to culminate a relationship sexually.

A nonsexual event can upset or even destroy one's sex life. Tamara was betrayed in business dealings by her employer after she had given him nine years of hard work and devotion. Her trust in the human race evaporated, making sex too scary a proposition. Using this rite, she presented to God her desire to regain trust so that she could become sexual again. Another example: Bettina's parents verbally assaulted her, so she avoided any intimacy. Bettina's solution: she presented the desire for intimacy to God.

Step 6. Imagine the Goddess says of your hope, need, or desire:

I bless this part of you, just as I bless all parts of you.
This part of you is a god-given gift, healthy and sacred.

This ritual can be adapted to apply to any need, hope, or desire for self-fulfillment—whether a longing for a happy home or a desire to learn to dance—and will always help you overcome shame. Instead of a focus on the sexual in step 5, simply insert another hope, need, or desire. But pick *one.* Examples: the desire to start your own business; the wish for more money; the need for solace, support, or other care after a tragedy, such as rape or a death in the family; the desire to reunite with an exhusband.

Don't reserve this spell only for wants or needs of which you feel ashamed. Any goal, the desire for which is presented to the Goddess in this rite, can be more easily achieved. This is a spell you can apply throughout your life.

The Goddess may not give you all you hope for; this ritual is not a spell whereby you get all wishes fulfilled. Life is not like that, and thus neither is magic. Magic is a natural thing, a part of natural life. Also, tragedy is a fact of life; sometimes your needs go unanswered; you might think it is because God has deserted you or that your needs are just too selfish. Neither is true.

You might be asking, "How *do* you explain unfulfilled needs?" When I have an unfulfilled need, I don't always understand. But, eventually, I remember that I might need to do without something important because life, despite all its possibilities and joys, is limited, imperfect, even awful in some ways. I come to realize that in the final analysis the only thing important is that I *strive to follow the Goddess's moment-to-moment plan for me.* As my day progresses, I try to perform each activity on Her divine agenda for me, one undertaking at a time, whether that is teaching a class, making my next meal, watering my garden, meditating, holding my tongue when I want to let my temper get the better of me, letting myself feel unpleasant emotions that I would prefer to ignore, getting to bed so that I get a good night's rest, or going out dancing. At the time, I might be blind to how performing Her requests can add up to a lifetime's accomplishment that I consider important, but I remind myself that life's ultimate achievement is to follow her guidance and that doing so *will* eventually make me happy.

Don't get me wrong when I talk of limits and tragedy. I believe in miracles, I think magic is one way to make them, and I live in the realm of miracles on a daily basis. But this is The Third Road: contradictions— both sides of the picture—are considered equally by a shaman because the two sides together create the most power and happiness. For example, a shaman does not run from facts; in acknowledging that tragedy is a part of life he then faces it and is thus in a position to overcome it and maybe even create a miracle regarding it.

It is important when you face tragedy to have tools. Because this spell increases your ability to go after what you want and need, it helps you avoid, overcome, or better cope with a tragedy. And though there is no way to eradicate the hard fact of life that sometimes one is truly deprived, we should try to avoid that happening to us as much as possible. Using this ritual is one way; since it gives you power to strive for what you need, you are more likely to achieve it or at least cope better when you fall short of what you need. Life may be hard, but we can do everything in our power to make it easier except pretend that things are perfect.

This spell might even bring a miracle to you.

Assignment: during week 3, do the exercise twice. I strongly suggest you use it on a sexual issue the first time.

Francesca's Helpful Hints for Better Magic

An imagined experience or picture in a ritual, such as in the above rite, is often called a visualization. Don't be misled by that term. A visualization can be a use of imagination that encompasses the four senses other than sight. In fact, try to use as many senses as you can when you imagine something in a rite. A visualization can also include imagined emotions and intangible impressions and may be all the more powerful for it! Add emotions to your visualizations. For example, in the above rite, when imagining yourself in the presence of a loving, accepting Goddess, pretend you feel happy and content.

Depending on your personal style, you may *see* nothing in your mind's eye when you do a visualization. You may only imagine some almost-intangible but striking and useful *sense* of the event, scene, or object that you are supposed to be visualizing.

Don't feel you are failing if you are not visual in your visualization. Just keep trying. If, after lengthy practice, you find it is still a no go, it may be that your visualization strengths are not visual. There is no one best way to do a visualization—or to imagine something when I ask you to use your imagination in a ritual. Just repeatedly bring as many elements as you can to your visualizations, knowing that one can only improve magical skills over time. Eventually, the styles of visualization and of imagination that don't work well for you in your rituals will just naturally fall by the wayside, while those that really do the trick will automatically come to dominate.

The Wounded Healer

I said early on, in ancient times it was only after the shaman's own terrible collapse that he found his powers. That generally is misunderstood in this culture as a complete triumph over all his inner turmoil. Not so. Though his triumph was often nothing short of miraculous, a shaman's power continued to come from his wounds. The Wounded Healer, the traditional name for this type of shaman, is one whose constant, conscious awareness of his human fragility and limits keeps him in touch with God, the source of all healing. Only in acknowledging his limits can he fully acknowledge his need for God. Only when faced with the consequences of doing things all on his imperfect own is he motivated to turn humbly to God's help. Also, in continuing to treat his wounds—this includes emotional or spiritual pain—throughout a lifetime, he learns new ways to heal others.

How unlike the Western medical model of the doctor as god, perfect in all his arrogant declarations, or some religious leaders' supposed infallibility! Do not be surprised when meeting a teacher to find he has many illnesses or is quite odd. His limits are what make him a better teacher and spiritual healer than one who is "perfect." If you have a spiritual teacher who seems perfect, run! I am not joking. Very bad things are hidden somewhere.

When I say *spiritual healer,* I am talking about one who heals the spirit, not one who cares for the body or the psychological aspect of a person. I do not see the lessons I give as spiritual tools to heal the body or psychiatric disorders, even the mildest of either. I leave care of the body to a qualified physician, whether that is a Western doctor, acupuncturist, or whoever is best suited to treat the illness in question. I leave care of psychiatric disorder and other psychological aspects of a person to a therapist. I take care of the spiritual and psychic facets of a person. I am not a substitute for a doctor or therapist. To use a psychic or spiritual healer as such is an unhealthy and foolish decision. This includes prognosis!

However, everything has a physical, psychological, spiritual, and psychic aspect. When one has a medical problem, one uses a doctor; and when one has distressing feelings, one uses a therapist. In either case, one can also work on the spiritual and psychic aspects of the problem at hand, either on one's own or with help. Approaching a problem from all directions can yield amazingly effective results. You may wonder why, if I do not address one's psychology, do I talk about feelings like anger, fear, and love? Feelings not only are part of our psychological character, they're also part of our psychic and spiritual makeup. While a shaman is not a substitute for a therapist or doctor, a therapist or doctor is no more a substitute for a shaman than for a Catholic priest.

Avoid perfectionism in yourself. We all have a bit of the Wounded Healer in us, to draw on for his power. One of the problems with some religious and spiritual leaders today is that they pretend to be perfect. They will not admit they have the same failings, doubts, and quandaries as everyone else. And that they have them to the same degree. The message this gives is: Be perfect like me. Another hurtful message this gives us is: All of your daily confusions, disappointments, outrage, and legitimate anger for wrongs done would cease if you were truly spiritual, but since they don't, it is clear you are not a good person. This message makes folks think they are spiritual only if they act in a fake way, ignoring god-given feelings and inevitable human limits. But this mind-set causes them to hurt themselves and others.

Show compassion to everyone, including yourself, for their faults. That doesn't mean you have to put up with abuse or not stand up for yourself. That doesn't mean you should let someone's shortcomings be used as a business ploy to keep you from competing in the workplace. But, in the midst of all the struggle, competitiveness—both healthy and unhealthy—sadness, loss, worry, anxiety, and anger of our own lives, if we remember that everyone else is going through just as much turmoil and facing as many internal limits and external challenges as we are, we may not judge them as harshly. If I can remember that everyone else is just as puzzled, unable always to figure out the right thing to do, just as rushed when they make a decision, just as short of time, I am more likely to understand better when they make a hurtful choice.

This applies to your attitude toward your teachers and leaders. A way to break the cycle of perfectionism demanded of leaders is to realize that everything you go through—all the hopes, frustrations, disappointments, confusion, losses, and challenges—may also be happening to your teachers. That is hard to believe if you are part of a disenfranchised group. But it is usually true. Until you can believe it, you will lose great power because you will think there are not only spiritual heights impossible to reach but other ways to live you can never achieve. You are believing the latter when you think, "If only I get rich (become president, get famous, get published), my problems will be solved." Statistically, famous people live *far* shorter lives. It is also a Buddhist belief that being a spiritual teacher shortens your life. If one buys into the old saw "The grass is always greener in the other person's yard," one chases false power. I want to break the cycle of perfectionism demanded of leaders and everyone else.

In Earth-based spirituality, we drink wisdom from the trees' roots, enjoy love in the planet's rhythms. If we are holding ourselves stiff with a pretense of perfection, we cannot coil a relaxed body around a tree's base, we cannot lie with supple ease against the earth to listen to its heartbeat. The Wounded Healer, as wounded as he will always be, continues to create miracles in his own life and in those of others. Don't reject the part of you that is wounded.

Assignment: to be done during week 4.

An Exercise in Perspective

Step 1. Choose one group of people who play a key role in your life, like the folks you live with or the people in your office.

Step 2. Think of what they are like, in the sense of the degree and quantity of flaws they have.

Step 3. Ask yourself if you know anyone who is any better than them.

Step 4. Then ask yourself why you expect so much more of yourself than you do of everybody else.

This exercise may not be pertinent to you if you are not a perfectionist. But repeatedly clients are shocked when they see the degree of faults they lovingly accept (or at least acknowledge) in others as compared with the absurd standard they assume they themselves should meet.

It is necessary to have high standards toward which to strive. But join the human race: see how everyone around you has lots of faults; use them as a measure of what you can actually achieve. The ideal, absolute, and unrelenting goodness and irreproachable, ever-flawless behavior that you demand of yourself exists only in the mind of perfectionists and misleading spiritual teachers, and in God's perfection.

Assignment: during week 4, do the following three assignments in the order given:

1. After reading "The Wounded Healer," reread "'I Hate My Wife!' and Original Sin."
2. Determine one thing inside yourself that makes you expect too much of yourself. Ask God to remove it.
3. Recite three times in one sitting the last paragraph in " 'I Hate My Wife!' and Original Sin." The paragraph starts, "Every breath I take is sacred . . ." and appears right after Naomi's story. Recite softly and lovingly to yourself, even if silently.

If you can, do all three assignments in one sitting. Even completing two of the assignments in one sitting is wonderful, but if you can't, don't be a perfectionist. (A little joke there, but I mean it, too.)

I strive to tell myself in all things, "I do the best I can, but know I cannot do things at all well enough, and God will pick up the slack. I needn't be perfect, that's Her job." If you are a perfectionist like me, that attitude will definitely help you.

Table of Assignments

Do these assignments during the sixth month:

The first week:
- Write in your journal about pagan ministry. pg. 151

The second week:

- Strengthen your inner Good Faerie. pg. 153
- Say the "Prayer for Divine Help" three times. pg. 155

The third week:

- Write about any results you would like to see your initiation produce other than those described in this training. Also write down anything additional that you believe an initiation ritual achieves or should achieve. pg. 156
- Perform the ritual "In the Mother's Embrace" twice. pg. 160

The fourth week:

- Use "An Exercise in Perspective." pg. 163
- Reread "'I Hate My Wife!' and Original Sin." pg. 164
- Determine one thing inside yourself that makes you expect too much of yourself. Ask the Goddess to remove it. pg. 164
- Recite three times the last paragraph in "'I Hate My Wife!' and Original Sin." pg. 164

What Is Your Path?

Let's reaffirm that initiation is only one step on the path of power. To have an initiation without a path is silly. What is specific to *your* path?

Assignment: during week 1, take another step in defining *your* path by answering this question in your magical journal: (1) What are your life goals? In other words, why have you been put on this planet; what is your path? When you have written about that, answer this: (2) What do you need to do, ritually, spiritually, and mundanely, to follow your path, to implement your goals and visions?

Don't worry if some of your answers to "What is your path?" overlap with answers you've received from your previous work. They should, because they are all part and parcel of trying to live your ideal life. You'll likely get more information by addressing this question, since it approaches your goals from a different angle and you are coming to the question after having done lots of other work. Defining one's path is something that happens over time, and you will continue to do it all your life. If your mind turns blank when you are trying to do this assignment, that is fine. The attempt alone brings you closer to discovering what is specific to *your* path so that no matter how things seem you will eventually find the answer.

A Good Faerie might be a great help in answering the questions above. Don't belittle small steps toward your goal if that is all you or your Good Faerie can think of. Life is nothing *but* a series of little steps. Ever notice how quickly a toddler's tiny steps can get him into mischief?

I try to motivate myself to take my own small steps: complimenting myself for taking one, telling a friend I have taken one, and reminding myself that often the smallest steps are the hardest to take. These little steps add up and take me across huge distances.

If you can think of only one tiny step, that's all you need for now. The next will be revealed when needed. Some steps are impossible to see until you are ready to take them. Often taking one step unveils the next.

When answering the assignment's second question—What do you need to do, ritually, spiritually, and mundanely?—you may find some of the following mundane actions suitable:

Consider taking a class or going back to school. If you want your own radio show, maybe taking a class in broadcasting would help. If becoming a professional costume designer is your dream, you could look into what sort of college program might facilitate that. You can take a class on just about anything nowadays. If your life is centered on making a home for your family, and you're stymied because you're a pack rat who can't rid your home of clutter, there are workshops that can show you how.

Consider not going back to school. That was not a typo: often people go back to school when they already have what they need to learn on the job. This is especially true for women. And it can prevent a woman from achieving her goals anywhere near as quickly as she might. I have learned to achieve my goals without taking classes since childhood when, at age fourteen, without any relevant background, I started producing my own music shows in music clubs.

Read Games Mother Never Taught You *by Betty Lehan Harragan.* The suggested reading list at the back of this book shows how to acquire this out-of-print text. The book is somewhat outdated, but there is no substitute for it. I have seen other books with similar titles, but they were basically self-help books. *Games Mother Never Taught You* explains how corporate America works and how a women can succeed in it. The book contains straight-ahead business information that most men are raised with and most women aren't. It even discusses how going back to school often defeats a woman. If business skills are relevant to your goal, I cannot endorse this book enough.

If you are an artist who wants to earn your living with your art, you have to deal with business, even if not with corporations. *Games Mother Never Taught You* might really help you, too. Since the text helps women think in businesslike ways that are often foreign to them, you can adapt the book's lessons for the sort of business dealings an artist must learn to master. No matter how fabulous a person's artwork is, if she wants to earn her living with art, she needs effective tools to get ahead in a competitive market and to avoid the barriers that keep many artists from ever seeing their wonderful work sold.

Read other books. Read books relevant to your goal. Or inspiring texts; we need motivation to keep on going!

Ask a Good Faerie to be ready to convince you to keep going when things get scary or discouraging or otherwise seem too much to take on. It is frightening to go for your dreams. When an ABC radio subsidiary was training me to host an ongoing show for them, part of my training was to fill in for their absent hosts. The night I was about to host a show all by myself for the first time I momentarily panicked, called a friend up from the radio station, and whispered so that no one on site would hear me, "Get me out of here, what the hell do I think I am doing! I have to work the board, read the commercials, omigod, *read the commercials,* talk to callers, and do a zillion other things. The station's executive producer told me hosting is easy once you get the hang of it. But she also said that the first time is like riding a bike, trying to coordinate a million things. I am going to fall off the bike, I know it!"

He laughed and told me to go for it, that everyone gets stage fright. I am so happy he didn't say, "If you are that worried, tell them you can't do it." I went through with it, had a great time, and the station's executive producer said I did a fine job. And I will always be blessed with the great memory of filling three hours of air time exactly the way I wanted to; I got to say whatever I chose! Being a person who loves to talk and talk (and talk), I love that memory!

If you want to be an opera singer, don't ask your mail carrier how. Of course a mail carrier or anyone else is capable of coming up with great ideas, just because they are thinking beings. I live with a postal worker who offers great advice on all sorts of things. But the nitty-gritty of any realm needs to be learned from someone who knows the ropes. I often see people ask advice from everyone but the very people who have the advice they need. That is self-defeating. As much as it would be easier to ask for the information you need from your brother, wife, friend, or lover, they can't give you what they don't have, and you should not expect everything you need to come from them. Find someone who has had some success with what you want to do, and ask them. It may be time to add to your Good Faerie committee. If you find that intimidating, you might pray for courage or do a ritual to cleanse away that fear.

I've found that people are honored and flattered to be asked how they gained their success. Don't be shy. This may be the only way you can get the information you need to live the life you long for.

This new (or old) support member needn't have succeeded at *exactly* what you want to pursue. One of my Good Faeries is a top saleswoman with a major American corporation. She has taught me how to navigate the corporate world, which is relevant to me because as an author I am involved with corporate publishers. Yet her company has nothing to do with publishing or any other form of media (other than using it to advertise their products).

Do not consider someone who has been unsuccessful pursuing your desired goal an expert. While they might have invaluable input, their *authority* has to be in question. They can give terrible but convincing advice. When exploring the possibility of having my own radio show, I talked to a friend who had tried radio work and never succeeded. A good man, making an authentic effort to help me, he had not gotten over his disappointment. Without realizing it, he painted me a picture of the broadcasting world that was less fact than justification for his inability to achieve his dreams. He also gave me incorrect data for another reason. Lack of education about how the broadcasting world works had contributed to his failure. In a sincere, loving attempt to help me, he gave me misinformation without knowing it.

Pray for knowledge of the mundane means to implement your goals. God is smart. She can come up with anything from marketing ideas to a lifestyle choice that supports your goals. Remember, her answer can come in many ways, such as a friend suggesting how to carry out your goal.

How can you discover the rituals and spiritual means discussed in the second question of the homework? There is a rite that works in any situation. It consists of asking God for help in a way that actually lets Her do so (as opposed to, for example, asking Her to help in ways that aren't in one's own best interest, though at the time it may seem otherwise). There is no spiritual practice more powerful.

PRAYER: STAND AT MY BACK AND FIGHT WITH ME

I believe I have chosen a goal you want me to pursue.
Give me the power to pursue it in the ways you choose
so that I do not foolishly defeat myself.

I believe I am following a dream you have instilled in me.
Give me the power to hold to my dreams
despite oppositions and obstacles.
Stand at my back and fight with me
when I must fight for my dreams.
But help me not defeat myself
by holding my dreams so tightly that I crush them,
by fighting shadows,
or by battling foes that I should leave to your might.

Protect me in this endeavor
from false guides and false pride.
Help me cherish my own wisdom
without turning my back on yours,
which can guide me through all things.

Give me the power to attain my goals
according to Your generous wisdom.
Thank you.

Assignment: during week 2, say the above prayer three times with your goal or goals in mind. Then say it as often as you want; it will help you achieve your goals. God is the most powerful of all your Good Faeries. She will get done the job of helping you achieve your dreams. This prayer is also useful whenever you are getting in your own way.

If in doubt as to whether your goals are really the Goddess's goals too, use the following "Prayer for Clarity" three times instead of "Stand at My Back and Fight with Me." Knowing whether your dream goals are what God wants for you is one thing needed to implement your goals. If you think I am implying that God wants you to suffer instead of getting what you long for, remember this is a pagan God: She wants you to have fun and pleasure! And being very smart, She knows the very things that will give you the most fun and pleasure, things you might not think of or might dismiss when you first encounter them.

PRAYER FOR CLARITY

I hope I have chosen a goal you want me to pursue. Let me know.
If I am misled, show me what to do instead to be happy.
I know you know the best way for me to do that.

Give me the ability to turn my back
on that which may tantalize and promise much
but will only lead me away from fulfilling my deepest longing
and enjoying this heaven on earth you have created for me.

Help me let go of dreams that crush the better dreamer in me.
Give me dreams that lead me
to whatever pleasures your garden offers
that are the most delicious ones for me.

Protect me in this endeavor from false guides and false pride.
Help me cherish your wisdom, which can guide me through all things.
Thank you.

More explanations about the first week's assignment: Part of that assignment was to find ritual and spiritual means to implement your goal. Though the above prayers satisfy that requirement, I want you to go a step further: find at least one other ritual or spiritual means to help you move toward your goal. There are several ways to do this: search the lessons we have already had (or search *Be a Goddess!* if you did that training) for one thing you can apply to your goal. Maybe something internal is blocking you from even starting to pursue a goal. Cleanse that block away with "Kissed by a Star." If you are nervous and feel alone about pursuing your goal, you could do a cleansing or do the spiritual practice "The Goddess's Face" or do both.

Once students have been taught lots of Third Road techniques, they often do not see the many ways these tools can be applied. In regard to this assignment, and to any situation in which you want a tool but don't know which one is appropriate, I suggest you just pick one, use it, and see if it helps. The spell or spiritual idea you choose might have powers you have forgotten or not yet experienced. As an experiment, it might end up not being useful to the matter at hand, but (1) the Goddess's use of coincidence being what it is, there is a good chance the ritual or practice will help; (2) a person is of such a tight weave that almost any action you take can help; (3) if the spell is irrelevant, your willingness expressed in taking action helps in and of itself. In this way you discover, bit by bit, new aspects to rituals and spiritual tenets and new ways to apply them. You are working hard in this training; I want you to get the most return from your labors by discovering as many ways as possible to use what you have learned. I am showing you many applications, but these rites and tenets have so many uses that only time and your own experiences can show them all to you.

If you know rituals or spiritual practices other than those of The Third Road, whether shamanic, Wiccan, Buddhist, Christian, or others, use of them fulfills this assignment. I encourage my students who want to integrate their other practices into The Third Road work to do so. It *is* Third Road of you to use whatever it takes to get the job done.

Or if you write rituals, here is a chance to write one.

Assignment: during week 3, use at least one of the rites or practices you have come up with.

Assignment: during week 4, take one mundane step that was written in your journal during week 1.

Assignment: long-standing. Over time execute all the actions—mundane, ritual, and spiritual—that you wrote down. If you wrote down few ideas, you may eventually have to find more and execute them. Do this all at a snail's pace! Life moves far more slowly than one wants to believe. It carries us forward at a pace that can seem useless and absurd but actually does get us where we want to go. Ever been on a plane trip and felt you would never get there?

Initiation as the Goddess's Child

A priestess has healthy pride. But a Faerie shaman's particular style of powerful, safe magic, as well as sound spirituality in general, demands a difficult balance between self-respect and ego reduction. This odd counterpoint is necessary to safely walk the Fey path in terms of both its magic and its spirituality. Humility is not about groveling but about knowing one's limits, both those specific to one's self and those shared by all humankind.

Please always remember that initiation's capacity to lead us into priesthood is no more important than initiation's power to bring us more fully into the Goddess's care: we are not only Her priests but also Her children. On the one hand, we are, every one of us, truly Herself, able (like Her) to create the world of our own choosing, and boundless in our capacity for realizing our dreams. On the other hand, we are a living contradiction in that we are also limited, fragile, human, needing to recognize that we are made of dust.

In relationship with our Divine Parents, we can put ourselves not only in Their service but in Their care. This is our covenant with Them, and They will uphold us.

If, however, we are only Her priests, we are crippled. For instance, our strengths as priests can betray us if they blind us to times when we must surrender to Her divine, if sometimes puzzling, will and to Her ever-present guidance. Our priestly power can also hinder us if it makes us ignore our faults or our need to listen to the guidance of elders, peers, and those whom we serve as priests.

At other times we might so focus on *serving* the Gods that we overlook occasions when we must put aside our priestly responsibilities to be like a child and focus on our own personal healing and needs. Or in pursuing such self-care we might forget that God may have a better way to do it than the way we choose. Priestly arrogance can keep us from taking care of ourselves or letting the Gods do so; it can also keep God out of our lives in other ways. Despite our sometimes awesome power and knowledge when we serve as Her priests, as Her children we sometimes must instead rely on *Her* power, knowledge, healing, and care. If it is help we need, then we should become still, doing no more than simply dwelling within Her motherly love and care. It is a lush love She will give. Living as the Goddess's child is a blessing that only gets bigger and bigger over time!

Knowing when to be priest and when to be child is part of living the contradictions of The Third Road. Regarding *all* the shamanic contradictions I teach, it is hard to know at any given moment which side of the contradiction is the appropriate one to embrace. For example, I am a warrior: my spirituality tells me to not be a doormat but to fight opposition with God by my side. Yet sometimes the Goddess places a wall in my path that I keep banging my head against for no good purpose. It is hard to know at times whether to fight or to surrender. In one instance, the situation requires surrender, in another, the exact same situation should be fought against.

My healthy pride (one side of a Third Road contradiction, the other side of which is healthy humility) gives me an accurate assessment of my capabilities—I am a good fighter!—but can make me forget there are battles I cannot win. (When I am forgetful this way, I am lacking healthy humility.) Or my sound spiritual belief that I deserve to have a rich, full life can blind me to certain facts: that sometimes we must accept far less than is our due; that life is not always fair; and that part of spirituality is accepting loss, failure, and tremendous disappointment. Then again, a belief that one must learn to accept loss can blind one to times when low self-esteem is driving one to do without before considering other options. Or I might think I am being loving by making a certain sacrifice when instead I should be taking better care of myself.

It is mind-boggling how confusing it is to know where to walk on a given day regarding The Third Road contradictions. (An aside about terminology: the contradictions that I designate as Third Road's are, in fact, usually the contradictions that are just a part of *anyone's* life.) But one risks the gravest magical and spiritual dangers by not making the correct choices. The longer one walks any spiritual path, the more those correct choices become vital. This is where elders, Good Faeries, and God come in. One must be as a child—in the sense of relying on God as parent—and pray for guidance, then ask someone embodied for input.

Every bit of one's being might point to a choice and it still be wrong. I train people to trust their inner voice and instincts and to develop these traits until they are enormously powerful and gloriously driving one toward a magnificent destiny. I counter that by saying that no matter how well developed, these traits can easily lead one astray and will always be very flawed. Remember Hitler: no matter how strong or driving an urge, hunch, or sense is, no matter how right that hunch, sensibility, instinct feels, it is not infallible. There is *nothing* that is anywhere near infallible. I deeply want you to trust your gut and hunches. But embrace contradiction as a shaman; don't be black-or-white about it.

For example, one's whole being, often with good intent, can put up a remarkable struggle to make a given choice when another option is actually right. A proper sense of anger as sacred, coupled with healthily strong survival instincts, can make one think it wrong to apologize for the wounds one has inflicted and decide to focus instead on the harm done *to* one. Sometimes focusing on the wrongs others do, *no matter how strongly you react or how great the damage done,* can be one's downfall; this is easier to understand if you keep in mind that, faced with the exact same scenario, you might just as often act correctly by focusing on the hurt that's been done to you and confronting your abuser or enemy. Again, living The Third Road contradictions is hard.

Multiple forces can cloud the mind. A healthy motive can disguise an unhealthy one. An enormous capacity for sacrifice might walk hand in hand with low self-esteem, causing sacrifice when self-nurturance might be better. My confidence—a positive trait—might at times disguise an unwillingness to face unpleasant facts that demand humility on my part, so that I forget I cannot always know the right choice and neglect to ask the Goddess and my elders for guidance.

Humility and requesting guidance will help you know which side of the road to walk on. That and purification rituals as long as you live, so that the harder the decisions get—and they will get harder the longer you walk any spiritual path—the purer the heart that is making those decisions.

Be proud of your strengths, but keep them in perspective: they are nothing compared to Hers. As Her priest, use your awesome powers with confidence. But as Her child, turn to your Divine Parents, relying upon Their resources instead of your own. Goddess is the ideal parent: She will always be there for you.

Assignment: to be done during week 4. Some spiritual disciplines can be maintained only when in an ivory tower, away from the stress and obligations of a typical daily life. Some of those practices are great when on a spiritual retreat but cannot be fit into one's everyday schedule. Other "ivory tower" exercises don't provide the help one needs while one is walking one's daily *path,* one's day-to-day life.

For example, Benedictine monks, living a reclusive life, can spend a large amount of time in formal prayer in chapel. That is wonderful, and it helps them with the stress and obligations of *their* lifestyle. But the monks' sort of practices would neither be possible for a working mother nor always be the sort of spiritual tools that would most help her be a loving, happy parent. I want you to have tools that can help you actually *live* as the Goddess's child *in your real life, as it exists today.* This said, here is your assignment: in your journal, answer the question "What daily disciplines on the *path* (as opposed to being in an ivory tower) can help you *live* as the Goddess's child?"

There are three means to finding answers to this question. Please use all three:

1. Look through this book for practices that are in keeping with this section's definitions of living as a child of God. You can discover many, though they are rarely described as the disciplines of the "child." Apply them over time.

2. It is important to try to find at least one answer yourself. We must be responsible for our own morals by thinking for ourselves. Even if

nothing comes to you when you try to answer the question, that is okay. All God asks of you is that you try. Practicing willingness by trying to find answers opens up the door to the Goddess's inspiration, and your answers will come eventually.

3.   Ask a Good Faerie for an idea or two.

It is important that for the rest of our lives we ask, "What practice will help me continue to live as the Goddess's child?" This book will always provide a way to do that, and you must always use your own hard thinking and support system. A theory is of no use unless it is implemented; spiritual practices must be done on a regular basis or they fail us when we need them most.

I have said that severe danger awaits when one fails while on advanced stages of the spiritual path. The warning might seem out of proportion in a religion that fears no hell. But keep in mind that Third Road contradictions can defeat a person if he doesn't know which aspect to embrace when. This becomes all the more true when one is advanced. The stronger each side of the personality gets, the more it can delude one about what is needed to be happy. For instance, a thorough awareness of oneself as God might convince one that one cannot be content until everyone on the planet treats one with a degree of respect that is unattainable. The more immense one's magical and mundane powers are, the better an arsenal one has to defeat oneself. If you believe that this can't happen to you, I hope you will consider thinking differently.

I've perhaps never seen an advanced spiritual seeker able to maintain a reasonable degree of happiness without having *daily disciplines that, cultivated by years of application, are ready to catch them at the moments needed.* Practice both sides of The Third Road contradictions in your life as often as you can.

As the Goddess's beloved child, you can talk to Her in your own everyday words. This is legitimate prayer. You needn't bow your head, burn incense, or do anything other than address Her as you need and as seems right to you. When I write the word *pray,* this is often what I mean. Go to Her as a child goes to a loving mother: fearless, knowing you are welcome. Tell her in your spontaneous words, or through prayers you learn or write, whatever you need or want to tell her; in the same manner you can ask Her for whatever you need. You can even tell God you are angry at Her; She will not punish you for your perfectly human feelings.

A child might dance for her mom and needn't have theatrical lighting or music to do so. Dance your prayer, and don't worry about adding any rituals or spiritual trappings such as incense, recitation, or altars (though these are all great if you choose to use them). All you need do is dance. If you are doing it for God, She already knows. She cherishes the dance of Her children. If you'd like, ask God for what you want by drawing a picture. Prayer is using whatever means you select to communicate anything you choose to God.

Here is a prayer you can use when bearing sorrow.

INVOCATION TO THE CONSOLING MOTHER IN A TIME OF GRIEF

Hold me, Mother, as I cry.
Walk with me if I must go about my day in grief.
Comfort me when I am numb or frightened.
Distract me when I focus more on my pain than is healthy.
And send me love to heal me.
Thank You.

Reminder: prayer is useless if mere words on the page. It will not reveal its true power until you recite it as a prayer.

When praying *for* something—let's say comfort—you might want to imagine that comfort is being given to you right then and there. An ideal way to do this is to visualize one line at a time. (Visualization should always be done in the present tense.) When you recite, "Hold me, Mother, as I cry," you can imagine Her loving arms encircling you and comforting you. Breaking an imagined experience down into bite-sized chunks adds up to something more powerful than if one tries to imagine the whole experience all at once. Doing a visualization in step-by-step pieces also builds strong magical skills.

Table of Assignments

Do the following assignments during the seventh month, except for the last one given, which is to be done over time:

The first week:

- Answer these questions in your journal: (1) What are your life goals? In other words, why have you been put on this planet; what is your path? (2) What need you do, ritually, spiritually, and mundanely, to follow your path, to implement your goals and visions? pg. 166

The second week:

- Use the prayer "Stand at My Back and Fight with Me" three times, or use the "Prayer for Clarity" three times. pg. 170

The third week:

- Use at least one of the rites or practices you came up with in the first week's assignment. pg. 172

The fourth week:

- Take one mundane step that was written down in your journal during week 1 of this month. pg. 172
- Answer in your journal the question "What daily disciplines on the path can help us live as the Goddess's child?" pg. 176

Long-standing:

- Over time execute all the actions—mundane, ritual, and spiritual—that you wrote down the first week of this month. You may eventually have to find more ideas and execute them. pg. 172

The Third Road Initiation Never Stops

Because my self-initiation and the work that led up to it were uncharted territory for me, I was motivated to write this book and teach classes offering support and information that were unavailable to me. I had intended my own self-initiation to be a minor rite, just a little something to make me a bit more of a witch. The writing of the script and other preparations were basically done alone. A few elders helped in a minimal way with the preparation, but no one closely supervised me. In retrospect, I realize the work I put into this rite made it anything but minor. The ritual's results matched that work, surprising and changing me in profound ways; had this self-initiation not occurred, I might not be alive today.

I met Victor Anderson two weeks after the ritual. I sat on his couch, amazed, when he announced that I deserved a feather in my cap for having pulled off, on my own, a highly touted form of Faerie initiation—the kind that supposedly makes you High Muckety-Muck Queen of the Universe.

That rite has several forms; according to Faerie lore, the one I underwent leaves you dead, mad, or a poet. Believe me, I had nothing at all like that outcome in mind when I did it. Victor said that doing it alone was very dangerous and that I was lucky to have emerged unharmed. In retrospect, I agree. Do not try to pull off whatever you imagine that rite to have been without extensive guidance before, during, and after. (An elder can and sometimes should be present at a self-initiation.) The ritual that I did is a very advanced magical form, one that needs support. Luckily, I found some before, and much support afterward.

Later Victor gave me his formal Faerie initiation. I was deeply grateful to have this spiritual link with him, since I respected him as a wise elder and spiritual leader.

Despite my enormous respect for him and the rite he led me through, despite my gratitude for his lessons, despite the fact that throughout the community Victor's initiation was prized and sought after, my self-initiation is in many ways far more important to me than his initiation of me. I hope my students feel the same about their self-initiation and the initiation I give them!

When I showed up at his home the day he was to initiate me, we visited a bit and compared notes about our perceptions of the magical realms. Upon hearing my opinions, he told me that he could not perform the rite after all, that he had been in error to think he could. But my self-initiation had already given me what I needed. Despite all my talk about self-initiation, I do believe in initiation passed from one person to another, and I needed an initiation from another person. But my own rite had made me realize I needed no person to stand between me and God and that I was going to be fine no matter what. I knew I did not have to feel bereft if Victor wasn't going to give me the initiation I had come for; if I needed something from human hands, it would come when God wanted, through whom God wanted. I was in no way dissembling when I told Victor his decision was fine by me. He then immediately changed his mind and did the rite.

As is often the case with Wiccan initiations, I am oath bound to share little of what happened in that ceremony except with someone who is undergoing that specific rite. But I entered Victor's sanctuary with him and his wife, Cora; he invoked the Goddess; and they greeted me as a member of their spiritual family.

By creating both a self-initiation and many of the steps leading up to it, with minimal human guidance or academic research I had produced a traditional shamanic process. Shamanism is naturally in our hearts, part of our human nature, and when we trust ourselves we find eternal truths and our innate mysticism.

Dead, mad, or a poet. That rite gives amazing power, so I was lucky it went well. The year I spent working toward my initiation, I should have had close and extensive supervision and a great deal of teaching to be correctly prepared. I now do such training with students who need that particular style of self-initiation.

A few of the many reasons that sort of guidance is needed: my natural psychic virtuosity could have caused me trouble. Sometimes the more talented students get into *more* trouble because they have powers they don't realize, and the unobserved—hence uncontrolled—magnitude of these powers causes real damage. For another, psychological preparation (including cleansing of many specific blocks) is needed to undergo the rite without losing one's mind. I was lucky: I happened to have done that work on my own and in collaboration with a few teachers I had studied with for several years.

Prior to the creation of The Third Road, contemporary Faerie Tradition generally followed the hierarchical system of initiatory degrees often used in magical traditions. I took that for granted when first developing The Third Road, but over time I saw the necessity of embracing an alternative view of Faerie initiation. This approach is taught by my Faerie elder Alison Harlow, who understood that traditional shamans get one initiation and view all initiates as peers; if you are an initiate you are equal to all other initiates. (Alison embodies all that a witch and elder should be. Her humility, wisdom, and loving attitude are stunning. Despite her profound magical powers, she lacks arrogance and lives the lesson of treating others as equals.)

When I was first teaching The Third Road, I trained a few students to give themselves a self-initiation similar to the one I had created for myself. These students had temperaments and needs similar to my own; they were people whose needs could not be met without facing the initiation that would leave them dead, mad, or a poet. (Don't let this worry you regarding your safety as a person in shamanic training: luckily, almost everyone can embrace tremendous power without undergoing that specific initiation. In fact, most people would be *disempowered* by that rite.) At the time I wrongly believed these students were "better" than my others. I thought, *if they were like me, they were better.* Good grief!

That *is* how I was taught, but I will not shunt responsibility: *I* accepted the Faerie Tradition lesson given in those days, which held that certain powers were "better" and those with them should feel like the elite. Thus I developed curriculum only for that style of self-initiation.

For the rest of this tale to make sense, you must know that in those days I also constructed curriculum for The Third Road initiation that I *gave*—and still give—to my students, a curriculum that bestows different powers and lineage than a Third Road self-initiation.

As I developed more Third Road material, I recognized that initiations—both those given to oneself and those given to one by others—continue over one's lifetime in countless forms that range from a mundane lesson in surfing to a deeply formal and highly elaborate Wiccan rite. I saw that all these steps were part of a larger process. I also saw that most of those to whom I had given initiation, as well as those who had received initiation from teachers in other Wiccan traditions, eventually moved through an additional gate, one of self-initiation, each having its own unique style and powers yet remaining a part of the initiation and training they had already received. (I'll give an example below to make this clearer.) Again, all these steps were sometimes clearly—other times subtly—part and parcel of the same thing. I realized this individualized self-initiation was a vital, valid initiation. I did a self-initiation and received two others, one from Victor Anderson and a Third Road initiation. (After I had created the latter and given it to twelve people, they bestowed it on me.) Each rite gave me a piece missing in the other two. Bit by bit I viewed the one traditional initiation as being made up of many rites or, more to the point, as one never-ending rite.

Here's the above-mentioned example: When my initiate Sara Robinson gave birth, it was clear that though I am her teacher, friend, and a mother myself, though I counseled her about how to become empowered by childbirth, though a friend stood next to her in labor holding her hand, ultimately childbirth is solitary, with challenges that can be met with no other companion than the Goddess: a self-initiation.

Yet her labor actually continued her Third Road training: by facing new challenges, whether I was there or not, she better applied lessons she had received from me, better embodied many of the principles I taught her, and gained remarkable insights on her own. Remember, this is a tradition not only of being taught but of always discovering your own truths.

Also, even if a student is long gone from my tutelage, forever becoming more unique instead of a clone following the dictates of a tradition that imposes behavior and ideas, The Third Road tradition is such that the student could rightfully claim that she is still practicing The Third Road because *this* tradition doesn't inflict mandates; Sara's childbirth had its own unique style and gained her her own unique powers: Sara is from American pioneer stock and is a down-to-earth cowboy-boot sort of gal. Another person to whom I had given Third Road initiation might have gone on to start a new dot-com company, and that would have been *his* self-initiation.

I learned, both from the painful falls my arrogance caused me and from observing many initiates and non-initiates become miserable, that the idea that one style of self-initiation is better than another defeats and hurts *everyone* involved. The alternate view keeps one free from false pride and helps one to be forever gaining power. Unhealthy pride would keep one from this ever-increasing empowerment. I created a training for my initiates who wanted to do a self-initiation in their own style as a means of attaining the specific powers *they* needed. I made that training multilayered and tailored it so that Faerie beginners and folks in other traditions could undergo it; thus the seeds of this book were sown, and now we can all become Oh-Great-Priest-Who-Knows-All-Wisdoms!

My motto became "The Third Road initiation never stops," which gave The Third Road community a model of an ever-continuing, personal growth experience without hierarchy, one that fosters individuality among us.

Assignment: to be done during week 1. What do you think of the phrase "The Third Road initiation never stops"? Does it help you feel more powerful, and if so, how? Or is it nonsense to you? Write down your thoughts.

I have seen how deeply ingrained hierarchy is in the American mentality and how hard it is to weed out of even the most egalitarian personality. The subtle ways it persists are extensive. And one's God-given instincts forcefully, and perhaps with great subtlety, urge one toward accepting hierarchy. This is self-betrayal. I want you to watch for it. You who are drawn to The Third Road's magic and spirituality tend toward that sort of inner block; it seems to be the flip side of a coin, the other side of that coin being your wonderful individuality. So after you write, check your journal entries to see if the child in you is being suppressed by unhealthy arrogance, fear, or other blocks. Of course, shortcomings are not the only reason you would disagree with me—it would be hierarchical of me to insist any disagreement means you have inner blocks—but it is always important to look at one's inner barriers to a spiritual lesson and see if they are healthy and justified or unhealthy. If the latter, ask God to remove them and replace them with whatever attitude would open you to the lesson.

The Goddess and the God

JOURNAL EXCERPT

I had a vision in which:

Goddess said to God, "I am complete without you. Yet, in birthing you, I bear the fruits of my self-development; thus I birth my self.

"The splendid, slow-moving cycles of nature are an eternal feminine repetition. It is good that this circling holds only the present and the past. But, like all things, the cycle is flawed—unless it births a future, unless I birth you, who sees visions of the future, who moves, not in circles but in straight lines, toward destiny. Thus I birth my own future, my own self, for you are part of me. Unless I give birth to the fruits masculine, I am not fully potent."

God says to Goddess, "In giving birth to you I am not completing myself, I am bearing the fruits of my self-development. I am birthing my self. Unless I harvest the fruits feminine, I am impotent. My splendid vision is not rooted in rich soil. The future will be bereft of the compassion and carefulness learned only in nature's slow-moving cycles. I give birth to you; my movement

toward destiny, being a straight line that never deviates from its
course, is too perfect. Please blemish that exquisite procession with
compassion for your children: make the straight line bend before
moving forward to tomorrow. In you, I birth my own cycles, my
own self; you are part of me."

The above myth is flawed. No human endeavor, including receiving
revelation, is perfect. While revelation is information received directly
from God (not through a book or a person), even revelation that inspired the Bible is flawed. Pagans believe anyone can have direct contact
with God: we all can experience revelation. A bard creates myths and
lore. A sane bard, knowing her limits, doesn't need to pretend to be flawless in her lore. My above myth is oversimplified and speaks in gender
clichés. For one thing, it implies men are without compassion, women
without vision. But, below, I am going to use gender clichés and oversimplify.

This is odd given that a main point of this section is to help readers
free themselves from gender bias. But gender awareness is a complex
issue, and the myth can serve as a jumping-off point: I will draw on
what truth the clichés *do* hold. I would rather garner criticism for offering this important, flawed lesson than not give it at all. So:

If you watch how the genders act in the animal kingdom, you see
that not all human gender differences are the result of socialization. Yet
we need not be bound by biology but can *draw* on nature, our own nature. We can find both male and female within ourselves and express
both so that we can be everything, do everything, enjoy everything. We
can be free to do what we want despite this culture's gender biases.

The pagan God and Goddess are not hierarchical. Each not only
supports and feeds the other but is ever creating the other anew, showing us how life moves through cycles. We move from masculine phases
of our life to more feminine phases and vice versa. We birth ourselves
over and over in different aspects, not only those that are defined as
masculine and feminine.

Feminine culture tends to be focused in a down-to-earth way on
present needs: as long as the children are fed and no one does without,

there is nothing else to do. Male culture tends to have a wonderful sense of possibility; male culture says, "Look at what we can create if we only build a city, if we only make a wheel." Feminine culture can get stuck in the moment, not create enough change. Male culture in its enthusiasm for a vision of future can forget that children must be fed. How much world hunger is caused by visions of an amazing future world free of hunger? How much world hunger is because some women once forgot to look ahead to the future?

It is easy to think that because the Goddess created God, She is bigger and better. But the first person who walks in the door is not necessarily better. Don't be polarized. Look at each thing in life for what it is instead of thinking only in the dualities expressed in hierarchy.

The Goddess and God are a model that refutes polarities regarding women and men. They can show us that women are *not* the opposite of men and men are *not* the opposite of women. They can show us, too, that if one person has power the other person need *not* do without power, that power is *not* dominance and dominance is *not* power. Free of blindness caused by the belief that life is essentially a set of polarities, we can more accurately perceive our own unique attributes.

Life is not a constant set of opposites. It is not even a spectrum of choices, modalities, realities, or personalities running along a spectrum between two opposites. Life is a grid of endless points, each one unique. Nothing should be treated as the opposite of anything or anyone but as a moment, person, belief, or choice unique in and of itself, maybe tangential to all other moments, persons, beliefs, or choices. I do not even see the two sides of The Third Road as opposites or even as true contradictions.

Assignment: optional, but an eventual necessity if you commit lifelong to the shaman's path. When you are three-quarters of the way toward one of your life goals, reread the above section, asking yourself, "How might I presently be keeping myself impotent and not fully realized by not cycling like the Goddess and God do in the section's myth? How, by keeping too much to the patterns of feminine (or masculine) culture, am I keeping myself from completing the last nine yards of my current goals and from doing so happily?" A woman may ask this in reference to the blocks she is having by living according to masculine culture and vice versa for a man. A woman can act too much according to male culture; the converse is also true.

Within the shamanic lifestyle, a predominantly feminine time should eventually birth a few male attributes if not a full-out male-oriented time, and vice versa. If this movement does not occur, problems ensue. Projects may not be completed, ideas may not be applied in a down-to-earth way, internal breakthroughs may not be followed through to outer manifestations, or a lack of compassion and happiness may occur during follow-through. This cycling back and forth eventually becomes necessary for a person who walks the shaman's path for life, and he must do this assignment occasionally.

Earlier I said that it is a matter of choice as to whether an individual shaman *needs* to experience both male and female deity within. That statement is true. But though he may not need to experience inner *deity* of both genders, if he walks the Faerie shaman's path for several years, he *must* strive to emulate the gods' alternating male-female cycling represented in the journal entry's myth. This cycling is another core Third Road contradiction and as such has endless ramifications.

I suggest to anyone who has many, many years along The Third Road: while doing this assignment, also meditate on or write in your journal about the myth. The cycling described in it demands a lifetime's exploration if you are to perceive all its aspect and benefits, all the reasons one should follow it, as well as all the problems that are averted by doing so. I added the passage from my Book of Shadows instead of only giving the lecture that follows it because, as a myth, it can continually reveal new wisdoms should you walk The Third Road for many years.

A Lovely, Good Darkness

Here is another absurd polarity: light is good, dark is bad. In many ways darkness is a virtue and wonder. You can learn one of these ways if you do the following ritual, which draws on an aspect of positive darkness: darkness as a safe place of healing.

Assignment: optional.

Exercise: Healing in Safe Darkness

INGREDIENTS

- A shroud (shawl, sheet, towel, old blanket, curtain); anything needed to make a dark room pleasant and cozy
- Optional: anything *desired* to make a dark room pleasant and cozy; warm milk

Bitching can be okay. It depends how you do it.

In this exercise, one bitches in the darkness, not to hide in shame, but to be in the safety of the darkness the Mother gives to us as yet another healing agent.

Step 1. Make sure that the room is comfortable and cozy and that it will be a lovely darkness, a good darkness, whatever that means to you. Make sure the room is warm enough. You may want to make the room warmer than usual to create an extra-cozy, womblike feeling. If during the rite you want candlelight and incense pleasantly scenting the room, light them now.

Step 2. Put the shroud over yourself in that dark room.

Step 3. Have a complaint fest. The point is not to figure anything out, make decisions, or analyze problems but to get things out of your system. Rationality can come after the rite, and you will become all the more reasonable for having had a good vent. You can drink some warm milk intermittently while you bitch, knowing it is *in fact* the Mother's milk.

This is a tricky rite to do in a group. I suggest if you do it, everyone bitches at once. It makes for babble that no one hears, and that is just as well. It can be hard to hear someone complain without trying to help them, analyze them, or notice if they are misled. And one is easily misunderstood when venting. When one needs to vent, and only to vent, one shouldn't be told, "That last thing you complained about, it didn't really happen the way you just said it did." The complainer may already know that, but when one is venting one might need to focus on how events felt, not on accurately reciting a history. Trying to portray things accurately can distract one from getting in touch with feelings. Even trying to portray one's feelings clearly can get in the way of venting: a person cannot let loose and express whatever comes pouring up from her soul if she fears that statements like "I hate everyone in the world" or "I feel lower than I've ever felt" will be taken as an absolute truth rather than as a figure of speech or the way she feels only for that moment. She needs safety; her sharp focus on pure emotional expression might distract her so much that her words say one thing when her intended meaning is another; it would be terrible if she were held to her words at such a time.

Once one has gotten everything out of one's system, it is easier to see and hear history for what it is, be open to feedback on how one might improve, analyze or hear analysis, see and hear where one is misled, and receive other help. When the tempest has died down, one is more able to explain feelings in ways people won't misconstrue.

One may not even want nurturance or consolation when venting. When someone needs a good tantrum—and this ritual is a way to have one safely without hurting anyone—solace may get in the way.

Ritual aside, when working in a coven in which someone can vent without hurting others' feelings—for example, no one present is involved in the situation the potential complainer wants to bitch about—you may want to agree simply to listen silently. You may also want to act in the spirit of step 3.

Step 4. Take at least five minutes to be silent. Start out by using the time to compose yourself, just by resting and maybe taking some deep breaths. You may have stirred up a lot of feelings that need to settle down. This—and maybe anytime in the next twenty-four hours after the rite—is not the time for a group to analyze anything its members have just expressed. In fact, the group needn't necessarily ever give feedback. But especially now participants may be too vulnerable, or, though intellectually knowing that their circle is a safe group, they may not yet know it emotionally. In the quiet time they can realize, "Wow, I said all *that,* and, look, no one is jumping down my throat."

After the silence has rested your mind and established a feeling of safety, continue in the quiet: ask yourself if you need anything. Usually one feels great after this ritual, but you may have to move on to this question without feeling reasonably safe yet. In which case the question to ask yourself is

"What would help me feel safer?" If your serenity is marred because you feel guilty for having expressed anger or longing or dissatisfaction with life, maybe you need reassurance that what you did is healthy. If feelings came up that were overwhelming, maybe a hug would help. In any case, even if you find a sense of safety before arriving at this step, still ask yourself if you need anything. You may need a call or visit to an old friend for comfort, a bite to eat, a glass of water, or to curl up and mindlessly forget your troubles with a sitcom on TV.

JOURNAL EXCERPTS

> *Dragon comes with his tears and wild laughter. A wonderfully insensitive laughter . . . Pegasus comes also. The wind blows, I encircle it, the Pegasus and dragon in my arms. They are gone . . . The sun shines. The earth is baked and cracked. Ghosts rise from the ground . . .*

> *I am told in meditation: take what you want from the earth but not what you don't want. I am to tell others this.*

Building a Community of Mystics

The Third Road material, as a shamanic path touched by the Fey Folk, attracts freethinkers, many of whom are loners. I created the curriculum to help people follow their stars and, to use the joke of one of my initiates, become "a cult of one." As of 1986, an unusual community sprang up, one we are very blessed to have: many mystics, a lot of whom are loners, all independent thinkers, somehow began coming together then wandering off alone on magical journeys. They reappear often—or not so often—to celebrate what they have learned and to glean new things that one can discover only through camaraderie, then they wander off once more. This odd community structure allows for both fellowship and the independence that can be crucial to the free spirits who are drawn to The Third Road.

You, too, can be part of this network, a loose network of people who love their independence but who realize that community, support, and camaraderie foster that independence. To do so, you don't necessarily have to meet one of my students face-to-face. You may never even e-mail a person who has read this book. But you can find those who are in the *spirit* of The Third Road community. Here's how:

First, you may already have one or more relationships that fit the bill. Likely, one of your Good Faeries supports you because she is independent and open-minded. See, good chance that you are already part of the sort of community I described above!

Second, read the rest of this section, "Building a Community of Mystics"; its entire focus is on, well, how to build a community of mystics.

It is often hard for folks like me and other Third Roaders—mystics, creative types, independent thinkers—to create community, yet somehow, mysteriously, I became the leader of a national community. I find this fact surprising, wonderful, a blessing, something that feeds me beyond measure, but also odd, because I am such a loner in so many ways: a classical shamanic hermit who spends hours alone in her cave. The odd history of The Third Road community taught me a lot about how Third Road types can build community.

When getting support, look for true mirrors of your uniqueness. Don't seek those who are just like you; look for those who are just like you only in the sense that they are just like themselves. A *real* mirror of your uniqueness will not be a person who provides an identical image but someone who instead is unique unto himself.

There's a saying that there are five honest people holding the cosmos together, and none of them knows who the others are. I think Annie Sprinkle, the performance artist, is one of those people. That is how much I admire her. While my sense of sexuality is far different from hers—we probably could not be *more* different that way; apples and oranges, and ain't diversity grand!—her total embracing of the sexual, her complete and loving acceptance and celebration of everyone's sexual preferences and quirks, her enormous integrity, all coupled with as loving a heart as you could ever meet add up to saint status in my book. Just knowing Annie exists, is "out there" in her own special, valuable way, keeps me going because I feel less lonely when I face the challenges I meet on *my* own unique path. A friend says Annie and I are alike in that we are both completely "out there." Annie's existence inspires me to not worry about what others may think but just live my odd, happy life.

If you recognize one of the five honest people and know him personally, you might want to call him up and find out if you receive a boost just from hearing his voice. If so, you might phone him now and again when you want to feel more motivated about your goals. If you don't know him personally, you can put his picture up on your refrigerator. We all have spiritual links to people we may never meet face-to-face or even by mail; reminding ourselves of these links helps us be inspired and nourished by them.

It is hard to find communities that support the commitment of their members not to follow a herd mentality but to live life in the way each member thinks is best. You've seen teachers who declare, "Reject conformity. Be yourself!" then ostracize a student if she is herself instead of imitating the teacher. That reinforces the student's belief that she cannot become part of any community if she follows her star. Many alternative movements are made up of people who say, "I throw off the shackles of following the crowd," but who act exactly like their leader. (I once joked to a member of the self-described anarchist community that I almost never hung out in that crowd because its dress code was too strict. The poor fellow got very flustered explaining how they really did all dress their own way.)

But I have no doubt you can find wondrous individuals like yourself because there are many more such people than our society realizes. The world is filled with unique, special folks who others may dub odd but who know that odd is good. I also know you can find camaraderie because The Third Road community proves such fellowship is possible, embracing the odd and rich with diversity. Students—wondrously mad, often politically motivated, representing everyone from lawyers to bike messengers, a vibrant rainbow of races, ethnicities, and lifestyles—join together to work and play. Someday, this type of small, intimate, yet empowered community will form the basis of the global village. Make your village! Be open to those who are not like you; you will be surprised to find comrades.

It is sometimes hard to be open to diversity. People who are mystics or freethinkers are often cranky (I can say that, I'm a cranky mystic), so they can be hard for you to tolerate. They are often injured from years of being misunderstood, so they may view you suspiciously or be quick to take offense. Your own similar injuries may make you quick to take insult or to believe too easily that once again no one understands you. Two such people might end up staring each other down, each thinking, "This person is just another conformist, just one more person not like me." Often freethinkers have their own rhetoric, which is great until one says "blue" and the other hears "green" and a fight ensues. But it is worth the struggle. Because you need other people's uniqueness. Remind yourself that in shamanic society, each person is important, their unique needs and potential affirmed and supported.

Some readers may benefit from examining themselves for wounds they carry because no one understood them when they were a child or an underlying hurt that causes them to be cynical, easily insulted, or always ready to feel indecipherable to *everyone*. If you find unhealed wounds, you can recite "Invocation to the Consoling Mother in a Time of Grief" (taught in the seventh month's lesson and easily found by referring to the table of rituals).

Many free spirits disguise the unique gem they are with a protective layer of conformity. Some do it to avoid being ostracized, others because they are under cover, doing all sorts of amazing work that's possible only because they are blending in. Look closely at those around you.

As to there being far more unique, extraordinary folks than most unique, extraordinary folks think: take that one on faith as an experiment. After years of teaching and counseling folks all over the world, I who was once *sure* there were so few of "us" have done a complete turnaround. I now believe there are innumerable throngs of us, tucked away in all sorts of unexpected places.

If a person doesn't have every quality you think you need, she or he can still have an attribute or thoughts that support your way of life. Many of my nearest and dearest are not shamans. I look for friends who have integrity, are lots of fun, are driven toward excellence, have a glimmer in their eye that speaks of healthy madness, and, of course, live life in their own way. Such folks are hard enough to find without demanding they also be witches. Some of these friends don't consider themselves spiritual, which I find funny since they are among the most spiritual people I know.

Assignment: during week 2, say the "Prayer for Divine Help" three times. Reminder: the page on which the prayer can be found is shown in the table of rituals.

A Shaman Is a Healer

All shamans are obliged to serve others. That may mean raising your family or being a professional basketball player, as opposed to acts more typically seen as service, but no one can live happily without doing service. The classical Celtic shaman, as distinct from my adapted modern version, primarily served as a healer. A great deal of her training was focused on making her into a healer, and she was well paid for her healing work because the importance of a healthy spirit was well understood by the Celts.

Here are two methods you can use if you want to do spiritual healing on others. I will also teach you another one later, called "A Spell to Get Just About Anything." These three spells encompass secrets Celtic shamans used to heal someone's spirit from overwhelming grief, discouragement, heartbreak, trauma, suicidal impulses, alcoholism (though it wasn't called alcoholism then), and many other soul sicknesses, as well as to heal the body. Do not use these spells until you have read this whole section. Be sure to apply "The Magic Formula" to all of them.

The Secrets Shamans Use to Heal

I feel vulnerable writing background for the following rite, for it is not only personal but also brings the personal together with the political and spiritual. Some people feel threatened when those three join, and they will attack.

We all know that those who hold alternative views can suffer harassment. Late in 1995, my media and other ministerial work drew the attention of someone who made a death threat to my face. Over a year's time, I also received, from other people, filthy letters and many crank calls. I was terrified when a crisis expert told me to keep a witness with me, on and off for five weeks, because of the death threat.

People often ask, "Why did he threaten you?" Ask him! I barely knew him. We had a minimal connection; I was traveling around the San Francisco Bay Area doing my professional work as a shaman, and he was working at one of the sites I visited. All I can determine is that he was mentally ill and apparently wanted to stop my work. Past that, it is conjecture: I suspect he felt he could intimidate me.

I continued to do my work in the community, knowing that this necessitated often being in the vicinity of the man who had threatened me. My profession demanded I attend events at which he would be present. I am no hero: I was terrified to do this, I whined and complained to friends and got mad at God for "putting me in this position." Yet I try not to back down from work the Goddess gives me, which is to heal and educate others. I am not saying that you should do what I did; we all have to make choices according to our own unique destiny. Perhaps if my daughter had still been young I would have chosen otherwise. But my destiny was to stay put and not run from the danger. While I am not a very strong person, I am a stubborn Sicilian, triple Scorpio.

I did survive, thank Goddess! But one morning during the year all of this happened, I received a cruel e-mail message. This one was not from some bigoted, so-called Christian who thought that in attacking me he was taking the moral high ground; it was from a close-minded witch thinking she was taking the moral high ground. She wrote to me saying that I was utterly immoral and only out to make a buck and that Goddess spit on my fraudulent endeavors as a healer. Sadly enough, the pagan community is not free from infighting or from thinking it is okay to verbally attack someone in the name of moral concern. I read the letter. I was tired and sad. And I hungered for the healing we all need from life's battles.

The harassment of that past year had caused me fear, anger, and disillusionment. While it is important to have a few close friends with whom one can privately share the details of life's struggles, the strongest form of healing I know is to serve and heal others. This has always gotten me through hard times more than anything else. The balm to my despair during that period consisted of my deepening my commitment to minister to, and heal, trauma survivors.

In the same vein, the following prayer was my solution to that morning's disturbing letter; I wrote it in hopes that it would give a tiny bit of love and healing to others. I included lines I had written years earlier. Discouraged by and disappointed in my species, I needed to reaffirm my primary spiritual truths and weave them together with new relevance.

PRAYER TO HEAL OTHERS

Mother,
kind Mother who embraces us with love,
keep us mindful,
and stay with us in the union of all things.

You always bless me
with your kindness, power, and protection.
Now I send you my own kindness, power, and protection.
No god is invulnerable.
All gods need our care.

Mother, keep us mindful,
and stay with us in the union of all things.

Mother,
You were the first of all witches,
spinning a universe from Your passion for our good Father.
So I now spin this wish from my own passions:
may your universe be as Your most loving dreams imagine it;
may I help build a kind, healthy world.

Mother, keep us mindful,
and stay with us in the union of all things.

Mother,
grant me the power
to bless your children each day with your healing grace:
keep me from reciting empty words and puffed-up pledges;
help me instead to perform concrete acts of love and duty;
give me an ability to listen to sorrow,
the knowledge that a hug is a potent healing salve,
and the power to heal others in whatever way you deem.

In the health of others, I find my own health,
for no one stands apart from life's weave.

Mother, keep us mindful,
and stay with us in the union of all things.
So mote it be.

This prayer can help humans as well as God's other children: animal kin, a specific piece of land such as a forest, or the planet as a whole. Just reciting the line "may your universe be as Your most loving dreams imagine it" will heal someone or something somewhere though you may never know who or what. You can also use that line with something (or someone) specific in mind, whether spiritual, emotional, psychic, or physical health is the issue. But let the Gods decide the healing needed and the best way to accomplish it. Leave the details to God. For example, if you say the line for a friend with a serious illness, the Gods will apply your prayer as is best. Sometimes someone needs to die; that is a healing.

I had a severely disabling injury in 1997. For six months I had only about 15 percent usage of my hands, arms, and upper back, and then the usage came back at a snail's pace. Friends were horrified on my behalf. I could tell them, in sincerity, that the injury was the best thing that had happened to me in twenty years because it taught me things I could not have learned otherwise. I would not wish injury on anyone. But for me there was no other way I was going to change things in my life that desperately needed changing. My existence is a million times happier because of that injury, though I struggled with that affliction for a long time. Sometimes we cannot get healthy in spirit, or even eventually fully sound in body, until we face a devastating illness, and I would not have wanted anyone to pray that life-changing event away.

Please do not interpret that last sentence as implying that there is a war between body and spirit and the body must suffer for the more important spirit! I was only referring to how an event *sometimes* occurs. Part of leaving the details to God means that when you let go of an agenda that, for example, someone's illness be cured so that he can live free from physical complaints, you do not get caught in the opposite, morbid extreme—the belief that suffering is the inevitable healer of the spirit. Check yourself to see if somewhere, hidden away inside, you feel that to be really spiritual an ill person must suffer deeply or even die. If so, rid yourself of that belief in your pre-ritual cleansing. Joy and pleasure heal the spirit (and body). Try to pray without biases. *Completely and fully* leave it in God's hands. If a place rather than a person is ill with an environmental problem, do the same. No matter how serious the situation, let God decide. The more serious, the more Her wisdom is needed and the more one can be misled by one's own deep concern.

You may ask, "Then what am I praying *for?*" Ancient Celtic shamans understood that a prayer saying, "Goddess, do as you will," actually adds to Her power to do Her work well. Your prayers help God!

More examples of bias: If a friend's husband has died, and her grief is so extensive that you are worried for her, don't assume that the only healing she needs is to cry it out on your shoulder. Maybe after many months of tears she needs a new lover; love and sex heal in amazing, sacred ways. Maybe one person terrified from having been raped needs to be left alone so that she can get clear about how she feels; another might need to sleep on your couch until her fear of being alone ends.

Praying for healing of the body does not contradict leaving physical healing to the physician. *Prayer* for physical health—as distinct from psychic healing of the body—is fine if when using the above prayer you follow the instructions; if the ill person is getting all the medical care he needs; and if it is clear that divine help of *any* kind is in no way to take precedence over *any* of the physician's decisions, including diagnosis, prognosis, and treatment.

After reciting this prayer, even if you have no one or nothing in mind, the Gods will send you an opportunity to help or heal others, in whatever way is best. You might interpret this to mean that you will be shown a ritual to perform. Not necessarily. As I said, you'll be given a chance to lend a hand in *whatever way is best.* It might mean being extra patient when listening to the problems of a depressed mate. Or telling an alcoholic about Alcoholics Anonymous. It might mean massaging a sick parent or despondent friend. Or running to the pharmacy to pick up medication or cleaning a polluted beach. It might mean doing nothing, because sometimes the only way a person will heal is when we leave them be. God will let you know what to do to heal your loved ones or the planet. It may be very indirect but effective: you might end up healing the environment by telling jokes to an environmental activist who has been so spiritually beaten up by the opposition that he just wants to turn his back on his life's work. Humor can cure us of many spiritual ailments! Or you might facilitate a healing by driving someone to a doctor when she is too frightened to go alone or has no other transportation.

RITUAL

Love Renews Our Planet's Health

The ancients would make love in their fields to ensure healthy crops and make the planet whole. I encourage you to practice that old way: make love with someone you care about—you can make love to yourself— and while you do, offer up the sexual act as a prayer for the earth's healing. That is not difficult; simply say, "I offer up this lovemaking for the earth's healing." If there is a specific area you want to help such as rain forests or a local wetland, add, "I also offer up this sexual act for the health of the rain forests (local wetland, whatever)."

If this rite has no appeal, note that I only *encourage* you to do it. But it is a wonderful experience and one that might surprise you.

Ultimately, spirituality is about love. The Goddess expresses her love in a father's love for his son. Or even in a store clerk's warm courtesy when she listens to a customer's confused, rambling query. God's love is also expressed through recycling or donations to a charity or museum as well as in a postal worker's fastidious care to see that mail reaches the right destination. Sometimes the substantial effort it takes to do one's work well can truly be called love.

Just as much a part of spirituality is romantic love. Including sex. Love between two people, including sexual expression of that love, is that which creates the world and keeps it ever renewed. Sex is holy, as long as it is ethical and done with love. Whether between a man and woman or two people of the same gender or people of different races or two people of very different ages, sex is a holy expression of the Goddess's love.

There is an exception: a sexual encounter between an adult and a child is neither ethical nor sacred. Without exception, that is a heinous crime; without exception, it is spiritual assault. There is no circumstance—no matter how unusual or mitigating or *whatever*—that makes it other than rape. If you were sexually molested as a child, or raped as an adult, this rite offers healing.

Do this spell the same way you said the "Prayer to Heal Others": leave the details to God. Reread all instructions following that prayer before doing this healing, and apply what you can to the land. For example, our environment is sacred and should be protected. Yet deep concern, a driving force that God gave us to motivate us to help heal loved ones who are ill and to fight for the well-being of Mother Earth, not only can drive us toward the correct decision like an arrow to its target; sometimes it instead can make us feel sure we are on course when in fact that arrow is flying toward the worst possible target. This well-intentioned disaster comes about because the driving forces within us are so strong that they not only motivate us but also can blind us.

Despite what I have written about leaving the details to God, there is nothing wrong per se with doing a ritual for someone (or something) with a specific type of healing in mind. Theoretically you can do a rite to save a forest you love from extinction or to cure your friend of cancer. But to do such a rite powerfully and safely, Faerie-style, involves technical and ethical details not covered in this book. You cannot be specific in the spell and have the spell work as you intended without those technical and ethical details in place; with something as grave as cancer you don't want a spell that backfires. Applied to a minor ailment, a mistake in your spell might be more damaging than the original problem. Leaving details to God puts the healing in the hands of a powerful Healer who knows how to circumvent mistakes.

If you apply this spell to a specific locale, trust God to know whether, for example, to stop erosion in that place or to let it happen. In other words, use this ritual on a particular site the same way you would perform the rite on the earth as a whole: let God decide what constitutes the health of the planet and of the locale. Evolution is a complex science She has worked out; She understands very well how to apply it.

Ethics affect the technical effectiveness of magic. (Reminder: everything said in this book regarding magic, shamanism, and so on applies to the teachings of The Third Road. Whether ethics affects other traditions of magic is a moot point.) The state of your ethics affects whether a spell works because ethics and morals are not just mental constructs. The fabric of nature, the substance of matter, has ethics and is moral; to use magic wrongly, no matter what the excuse, is to try to trick nature. Forget it. Nature will win. As the ancient Celts realized, the Goddess and God are in—and act through—all matter. Furthermore, shamans understand that all things—*all* things: every atom in every tree, animal, grain of sand, page of a book, folding chair, or piece of plastic—is alive and cognizant and cares about what happens around it. Nature has honorable principles. In the same vein, I cannot educate you in this book on the ethical details needed for certain spells; leaving those out of the spell through lack of education can still make the spell backfire. Nature and all matter will do what they must to follow their innate ethics and morals, and who knows how that might affect the results of the spell?

Magically leaving details to God does not imply one shouldn't fight on a mundane and spiritual plane to save our planet. If you are a warrior, it is fitting to fight for good on the material plane, as long as you assent when the Gods want you to back down. (It is good military strategy to go with the Gods' plans. They are smart generals.) Magically, leave the details to God in Faerie rites unless you have a face-to-face teacher.

If you want to use magic as a warrior, apply cleansing rites to qualities in you that keep you from fighting on the mundane plane: fear of mockery; unwillingness to stand out in a crowd; a belief you could never win any battle; and the like. Until relevant blocks are cleared, a shaman warrior does not have his full power. Clear only those things that stand in the way of *your* battle style. For example, some warriors fight best if they don't stand out in a crowd; to show their hand would ruin their strategies. Remove the inner impediments relevant to your fighting style. Whenever removing blocks regarding any goal in life, it is usually best to remove one block to a specific goal at a time; go at the same slow pace that we have been following in all our shamanic work. Steady and slow is the best mode of shamanic transformation. Be patient, warriors.

Whew, we've gone from a spell that heals the planet through love-making to ethics to the cognizant nature of all matter to spiritual warriors. That's a living example of how all things weave with one another! And now, back to that sex spell:

Leave technical magic out of this sex spell. There are two reasons.

1. It is an inner block to think that sex needs ritual trappings (such as candles and incense) to be sacred or magical. Plain old sex, done as one usually does it, is all it takes. After all, there is nothing plain about plain old sex. Have fun, enjoy being orgasmic, and know that that is of itself sacred and magical. If you feel odd about that, before you do the spell you may want to perform a cleansing on the inner things that make you feel odd.

I wrote *orgasmic* and *fun* to get the point across that one needn't be pompous or self-conscious or change one's usual sex style. But if you don't happen to reach climax, never have orgasms, or experience sexual problems that are typical to you or that happen just this once, the spell still works quite well. Sex is magic. For example, maybe you are an incest survivor who enjoys making love but you never feel quite safe because sometimes old feelings of violation surface. If you want to do the rite, let yourself enjoy it without pressuring yourself to be suddenly free of all fear. And who knows, you might even find the safety you have long gone without.

2. This is a powerful ritual done safely if you do it as written here. Do not bring in technical elements, such as visualization or methods for altering one's consciousness—but *do* perform "The Magic Formula"— for in doing so you also bring in many conditions that, though powerful, have ramifications that can adversely affect safety. Such conditions may also affect whether or not the spell works the way you want. Navigating the spell once technical aspects are added requires lessons from a Third Road instructor who can teach you in person. Just make love, and know you are deeply blessing the earth in one of the most profound rites you might ever perform. Technical elements are not needed to make this rite powerful and great fun. You may have the best sex you've experienced.

This ritual automatically heals you, too. You are a part of the earth; without adding or changing one thing in this spell, you are automatically healed of something. It is likely you will feel something profound happen to you in the middle of the rite. Or you may not feel the healing or see the results for a long time. You may see results later and not think they are related to the rite. The rite might heal a wound from the trauma of childhood molestation or mugging or heal a block to abundance or inner wisdom. You might finally realize, or come closer to seeing, your inner and outer beauty. You might gain confidence in your anger as a source of power. Or an anger that depletes you of energy might disappear. A blind spot that keeps you from career advancement might vanish. Healing one part of you heals all parts of you, even your deepest wounds, even if the obvious part of the healing seems too small to be significant.

"Prayer to Heal Others" and "Love Renews Our Planet's Health" are powerful rites. As always, use them exactly as given. Shamanic healing, being as real as a knife—you don't think a knife is only a metaphor— and as powerful, and being an effective form of touching another person, can cause great harm if done improperly. This same advice applies to "A Spell to Get Just About Anything," which you will learn later.

These three dynamic spells are the stepping-stones to even more powerful Third Road healing methods, which you may need face-to-face training in order to do properly. Doing psychic healing of a person or place, and having a specific result in mind, is highly advanced Faerie work. When training semester-long groups, I tell folks for the first two years, "If you feel you *have* to do a spell on someone or something, with a particular outcome in mind, use a rite in a tradition you already know." Readers, this is an option for you. I always add, "If you have no tradition that has a spell you can safely use, talk to me and I will show you the details needed for that specific spell in the exact circumstances you are using it in." You and I don't have that option; this is a book. But all is not lost! You can get ideas from your local metaphysical bookstore, a psychic consultation, or a Good Faerie who's pagan. More important (note well): I finish off my little speech to my students this way: "Most of the time, no matter what people think, it is better to leave the details to God until one is an adept, and, even then it's a good policy a great deal of the time. I cannot tell you how often someone really thinks they have to do it their way, when they are subtly sabotaging their very goal and/or working against the best interest of everyone involved."

I will admit it is even fine to apply Third Road magic to a physical ailment and select a specific outcome, but that takes years of study, and it is too dangerous without in-person tutelage.

Table of Assignments

Do these assignments during the eighth month, except where otherwise specified:

The first week:
- Write down your thoughts about the expression "The Third Road initiation never stops." Then examine your journal writing to see if it expresses unhealthy arrogance, fear, or other blocks. If so, ask the Goddess to remove them. pg. 184

The second week:
- Say the "Prayer for Divine Help" three times. pg. 195

Optional:

- Perform the exercise "Healing in Safe Darkness." pg. 189

Optional:

- Recite "Prayer to Heal Others," pg. 197 and enjoy "Love Renews Our Planet's Health." pg. 200

This assignment is optional now but an eventual necessity if you commit lifelong to shamanism:

- When three-quarters of the way toward one of your life goals, reread "The Goddess and the God," asking, "How might I presently be keeping myself impotent and not fully realized by not cycling like the Goddess and God do in the section's myth?" pg. 187

How to Avoid Dangers and Problems Before, During, and After Initiation

JOURNAL EXCERPT

Though D. doesn't know any of the people involved, I thought he would be a good person to talk to about the anger I felt because I hadn't yet received the initiation I wanted. He said, "Good. A chance for humility." I kept saying how angry it made me, and he laughed and said that sometimes criticism is more important than praise. So I am feeling better about this. Not completely, but considerably . . .

Throughout this training, we have routinely and rigorously discussed solutions to the dangers of both the shamanic journey and magic. Often this instruction might not have been apparent. It is time to address these potential problems in a new context. The dangers and solutions discussed below are relevant to any spiritual path, even the most mainstream religious one.

Since initiation is not a moment in time, these problems can happen at any time. Sometimes, the exact moment known as initiation exacerbates these problems or can even contribute to our getting lost in them.

No book can mention all the dangers of any spiritual path, whether pagan, Christian, or any other spiritual tradition. Nor can it give *all* the solutions to the dangers mentioned. I would be put off by any book or person who said they provided answers to all the difficulties that might arise on a journey to the grocery store, let alone on a spiritual or magical journey.

Having done the work in the seventh month's lesson, "Initiation as the Goddess's Child," you are ready to explore some of its issues more deeply by examining spiritual and magical pitfalls and their solutions. Some of these are linked to and/or feed each other; others are variations on a theme. Here are the pitfalls:

Unhealthy pride and false ego. I've discussed versions of this, such as Hitler's believing so strongly in his inner voice that he devastated the world. In my case, it was arrogance that made me feel morally superior to an elderly woman in the grocery store, when *I* was the one who was being selfish. Let's explore it further:

Self-justification regarding an unhealthy ego. There are many versions. In the grocery store I pumped myself up with "righteous" indignation and looked down on someone who was not even in error instead of looking at *my* error. Watch out if you ever feel high and mighty. Feelings of moral superiority often precede one's downfall.

If one can face down one's unhealthy ego tendencies, including self-justifications, the other dangers along a spiritual path are more easily avoided. This sort of humility is hard to achieve some days. We forget the importance of it or even fight it. Our very survival instincts might battle against humility. I am not denigrating survival instincts; they are a wonderful gift that help us persist and fight for our rights. But even our most potent attributes can be a double-edged sword; there is nothing that can not be used to gain victory or defeat. And any positive attribute or inner shortcoming that blocks true humility will often feel oh-so-right. Your survival instincts might go into overdrive and convince you that you will lose all if you do not desperately cling to your unhealthy ego.

Thinking oneself immune to spiritual dangers. I want advanced practitioners to pay attention to this section. It is easy to think oneself immune to the dangers listed here. That, of itself, is one of the biggest dangers an adept faces. Also, you face pitfalls that occur specifically when you're on your own in your advanced work.

Pomposity. Earlier, I wrote of the initiation that Faerie lore says will leave you dead, mad, or a poet. I've realized that to help the supplicant (one seeking initiation) go safely through this particular initiation, the teacher has to build the student's ego up to fevered pitch, a state that would truly be megalomania in another context. After initiation, it is required that the teacher immediately knock down the new initiate's ego severely (not cruelly or without warning). Only through this process can the student learn to walk between the two ego states the rest of her days. Getting someone through that particular gate requires building her ego up to mythic proportions. Navigating life on the other side of that gate requires the ego often return to that state. Yet this causes trouble if not balanced by recognition of human limits. This is a necessary contradiction. Otherwise one gets a fool who thinks she's a sage and who ruins everything in her path and in the lives of those around her, all the time truly believing she is holy, above reproach, and doing what is ethical.

The more advanced you are, the better your self-justification for unhealthy ego can be. And the more dangerous it can become. The more any side of The Third Road contradiction is developed, the more the other side of that contradiction, its so-called opposite, must be developed. This can only be done through daily disciplines, consistently maintained. (If *disciplines* calls up images of behavior that was forced on you and that suppressed your spirit and joy, use the word *practices*.) Just making a few or occasional stabs at humility—or any other trait you want to develop—won't do. But you don't have to practice all those disciplines right now, today. One shouldn't. Add them over time, slowly, at the same pace that the rest of this training has been done.

Here are some daily disciplines to keep the unhealthy ego down and avoid false pride: surrender to life's flow; listen to feedback from embodied peers, elders, therapists, and the like; constantly recognize and accept one's human limits. These disciplines, like all Celtic ethical disciplines, not only help one remain principled and safe but also allow you to experience the ultimate happiness, in the most mundane sense, the way you feel after a massage or during a concert.

False humility is just as dangerous as false pride and can be a form of arrogance. The next assignment discusses its antidote.

Hiding self-knowledge too deeply in the unconscious mind. Both healthy and false humility can make us hide our attributes and faults. There is another cause: our strengths as well as shortcomings can be hidden too deeply from our conscious sight.

A shaman learns to do what I call "bringing the dream into the waking mind." That dream includes the wisdom of the unconscious mind, which is filled with gems of self-knowledge, creativity, solutions, and powers unique to each person. Victor Anderson taught me that the unconscious speaks directly to God. Yet the unconscious is often feared in our culture, viewed as the repository of evil impulses that need to be repressed as they sit in waiting, ready to pull us down into a mire of depravity. Ick!

There are many reasons that our faults and fears as well as much that is brilliant and good in us becomes submerged, hidden in our unconscious. Repressive religious messages make us ignore our passions until they become hidden even from ourselves. Or one might blame oneself for a trauma that someone else perpetrated—for example, the suicide of one's parent when one is a child—and the guilt is so unbearable that if it is not healed it is driven further inside. There it continues to press upon one with vague confusions and terrifying, unnamed pain. Modern life, from childhood to adulthood, repeatedly drives both the good and the bad of oneself into the hidden recesses of one's being: everything from stifling disciplines in school to the homophobia that makes a lesbian lose touch with her desires to mind-numbing drugs that mask rather than heal our fears to extreme financial pressures that make someone throw up her hands and think she means it when she says, "I never really wanted to do anything with my life anyway but earn enough to pay the bills." By the time we become adults, we have lost touch with an enormous part of ourselves.

This training, in all its parts—from precepts to rites to lectures—helps bring our dreams up into our conscious minds. A person committed to lifelong shamanism always does the better part of these rites or carefully adapted versions thereof and adheres to most of these precepts so that the unconscious keeps divulging new gems, new solutions to new problems, new powers, and new creativity. Wounds healed, and faults that have been overcome, often later reveal new layers that need resolution; a person who chooses the shamanic path for his whole life finds solutions to these deeper wounds and returning faults because he continues to bring the dream to the waking mind. Thus he stays happy and does not fall back into old patterns of self-defeat or hurting others.

The curriculum weaves together as a whole to bring us in touch with the dream in a useful, safe way; doing only some of the lessons might not help you to safely uncover the dream or interpret it accurately. I'll give an example of this weave. During an ancestor ritual one might hear messages from one's unconscious. Great! But adding an exercise that increases self-esteem makes one more open to, and able to hear more accurately, the messages of the unconscious as revealed in the ancestral work. A further weave offers even more benefits, as the self-esteem and ancestral material, working together, help one honor the beauty one discovers buried deep within the unconscious and bravely face the scary faults one finds hidden in one's self. But one's conscious mind might do an about-face and make excuses for the self-defeating or hurtful actions revealed; more weaving, in the form of ongoing rites of surrender, keep this from happening. And so on.

Psychic fracturing is another risk. When an event is tremendously joyous or painful or causes a major inner change—whether for the good or bad—one can be overwhelmed and the conscious mind can become more separated from the unconscious mind than it should be. This psychic fracturing is already somewhat the case with most people nowadays and is the very thing discussed above. Initiation without proper preparation and follow-up can seriously exacerbate the problem.

Max's Follow-Up Ends His Spiritual Wild Goose Chase

Max came to me for counseling because he was very spiritual yet very unhappy. He was gay and felt guilty about it. In telling me this, he happened to mention that he had had a vision of a group of men sitting in a circle talking about their love of God and hugging one another, and when the circle was over two of them went to a home they shared, where they curled up like two happy puppies and slept. Asked what this lovely vision meant, he told me it was "a sign from God to be nice to all people, never angry, and to always treat others as equals."

While that *sounded* good, I suspected that God had sent Max a vision that his unconscious offered up to him, and his conscious mind could not believe the vision's *true* meaning. So his conscious mind disconnected itself from his unconscious as well as from his feelings and his common sense. Max truly wanted to serve the Goddess and the gay community but became caught up in spiritual razzmatazz: by trying to "be nice to all people, never angry, and to always treat others as equals," he repressed his feelings and passionate desire to integrate his spirituality and loving desire for other men. Of course, an intention to be "nice to all people" needn't indicate a suppression of one's feelings, but *Max* had unknowingly fixated on that goal as a means to suppress his authentic feelings and the true interpretation of the vision; only in the psychic fracturing of suppressed feelings could he maintain the false interpretation. His understanding of the vision sounded great but felt all wrong to me; Max was all white light and unicorns, miserably chasing after a phantom dream he thought God had sent him. I am not denigrating unicorns, white light, or a person's revelation when it is one of innocent sweetness. But his was sweet like a diet of only cotton candy, a forced innocence that to my psychic perceptions felt inauthentic. I gently told him all these things, adding, "Only you know what your vision meant, but I suspect it really meant that you might enjoy starting a pagan group for gay men."

He insisted, "Oh, no, initially I had thought so, too, but I realized I had misinterpreted the image. I was overjoyed at the thought of a gay pagan group; our town needs something like that! But then I realized that it is more important to always be kind than to just form a group. It was arrogant of me to think otherwise."

I said, "Max, that might be true for some people. I don't think it is true for you. Besides, why choose between kindness and a group? And why not *humbly* start a group? I think that what happened is that your guilt about being gay kicked in. You had not sufficiently cleansed yourself of shame about your sexuality. So you started reinterpreting the vision." Seeing him shake his head no, I quickly added, "Let's get rid of that shame and then see what you think."

Over a few months we worked through his shame. Once he gained pride in his sexual preference, he also accepted with pride his desire to serve the gay community as a priest. He stopped his spiritual wild goose chase. His pagan group for gay men thrives today. His story is an example of someone overwhelmed by what should have been a groundbreaking healing experience—his vision—that instead became psychic fracturing. The antidote is: follow this training.

Embracing pseudospirituality by rejecting the body and physical pleasure is sometimes a form of psychic fracturing, but other things can cause it. An antidote to this problem, whatever the cause, is to continue one's purification work on those things that stand in the way of self-love, self-care, and sexual expression. (You don't need to worry about suddenly beginning that work. You are already doing it! Later we will discuss what special work you might need to do right before the initiation rite with regard to psychic fracturing. Unless you feel very pressed, don't worry about it for now.)

If rejecting the body and its pleasures is caused by psychic fracture, one actually feels separate from one's body.

Rejecting the body or material world can lead to all sorts of problems, such as physical illness or running short of money. God doesn't want that for you. She loves you and wants you to take good care of yourself. A habit of doing otherwise can be caused by false ego, as in, "I am the omnipotent priest of God; I can work three full-time jobs and never lose my temper with my family."

A fixation on self can make one miserable. Much as I emphasize self-care, self-expression, self-fulfillment, self-healing, and self knowledge, one can go too far, with the best intentions, and not even know it. For example, one can be so preoccupied with job security that one is always living in fear. Or one can focus on self-healing so much that one never goes out to have fun; even recovering from tragedy cannot happen without a degree of enjoyment in one's life. One can examine one's feelings unremittingly so that, without intending to be hurtful, one forgets to take other people's feelings into account.

This can be made worse by another fixation on self: a person may forget that *many* people live their days dealing with intense sorrow, pain, or loss. Thus he comes to believe that his own unhappiness is far stronger than that of most other people. Holding this belief, he cannot notice when other people are just as vulnerable and in need of a sensitive response as he is. Ultimately, we are on this planet for two things: to have fun and to serve others. That is the crux of The Third Road contradiction. Without pleasure in our lives, we can serve no one; unless we serve others, we do not find fun, do not heal our worst injuries, do not find our truest self. The solutions to fixation on yourself are to help others and to have people around you who will tell you when you are unknowingly overwhelmed by a focus on yourself. Those who commit to shamanism as a lifelong path must also continue purification work to be free of the inner elements that lead one to becoming overly preoccupied with oneself.

Disruption in one's life during the year after an initiation is to be expected. Change, even a wonderful one, jumbles up one's life for a while. For example, when you gain self-confidence, friends might be temporarily afraid, thinking that your new poise means you are going to desert them. There may be stress and struggle in your relationships until your pals see that your new faith in yourself can only make you a better friend. Another example: after clearing inner blocks to going back to school, during the first semester one still might face fear of meeting new people in classes, not to mention a lower income while school is a top priority. Changing for the better has a domino effect. Your environment shifts, and it takes time to get used to it. Wonderful new choices bring challenges that also aggravate unresolved fears, angers, and self-defeating beliefs; these traits surface and need to be dealt with. But it is worth it, because in the end you not only feel a great sense of achievement but you also have taken the steps to happily live the life you dream of. Antidote: keep using the tools and ideas in this book, including getting support when needed, and you will be fine.

When one gains power and does not use it, or uses it incorrectly, acci-

dents can happen. Eliza never stood up for herself. When she finally had the confidence to do so, she wanted to storm unannounced into her boss Jack's office and tell him, "You are a jerk!" Needless to say, Jack would not have understood that Eliza was upset about not having been paid sufficiently after many years of excellent work. Eliza had gained enough self-esteem to do the right thing, but she didn't have the skills she needed to do it correctly. When she came to see me, we discussed ways in which she could calmly tell Jack that she loved her work but could no longer stay with the company without a pay increase. She resolved to explain to him that her needs were now greater than could be met by her current wages. This scenario worked, and Eliza didn't have to insult Jack or risk leaving her job without a good reference.

Someone might also bring in psychic power and not know how to use it. If your cat is knocking more things over than usual, or a few things in your environment mysteriously fall from their shelves, you might be gaining magical power that you don't quite know how to use. Usually, if you just continue your work, the cats will settle down and accidents will stop. As you keep at your magical efforts, you come to use the new power more effectively, and thus the "fallout" ceases.

However, some extreme versions of psychic disruption in one's environment do require support. You may need to contact a reputable professional psychic or shaman for help. Or look to a nonprofessional: a longtime witch or person who does psychic work exclusively for friends need be no less an expert than those who earn their living in the psychic realms. You might find nonprofessional help in a local pagan group or an on-line chat room. Don't let morbid fear of psychic disruptions in your environment stop you from becoming the magical person you are. Power unused can be all the more problematic. On the other hand, one can have huge magical potential that one rightly decides to leave untapped. One need not become a witch just because one has the ability to do so. However, having a realistic fear that results from knowing you are by and large not suited to do magic is different from having morbid fears that keep you from doing what you love.

Kundalini blocks are a possible problem. When one participates in a shamanic training, energy flows into the body from all directions. Some of this power climbs up from the base of the pelvis to the top of the head and past; this progression of energy is called kundalini. The kundalini can meet obstructions at any point. These obstructions are usually caused by one's inner blocks. If you feel energy stuck at any point along your spine, ask yourself what outer goal in your life is blocked right now and what inner factor might be contributing to it. If you discover an inner block, it might be the kundalini block. Cleanse it away. If you discover no cause, ask the Goddess, "What is causing this block in my energy flow?" As always, Her guidance can come in any and all forms, so stay alert for the next few moments or days after asking the question. If She reveals the block—too much fixation on one's own needs, suppression of one's feelings, confusion about one's obligation to one's family—cleanse it away with one of the book's purification rites.

Just as an extreme psychological dilemma might need the expert care of a therapist, so an extreme energy problem, such as a kundalini block that is very troubling, might need the help of a longtime shaman.

Assignment: during week 1, look through this book for premises, practices, and attitudes that develop healthy ego and pride. You may want to fulfill this assignment by perusing the second month's lesson's second section, "What *Is* a Priestess?" or, in the same month, "'I Hate My Wife!' and Original Sin." Or you might look in the first section of the fifth month's lesson, "If You Walk the Path, the Initiation Will Happen of Its Own," or the same month's "Bardic Brats." Or you may prefer to explore the volume at large.

This lesson has designated false humility as dangerous and as needing an antidote. Anything that cultivates wholesome self-respect also reduces false humility.

After doing the above, do a lengthier assignment. Think of examples of healthy ego and pride. Do this by asking yourself the following questions and giving very concrete, specific answers:

Ask: "How might I take pride in myself and my accomplishments?" Your answers should be *actions* you can take and *concrete, clear-cut* actions at that, such as, "I can tell a friend what I've achieved" or "To treat myself as the precious child of God, I will buy myself a pretty scarf I've had my eye on." Vague responses like "I can value my work as a parent," or "I will honor myself" aren't always as useful. If you only find such inexact measures, follow through on them with a further query: "What *specific* thing can I do to value my work as a parent (honor myself)?" You can value your parenting by, at the end of every day, telling yourself one thing you did well as a mother or father. You can honor yourself by spending a few minutes every day relaxing over a cup of tea.

Ask: "What does taking good care of myself mean?" Again, you'll want to ascertain a specific, concrete response such as eating nutritious food or keeping a sane work schedule.

Assignment: to be done during week 2. This chapter has discussed various forms of pomposity—for example "righteous" indignation—as well as how one might lack recognition of their human limitations. But we all have to think and work for ourselves, so take the discussion a step further: think of another form of spiritual pomposity. Then come up with a practice that keeps the ego down to a healthy size. To fulfill either part of this assignment, search for answers in this book, or look through the database that is your mind, or ask a Good Faerie his thoughts, or ask God for an insight. Note I said "practice." Be concrete and specific; find something you can *do*, even if it's an attitude you can practice having.

Assignment: during week 3, analyze: What in this training prevents psychic fracturing? You need not spend more than three minutes on this exercise!

If one walks the shaman's path for life, one must eventually follow all its disciplines or carefully constructed variations thereof. One might need all these disciplines—for example, self-examination regarding unhealthy ego, pre-ritual cleansing, and honoring oneself as a child of God—even if one chooses another form of psychic work or spirituality or if one chooses to create an amalgam of several paths. The greater any power, even the highest spiritual power or the most ethical magic, the more potential for negative damage. However, don't get overwhelmed. This section's solutions and suggestions for avoiding dangers and problems before, during, and after initiation need only be introduced into your life over a long period of time. Maybe over many years. Bit by gentle bit, add them—and the other disciplines that will develop both sides of The Third Road contradiction—to your daily, or at least your frequent, practices. At the same snail's pace, come to maintain these disciplines in an ongoing, consistent routine.

If any of the dangers in this chapter appear in your life in ways that are puzzling, remember to pray for guidance or ask for embodied help.

How to Have Great Sex

If you improve any part of your inner landscape, your sex improves. For example, when you enhance self-esteem or communication skills, you enhance your sex life. So any ritual or lecture we have done to bless or empower any part of your life helps you have better sex. "Prayer to the Loving Father," in freeing a person from the fear of being all alone in the world, might also give her the sense of safety she needs to express her pleasure-seeking nature. The section "Our Journey to Ourselves," in the fourth month's lesson, promotes self-defined spirituality and thereby encourages a student to develop her lifestyle in accordance with her specific sexual needs. "Prayer to Find and Celebrate the Self Through Selflessness" helps one serve others; when one gives of oneself earnestly, one becomes fully engaged in life and thus has the capacity to experience intense sexual pleasure.

But it is great to emphasize sex all by itself. Cleansing away a sexual block is very much in keeping with pagan spirituality. Don't feel guilty for doing so. Plain old sex, without ritual trappings, profound thoughts, or an attitude prescribed by a religious group, is holy.

However—and I can't emphasize the following strongly enough—if you want an ecstatic lifestyle, focusing only on improving your sex life will defeat you for two reasons: the sex will decline, and the lack of integration will defeat you. Sex is not distinct from the whole of you; neither is finding satisfying sexuality separate from improving your spirituality. For years, on a consistent basis, I've had amazing, mind-blowing, soul-fulfilling sex, sex so great that I feel I can die without ever having sex again. (Not that I'm planning on that!) I *know* that the reason the sex is so good is because I have learned about serving the cosmos.

Prayer for Great Sex

This prayer is a sexual healing and an empowerment of one's sexuality. It is also a spell to improve one's sexual pleasure.

"Prayer for Great Sex" can be used several ways. Done right before making love, it will heat things up! Or you can recite the prayer even if there is no lover on the horizon so that your sexuality is in better shape when love eventually does arise. It provides valuable healing for anyone, from those who are already sexually fulfilled but want to make it better to the nth degree to people whose spiritual wounds cause them profound sexual frustration. The prayer can also be used solely for the sake of feeling sexy and vital even if one is committed to celibacy; it just feels good to do the prayer!

There is great power in our sexuality. When we feel free to express our sexuality—even if the way we do so is celibacy—we can express many other parts of ourselves, such as our healthy drive to succeed in business or our profound urge to be creative.

Use this prayer once as instructed, then as you wish; if you use it a lot, make sure to return to the instructions now and again, and follow them exactly.

This prayer repeats the line "Purify me sexually" three times. Making that request may bring up your blocks to your ideal sex life. Every time you ask "Purify me sexually," check for such blocks. Examples: When you ask Her to purify you sexually, do you hear within yourself a self-abusive or defeating thought like "To be pure means to be alone," "I am bad to care so much about my own needs," or "God's too busy to care about my sex life"? Each time you examine yourself, if a block(s) is apparent, interject the prayer "Please purify me of this/these thought(s)" right then and there.

More examples: Maybe at another point in the prayer, when you ask the Goddess to purify you sexually, you may become afraid that She will punish you for wanting sex. Or some part of you starts thinking it is evil to love, to be held, to honor the pressing desire for a lover's gentle touch, to profoundly want one's own mate to lay against one in the darkness after lovemaking, to want to fall into an interplay of breath and sound and sigh as the two of you giggle and babble and share secrets before sleep. Pray to Her: "Please purify me of such fear (unhappy thoughts, etc.)."

More examples: Maybe after asking "Purify me sexually," while searching for blocks to great sex, you realize that you think that no one will love you. Pray, "Please purify me of this block to great sex."

After the prayer's three repetitions of "Purify me sexually," continue on with the prayer, checking in every few lines or so to see if any of these additional lines bring forth similar resistance to your sexuality, sensuality, pleasure, and sexual gratification. If so, ask to be cleansed of the resistance.

Dear Goddess,
Purify me sexually.
Purify me sexually.
Purify me sexually.

Please, Goddess,
help me allow the sex to flow through me,
sweet like coconut milk,
sweet like honey, sweet like love,
rising from the earth with its green pulse, mud, and blue waters,
rising up from my crotch into my lungs, into my breath.
Let my breath weave sex with the air,
with the very molecules that dance around me.
Let my sex rise to greet and mirror
the arching blue sky above me,
the endless pulsing universe,
and your timeless, perpetual, never-ending union
with yourself and your darling God.
Let my sex be in union with your joy.
Let my sex be in union with your divine and sensual will.
Help me realize that you take joy in my pleasure.

Help me remember that you created my sacred body.
Help me remember that I am God.
This is truth I have spoken, and thus it is and will be.

Assignment: during week 3, do the prayer at least once. If you need healing or want great power, spiritually or sexually—or otherwise, for example, the power of negotiating well in a business deal or of calmness during a crisis (remember, in the Goddess's mysterious weave, *any* empowerment helps you find strength in other areas of your life)—use it three times over the month.

The first time you say it, refrain from making love immediately afterward. This prayer can be a very powerful healing; extensive shifts can happen. In one sitting it can clear away many blocks and improve one's sexual state of being powerfully in many ways that are visible right away as well as in others that are not. The prayer can also touch hidden feelings or parts of your "spiritual anatomy" of which you are unaware, having more far-reaching implications than some other rites in this book. By not using the prayer right before lovemaking, you allow time for absorbing the large shifts or intake of power that can happen; these shifts and powers can be disrupted or cut off or overwhelmed by immediate lovemaking. Use the rite once, and give yourself time to see how you feel for awhile afterward. Then you'll have a better sense of what the rite does, and in the future you can check in with yourself about whether you want to use it right before lovemaking or not. It *is* great that way, and I strongly suggest you try that, but at times it is best done on its own. Then the lovemaking that follows hours or days later will be even better.

A discussion of the sacredness of sex must touch upon AIDS and other sexually transmitted diseases (STDs). We honor ourselves and our partners as gods when we protect ourselves and them from STDs. We show healthy pride, enjoy the full magic and joy of sexual pleasure, and heal the planet when we shield ourselves and our partners from STDs.

Do not let anyone's spiritual double-talk—including your own—convince you that avoiding STDs is ever unnecessary. Misleading excuses include:

- "This is sacred, so we can't get hurt."
- "It's just mind over matter."

- "You're in circle, so you are protected from anything we do causing you illness."
- "I really love you (honor you, want you, am so turned on, know deep down that we've nothing to worry about)."
- "If you loved me (trusted me, honored me, wanted me, were not frigid, weren't so negative), you wouldn't worry."

If you find yourself unable to follow guidelines for avoiding STDs, find the inner blocks to doing so and purify yourself of them. You might also talk with a Good Faerie, therapist, or spiritual counselor. It can be very difficult to say, "I only make love if it is safe sex," or, "I have a herpes outbreak so I can't make love today," but you'll thank yourself for doing so.

If you do not know safe sex guidelines or how to protect yourself or your partner from herpes and the like, go to "Supplementary Magical Resources," which has contact information for the free, confidential CDC National STD and AIDS Hotline.

What Does It Take to Be the Fool? and Other Lessons in Group Dynamics

Assignment: during week 4, read the following material. You will see that your next assignment will be to write down your reaction, but read the material below for the first time without an eye to your writing. Do not worry about whether you agree with everything written below: I don't, and I wrote it! Perhaps I only meant it for the moment we are sharing this specific lesson. If, as you read, you pretend the material is a song with a melody you enjoy, you might avoid reading with half your mind on the writing assignment and analysis and be more able to enjoy the spirit of the piece and discover what lessons it has for *you*.

Read to yourself in a gentle nurturing manner:

The Hopi shaman always works side by side with a fool whose job it is to disrupt any ceremony the shaman leads. So important is this foolish role that the shaman splits his fee for the rite with the fool.

Leader, fool, lost soul—there are many roles in a ritual, and everyone has their own. Sacrifice, witness, beggar. Make up your own role.

Any gathering is a ritual. Be a fool only if you are willing to take responsibility for the clothing, shelter, food, and souls of the group you disrupt. Be a fool only if you are willing to become *the* leader of the group you disrupt.

Be a fool only if and when your heart is bigger than everyone else's in the room. Otherwise your chicanery—for example, disrupting others by arriving late—is not informative or liberating but petty and annoying. If your heart is not bigger than everyone else's in the room, do not be a fool. You might sit on your hands instead; perhaps learn the role of witness. It is good to learn many roles.

Being a leader is tedious. Once I was a fool. I was so good at my tomfoolery others followed suit. Being a leader is tedious, unless I use it to turn the lives of my followers chaotically fruitful so that they become happy. Unless I use it to train fools.

Be a leader only if you are willing to be sacrificed. Because the leader, the king, is inevitably sacrificed; it is part of the job. I speak here of true leaders, not tyrants who wrongly sacrifice the lives of people less fortunate who should instead be served by their leaders. A king's blood eventually floods the land, his very life a gift from him, pouring red as it blesses the earth and makes it fertile, that his people may enjoy bounty. They cannot prosper without the king's life forfeited. The king's body is stepped over and upon by those harvesting his crops; that is the definition of sacrifice.

Be willing to pay the cost of any role you choose.

Assignment: week 4. Having read the above material, write about it, even if only a line. Here are some questions you might find useful when writing: What in the material do you agree with? Disagree with? How does the material relate to you? What does your role in groups tend to be?

By the way, I strongly identify with the Fool—also known as the trickster—and everyone attracted to The Third Road seems to have a bit of the trickster in them.

We all have different needs that, when met, let us fully express our special gifts and enjoy ourselves for who we are. Therefore:

Assignment: during week 4, do the following ritual:

RITUAL

The Fool's Home: A Meditation

I use the term *fool* in this rite, but substitute any role you desire wherever *fool* is used, as long as the role you choose is one that is part of a group dynamic. King. Hero. Helper. Nurturer. Warrior. Mediator. Loner. Even a loner relates to a group by *not* being part of it. There is no limit of roles to choose from. It is fine if you determine a role for yourself just for the duration of one usage of the ritual; you can always change roles later.

Step 1. Find a part of your body that feels powerful, either physically, spiritually, or otherwise. Maybe you have strong arms that can carry heavy objects. Or your lap is always filled with children who seek its broad comfort. Maybe some part of your body seems more stable or pivotal than others—such as a dancer's feet or writer's typing hands— or seems a motivating point of physical movement, spiritual thought, or political action. Maybe dwelling in some part of your belly or chest or calves is a spark that initiates hope, commitment, or service to community. Or some part of your body holds your deepest dreams.

Step 2. Close your eyes. Focus on the darkness that is automatically there on the physical plane when your eyes are closed.

Step 3. Imagine, visualize such darkness filling the part of your body you've chosen to work with.

Step 4. Imagine that darkness is a theater's stage.

Step 5. On that stage, in that darkness, imagine yourself standing, dressed as a fool. Visualize yourself as vividly as possible in that darkness in a fool's costume.

Step 6. Imagine that fool, who is yourself, being asked, "What do you need and want right this minute?" Let yourself answer as the fool. Try to let your response come easily instead of worrying it, forcing it, or even caring if it is correct. Remember the answer, even if it is something nonsensical that pops into your head.

Step 7. Even a fool has and needs a home. Imagine the fool's home is next to you . . . Also imagine the fool's home is in that safe, dark place within your body, within the part of your body you are using as the pivotal point . . . Imagine the home in as much detail as you can. (Reminder: when three dots appear in the instructions, do what precedes the three dots before you go further.)

Step 8. Now enter the home.

Step 9. Ask yourself what you need from your home today: To be nurtured? A time of rest? To dance? A time when you feel especially safe? (This is a different question from the one you asked yourself a few steps ago.) Whatever it is, take five minutes in the dwelling place to receive it.

Step 10. Clear your mind's eye as if you were erasing a blackboard with an eraser until there is nothing except the darkness made by closing one's eyes.

Don't forget to ground yourself! The ritual "Grounding" is quite necessary after the above rite.

Table of Assignments

Do these assignments during the ninth month:

The first week:

- Look through this book for premises, practices, and attitudes that develop healthy ego and pride. Then think of examples of healthy ego and pride. pg. 216

The second week:

- Think of a form of spiritual pomposity. Then come up with a practice that keeps the ego down to a healthy size. pg. 217

The third week:

- Analyze what in this training might stop psychic fracturing. pg. 217
- Recite "Prayer for Great Sex" at least once. pg. 221

The fourth week:

- Read: "What Does It Take to Be the Fool? and Other Lessons in Group Dynamics." pg. 222
- Then write about it. pg. 222
- Perform the ritual "The Fool's Home: A Meditation." pg. 224

The Goddess Offers You All Her Power, All Her Love, All Her Cosmos

As much as I fight to bring people out of isolation so that no one falls between the cracks of this poorly structured society, and as much as I hate isolation when it happens to me, there are times in most people's lives when there is no one to whom they can turn. Often this happens when a person most needs support, perhaps because a tragedy has occurred in her life. But at such times the Goddess is there, and all Her power, all Her love, all Her cosmos is at your disposal.

It might be hard to hear "Turn to Her." That can be misheard as "Do without real company, do without real nurture, forsake your real needs for an illusion." No. Instead, know that you are never alone, never at a loss, never having to be without hope.

When there is no other place to turn, you can say, "Mom, help!" and She *will* help. (I think we should all make that prayer even on our good days.) Of course, good day or bad, then you have to accept Her help. And you might not like it. I fight with God sometimes. She tells me how to do things in a way that will make me happy, and I say, "But I really want to do it *this* way instead." Then I do, which makes a mess of things. Eventually I do it Her way and end up really happy, because Her way was the method or goal that I needed to be happy. She is very smart!

People often ask me if spells always work or how to ensure that a cleansing ritual will work. Spells do not always work. Does anything "always work" other than God's never-failing love and care of us? (That was a rhetorical question, please don't answer it.) To me, that is the only "always." You may ask, "So, why do spells?" For the same reason you go to work or make love. You go to work in hopes it is the best way to earn money, you make love because it is fulfilling. But you have no guarantee that anything you do will work: the money you earn may not be enough, and you may get frustrated sexually because you cannot climax. Nothing in life is foolproof, but the smart person does every last thing they can do to ensure they live the best life possible—*and* to ensure their spells do work—then they trust that the Goddess takes over from there and does a perfect job of it. Reliance on an all-powerful deity never fails us. We are in a partnership with God in which She is delighted by our efforts, however limited, and makes sure that all Her powers—which are *all powers*—are at our disposal. She performed the miracle of creating us. She can perform other miracles for us. She is the miracle worker always by your side, helping you every step of your day.

Magical Style

By now it's clear that shamanism is a discipline. True spirituality entails an *applied* discipline. Another aspect of applied shamanic discipline is magic: in the same way that a Third Road shaman consciously builds spiritual skills, he or she also consciously builds magical skill. The key word here is *consciously*. Working randomly *is* fine; there is nothing wrong with learning a spell here and there, as much as you desire. In this tradition some students gather spells from many sources other than Third Road and expand their repertoire. But rather than working randomly, one can use a blueprint for developing psychic skills. In addition to the blueprint for training that is the basis for my teaching, some students create an additional blueprint for training themselves in magical skills. This may not be relevant to all readers at this point, or ever, but it needs to be explained so that you have a context for the lesson.

Learning face-to-face, some students request more and more technical lessons. Even so, those students might work out an additional blueprint that adds more elements to their psychic training. The Third Road is not just about following my style of magic but about adding your own style to it and using my style to reveal and empower yours. The Third Road says, Take responsibility for your path; only you can know ultimately what training you need for your magical power and psychic well-being.

When Victor Anderson offered me initiation, I answered, "I have my own style. I don't want to be stuck following the rules of a tradition." He explained he taught an eclectic tradition. I accepted his initiation. I followed his example but wanted to take it further. To help my students follow their own style of magic, I developed the material in this book. (This is not to criticize Victor's work; if he had not done his brilliant research, I would have had to do it. Instead I could go beyond, and now you can go further than I.)

The longer one walks The Third Road, the stronger the emphasis on selfhood. This focus can mean anything from developing greater and greater self-expression to taking more and more responsibility for one's actions. You can be always perfecting your own style of magic, which may include a concentrated effort in one or more arenas of the psychic realm. One student might concentrate wholeheartedly on giving psychic readings, another on magically healing the planet. Those readings or healings can be done according to one's own style. If your style needs a greater technical orientation—Third Road's emphasis on technical development is already strong, but some Third Roaders want to become more technically proficient than others—you have to find more technical expertise. I offer that greater technical training to my face-to-face students who need it, but I also might tell them, "No teacher's blueprint for your training can be enough. Add to it."

You might think I am saying that there are certain things you must now or eventually implement. Not so. Technical proficiency as developed by the training is sufficient for most folks and may always be. And some folks' own style of magic *is* to follow their teacher's style, to do the rites by rote, and never create their own way of doing things or be eclectic. The information in this section is given to provide a framework for what follows below and to tell those who wish to continue on The Third Road beyond this book how to do so.

In addition, if I am trying to model a way of teaching in which the teacher has no pretense of being the all-knowing, perfect guru, the student cannot take the counterpoint position—an unintelligent, passive follower who is incapable of a sound analysis of the world we live in. The student must take on the difficult responsibility of adding to the training herself when and if needed. That includes magical training.

Assignment: time parameters explained below. This training has presented everything a student generally needs at this point to be magically powerful, safe, and have her own style. In addition, from long experience with a wide variety of students, I have built in safeguards to take care of many problems that only occasionally crop up. But, ultimately, only you can be sure a magical training is thorough; only you can determine what is needed for your specific, unique case. So, ask yourself, "Is there a magical technique and/or discipline other than those given in this book that I need at this point in my training? Could my style of magic be strengthened by repeating, a few times, one or more of the rituals given in this book? Is there optional work in this training that I need to start using? For psychic safety, do I need to perform one of this book's exercises two or three times more?" Ask God to tell you. Sit down and think about your needs. You might ask friends for input, people more magically advanced than you; you might also look through books or Web sites to stimulate your thinking.

Here are some examples. Let's say you've already cleansed yourself of a morbid fear that you would be punished for using your psychic abilities. And you've also talked to a Good Faerie who reassured you that magic is a gift from God. But you still get too nervous about doing rituals. You might start using "The Mother's Cloak" to give added protection before starting a ritual and see if you feel better. Who knows, maybe for some reason *you* need an extra precaution.

Or perhaps you are struggling with an enormous depression, a tremendous lack of self-assurance, or an inability to begin efforts toward a desired goal. Strengthening visualization skills—by repeating some of *Goddess*

Initiation's exercises that use imagination—might be a good idea. Then you can sit down once a week for a month and visualize yourself as serene, confident, and happy. Not that you can't do so without improving your magical skills; but if you improve skills even a tiny bit, you are more effective.

Or maybe you want to explore a new psychic arena, like reading tarot cards or using spells that draw on magical herbalism—not because you are having problems but because you enjoy learning. Search out a book or Web page on the topic, or ask someone in an on-line pagan group how to get started.

If you decide to add something to the training, here are more ideas about how to do so. "Supplementary Magical Resources" and "Magical Reading" provide ways to obtain additional training. Also, you can give thought about how to connect with someone who might help you fulfill your goal. Plus, you can pray for a teacher, even if you need him for only one lesson. Be willing to draw on traditions other than the shamanic; the very technique(s) you need might be known by a Christian psychic or Taoist; a shaman recognizes power whatever the source. Instead of looking only for something called *shamanism,* keep your mind and eyes open to the world around you, and you'll find the powers you need in everything from a Buddhist prayer to a class in swing dancing to an Al-Anon meeting (Al-Anon helps people affected by the alcoholism of a friend or relative). Lessons can be found anyplace.

You can obtain any training you need. But to do so, you might have to take initiative, which can be a frightening proposition. You might feel unqualified. But, in the final analysis, no one but you can see that you get what you need out of life and make the decisions that are a part of doing so. This is a chance to practice! This book has been helping you be up to the challenge of taking good care of yourself. Go for it! Take a deep breath, and pioneer on!

Time parameters: start this assignment week 1.

I am not asking you, *all in this week,* to determine and receive any and all magical training that you require or desire. The assignment can take as long as it needs to be done right and without frantic rush; it is a lifelong assignment! This is how one creates a blueprint for training oneself magically. If you want more training, add it in the tiniest increments; that is the Faerie nature of training. You needn't feel overwhelmed by this assignment. Maybe the next three weeks all you do is decide if you need to add something or not. Then you might take a few weeks finding out how to acquire that something, then a month slowly doing so. Or you may go far, far slower than that!

Those who want to make a longer-term or lifelong commitment to Third Road shamanism should do this assignment again after their self-initiation and continue to do it occasionally.

Applied Mysticism

It's hard for both adepts and novices to apply spirituality and magic to mundane life, though they might face very different challenges and confusions when asking themselves (or forgetting to ask themselves), "How do I actually use my concepts and magic in daily life?" Applied mysticism demands that both adept and novice work vigorously toward concrete application of spiritual principles and magical tools. This book has shown how to use both practically. Let's focus further on magic now.

Mysticism and magical techniques should lead us toward God, not away from Her. They should lead us toward our lives, not be escapism. To heck with all that magical wizardry and mysticism if you can't get your dishes done. And being a good shaman means getting those dishes done. I don't care how mystical your poetry is, you need to tend to your housework, too. (If you don't care about your dishes being clean, don't invalidate this whole paragraph or I am going to bounce you up and down like a beach ball. Okay, that probably isn't very compassionate. Let's start again! My point is that magic and mysticism don't free you from your down-to-earth responsibilities.)

We're never too advanced to be duped by glamour. Oh, it gets so enticing and deceptive at any stage of the path. (*Glamour* is an old term for an illusion, in this case a wondrous, compelling illusion of power and magic that one is sorely tempted to chase after.)

When one is coming to power, whether by working toward an initiation, college degree, or major business triumph, especially when close to the finish line, as in this training, it is easy to be sidetracked by poetry that doesn't get the dishes done, religious practices that isolate one rather than help one contribute to the community, or desperate quests that are a wild goose chase after glamour.

A person is perhaps caught by glamour if they are looking for too much training instead of getting on with the business of living. Mystics too often climb an ivory tower of training instead of being out in the world facing the challenges of life or serving community. Sometimes it is good to retreat, but there is a time and place for it. Overemphasis on training is only one type of ivory tower.

Faerie glamour can rob one of a real life. I know of the huge price from personal experience. I want you not to pay what I paid. Everything in life is a trade-off. You can't enjoy the benefits of being blond and brunette at the very same time. Likewise, the time you spend chasing glamour or sitting alone learning new spells cannot be devoted to other things. So be sure you're spending your time *living!*

Assignment: during week 2, find one thing inside you that makes, or might make, you want to walk away from following through on a specific project that you are close to finishing right now. Or think of a certain activity that you tend to start and too often not finish; then determine one thing inside you that feeds into that behavior. For example, some people sort their laundry then let it sit in piles on the floor for weeks before going to the laundry. It needn't be a big project. Apply the pre-ritual cleansing from "The Magic Formula": "Mother, if you deem it best, remove these blocks to love, joy, protection, power, and serving others." Change *these blocks* to *this block.* That cleansing is great to use whenever you need to remove *any* inner block.

You may have a valid reason for stopping a major project, but if you think that is the case, discuss it with a Good Faerie and/or pray for clarity. I remember several of my achievements for which I am very grateful. The reasons I gave myself for not finishing them at the last minute still seem sensible to me! Only in talking with others, and praying for the ability to keep going, was I able to go the last nine yards.

Assignment: during week 2. After doing the above assignment, find one inner block that makes, or might make, you want to refrain from completing this training, now when you are so close to your initiation. Then apply the pre-ritual cleansing from "The Magic Formula."

Again, if you have a reason for stopping the training that seems legitimate, discuss it with a Good Faerie and/or pray for clarity.

If you know that finishing is the right thing to do, you can pray for the power and willingness to do so. It might make all the difference.

Assignment: during week 3, then for as long as you practice shamanism, apply checks and balances regarding *authentic* spiritual power:

1. Question yourself: "Are my spiritual and magical practices improving my mundane life?" If so, your quests for power can be quests for *authentic* spiritual power, not, for example, misguided applications that waste your time or leave you feeling terribly empty.

2. Have folks in your life who will tell you when your life is getting off track. They need not be shamans or even believe in magic; they only need to be the sort who will tell you when you are not "taking care of business." They do need to be honest, forthright people who can tell you something about yourself that might be difficult to hear and do so in a kind, nonshaming manner. If you know no such person, pray that one appears.

    You may have such a person in your life and not know it. I once happened to mention to a friend that I appreciate candid, unpretentious pals who bring unpleasant things about myself to my attention in a compassionate, gentle way. She surprised me by developing the ability to speak her mind about me.

    For me, the second part of this assignment is part of a larger practice. Sometimes I blindly fall short of my standard for good treatment of myself and others. I would be lost without someone who points out such times to me. For example, I have blind spots to working way too hard. We can be unaware of any of a myriad of ways we might be failing to love ourselves and our fellow humans. Self-delusion is an easy pitfall for me, so I need input. I suggest you eventually embrace this practice; it can be a necessity for some, perhaps all, people.

Assignment: during week 4, do the following ritual, which serves as a model for realistically applying spiritual and psychic principles—and for getting down to living one's life instead of being waylaid by false mysticism and escapism. The exercise uses a typical shamanic symbol or totem, the eagle, to serve as an example. Substitute your totem animal or any other image within your personal mythos that is an image of yourself. Or use an image of yourself as part of your ancestral bloodline. If you don't have a favorite image, choose one that has some appeal right now; you needn't use it again.

This exercise helps you discover your truest, most spiritual self, the part of you that wants to live life joyously and in freedom, soaring like an eagle.

RITUAL

Eagle Birth

INGREDIENTS

- All the makings necessary to start a fire: a fireplace with log, kindling, matches, etc.; candle with candleholder and matches; a bonfire, ready to be lit; or ingredients all ready for any other safe fire.
- A snack, one without sugar. The food needs to be something wholesome like fruit, milk, nuts, whole-grain bread, or cheese.

Fire is used in a simple way in this meditation, providing a simple bit of magic. Therein lies its power. Though water is not used in this rite, it serves as an excellent example of my point: water is clear, simple, yet we cannot exist without it, both because we must drink it to survive and because the greater part of our human bodies are made of water. The same is true of the magic and soul of Faerie: simplicity, with its enormous power, lies at the heart of our tradition. The Faerie path can be a simple one.

No matter how complex one's early spiritual seeking, struggles, or modes of self-help, *eventually* it is usually straightforward answers that do the trick. It is also the simple things that make life worth living. And it's the plain, unadorned activities that help us grow spiritually because they can be so difficult—like getting to work on time or displaying basic courtesies to family members after a long day at work.

Shamans were the first scientists; simplicity is not at odds with a scientific mind. Faerie Tradition works with nature, the laws of which are called "science." Nature is ever shifting. So a Faerie shaman works with the Goddess's perfect gift—that which nature has shifted to in any given moment. If a specific moment demanded it, a well-trained Faerie shaman might work a complex spell that resembled the most advanced undertakings in physics.

It is part of a Faerie shaman's spirituality to analyze, explore, invent, and be creative, but all those things can also be used as an escape at times when what needs to be done in your life is simple—simple magic, simple solutions, simple actions.

There is an expression that recovering alcoholics use: Simple is not the same as easy!

Step 1. Choose an image to work with in this ritual, an eagle or other image.

Step 2. Light the fire.

Step 3. Sit with the fire. Let it work its simple, natural magic on you. Let it warm you physically, fill you with good cheer, lull your mind until you feel peaceful, whatever fire does for you when you do this rite. Enjoy it. What fire does might differ radically any time you do this ritual. Perhaps let the fire dance for you.

Step 4. To take this step, you need to understand the terms *imitation eagle* and *pseudospiritual.* In the context of this ritual, I use *pseudospirituality* to refer to actions done—and attitudes held—with the best, most sincere intentions that appear to move one toward spiritual power but actually, unintentionally, move one away from spiritual power. A caring employer can at times unwittingly lack compassion when he thinks he is doing the most moral thing possible. At such a time he is *pseudospiritual* and an *imitation eagle;* he's not "the real thing." (I do not use *imitation eagle* or *pseudospiritual* to denote a person who is intentionally deceiving others in the name of spirituality and trying to appear other than he is. That is a whole other matter, irrelevant to this discussion.)

More examples of *pseudospirituality:* You might try to help a friend in need, thinking you are being caring, and even if your concern is real, your attempt to help may be motivated more by unconscious desire to control the friend. Or you can do endless favors to help others, thinking you are being spiritual, when in fact many of the favors you do come from an unconscious lack of self-worth. Or you might imitate your teacher's magical style when to do so means losing your own style of power. Even choosing the wrong totem animal because your teacher has that totem can be a form of pseudospirituality.

These are all honest mistakes. There is no shame in pseudospirituality. Think of *pseudo* not in a sneering, insulting sense but as a technical—nonjudgmental—description: there is not a shaman alive who has not chased after the wrong image, totem, magical method, or philosophical construct. It is part of the learning and growing process, a necessary error on the road to power, and this ritual helps you get back on track. This rite also helps you realize when an excellent image, totem, method, or construct that is generally appropriate for you becomes pseudospirituality because you are using it at a time when you should not. It is great to imitate one's teacher or do endless favors, but not all the time.

So gaze gently at the flames. Let yourself stay in whatever relaxed, pleasant frame of mind you gained in step 3; do not try to become more alert, do not try to force anything or *make* anything happen; simply wait; you will find the imitation eagle. A thought might come to you about some way or ways in which you are pseudospiritual. Or a fanciful image might appear in the flame, in front of the flame, or in your mind. If an image comes, it will likely represent a form of pseudospirituality.

Note I asked you to "Gaze gently *at* the flames," not *"into* the flames." The latter suggests you strain, trying to find something in the fire. Nope!

Step 5. If you've found a way or ways you are pseudospiritual, allow them to drain away into the earth. The earth can transform them for you into what they should be, then return that power to you transformed. (This is another way to cleanse *any* inner block you might have regarding *any* issue in your life: let it drain away into the earth. When you do this, be aware that it will be transformed. This simple purification rite is called "Gaia's Touch.")

Step 6. Find an eagle in the fire: let the image come to you or visualize it. Either way, you may see it in the fire or in your mind's eye or between you and the fire. Or you may simply get a *sense* of the eagle's presence somehow; often in visualization or when something "comes" to one in a ritual, one gets a certain indescribable sense of the object, place, or person in question instead of through a picture or more expected mode of perception. This is legitimate.

Step 7. Find an eagle in the fire within yourself:

a. Picture a pleasant fire within yourself, either throughout you or in one place that feels appropriate. You might build this visualization by remembering the magic that fire spun for you in step 3; you can imagine that whatever simple, wonderful magic fire gave you in step 3 is burning—maybe even dancing—within you now.

b. Picture an eagle within your inner fire, or let an eagle appear in that fire. Again, it is usually fine when using imagination magically, perceiving otherworldly realities, or using psychic perceptions to sense something in an unusual or indescribable way rather than seeing it, hearing words, or the likes. Each person has his or her own way of seeing the invisible realm and of getting its messages.

After grounding, eat. You may find you need not a snack but a whole meal.

Wholesome food after ritual can be a way to bring your psyche back to earth. Henceforth, after any grounding following a ritual, check in to see if more grounding is needed. If so, food might be the answer. Also, ritual work and personal growth are demanding, so sometimes it is necessary to eat afterward just to refuel.

If nothing comes up in step 4, it might later. Then you can cleanse it.

This is a hard rite to do because it asks you to face the self-defeating ways you approach your spirituality, and you might hold such ways dear. The solution to this is to add something to "The Magic Formula." And at this point in your training, you need, henceforth, to always make this part of your "Magic Formula." Let us look at this addition:

Step 2 of "The Magic Formula," the pre-ritual cleansing, will now have an additional part. After cleansing away those things that would interfere with *any* rite you are about to undertake, use the same method to purify yourself of anything that might interfere with the specific ritual you are about to perform. If it is a rite for prosperity, determine what inner blocks to prosperity you have: A belief you don't deserve abundance? A fear that others will turn against you if you get what you want? A life-long anger at those who have more than you? Anger is a gift and can be used as such. But it can also eat away at us and at our goals.

If it is a spell for career success, determine what inner blocks could sabotage your career. Fear of the visibility that accompanies a victory? A smoldering resentment against an old boss that keeps you from having a clear head when you interview for jobs?

A spell for compassion can be blocked if you believe that kindness is the equivalent of being spineless. Or if you fear that goodwill might override your instinct for self-preservation.

Often several blocks relevant to whatever rite you are about to perform need to be cleansed away.

These blocks and fears are often hidden, so always look for what needs to be cleansed, even if at first you think you don't need to. Forsaking this step brings many spiritual leaders and magical adepts to their knees; they think they are no longer capable of self-deception or self-justification or that they no longer need to examine themselves rigorously. Moral indignation is often a justification for lack of self-examination.

Denise's story is an example of inner blocks obstructing magical achievements. Her unrelenting anxiety about an upcoming job interview would have made her appear too nervous for a prospective employee to hire. So Denise came to me for counseling. I told her what I read about her psychically: "You are highly qualified for the job! But as a child you constantly heard your father say, 'You're stupid!' Your anxiety exceeds the expected fretfulness one has before an interview because you are desperate to prove to your father you are not stupid."

Denise responded vehemently, "Nope! I proved my father wrong years ago. I graduated from college at the top of my class. Besides, my father died years ago."

Over the course of the session I was able to show Denise that she had never acknowledged that deep down she still believed her father. Denise was unaware that she was trying to prove herself to her dad by succeeding at the interview, despite her academic success or the fact that her father was long dead. I showed Denise that her anxiety and unconscious belief could affect not only the interview but also the spell she was planning to use to get the job.

In the case of "Eagle Birth," one can easily be fueled by unconscious blocks that are very hard to face. For example, surrendering control to God can be too scary if the god of one's youth—one's parent—was abusive. Or false pride in the guise of moral superiority can justify inappropriate spiritual modes. But your thoroughness in searching out your blocks to this rite can save your life. In fact, doing this ritual occasionally over the course of your life—should you continue to practice shamanism or whatever spiritual path you pursue—can help keep you whole, happy, and safe, in part because the pre-ritual cleansings specific to the rite help you avoid spiritual pitfalls. We are never free of the risk of such pitfalls.

This training is not always explicitly about bloodline, but it *is* always about authenticity, which will inevitably lead you to your blood. For example, in developing selfhood and creating your own world, your blood heritage automatically emerges.

Being initiated into your bloodline is not as complex as some think. An authentic *path* is hard, and therefore so is a genuine initiation, but authenticity, if you work for it as hard as you can, automatically leads toward bloodline even if you give bloodline no thought. When you pursue your self-determined goals, your blood is leading you to its own gifts whether you know it or not. This is true even if you never know your blood heritage by name. A gift that makes you happy, even if you don't know its name, is worth gold compared to calling yourself "Faerie" or "King" or "wolf" or "mermaid" when such titles do not truly represent you. False titles distract you from your destined happiness.

Some people do not trust that what they themselves do is important, special, or meaningful. You hear them say of something they wrote (thought, have done, want, own), "It is *just* something I wrote (thought, did, want, have)." Don't seek something named and titled just to feel a sense of self-worth. You'll defeat yourself.

Rosemary Replaces Titles with Compassion for Herself

Rosemary was a client who defined herself as gay, disabled, and poor even though she was married to a wealthy man and she was not disabled. It might be hard to believe that a person could think of herself as gay, disabled, and poor and be none of those things, but trust me on this. I realize that a woman can be married to a man and still be gay, but this was not the case.

Having dealt with severe physical disabilities in my own body, I know they are not always apparent. I might suddenly be able to dance like a wild woman for one night. Folks seeing that might say, "She is not disabled." But that might be the only night that year I am capable of dancing at all. Disabilities are misleading—for example, their severity might wax and wane—so some people might not give them credence. I do not readily discount someone's claim to having a disability; nevertheless, I did Rosemary's.

I was able to show Rosemary that she appropriated the titles of oppressed groups because she knew of no other way to feel special. Also, she buried most of her feelings, those feelings that we all have as part of being alive, the fear, angers, doubts, and such that are just part of life. Unable to face them, she was deeply unhappy and mistranslated that unhappiness as her "lesbian oppression." (Again, some women married to men discover themselves to be gay; this was not the case with Rosemary.) Having faced her false titles, her false sense of self, she was also able to face the fact that she had no authentic sense of self. Bit by bit, through the counseling we did over three months' time, she found her true self and the true titles that went with it. Part of one's authentic self are those everyday feelings, both pleasant and unpleasant, that all humans experience. And in Rosemary's case, she discovered her talent as a potter and was excited to begin developing that skill.

Coming to Power

Someone has said, "It is only after graduating from acupuncture school that one learns acupuncture." *Use* your training. Apply it to serving community and enriching your personal life. Live your life; then you'll understand what you've been taught. Avoid using workshops—this from a workshop leader!—or other forms of self-help as a way of neglecting your life. One way people neglect life is to take on challenges that are too costly or are irrelevant. An example of the latter is my client Ann. She decided to overcome her fear of singing in front of others because that was an enticing challenge. But in working with me she came to realize that she instead needed to learn how to stand up to her boss whose sexual harassment was making her miserable five days a week. She benefited a lot more by facing up to the true challenge life presented her. This was a proper application of her training because it enriched her life.

We all must face challenges. But to borrow a thought from Charles de Lint's *Moonheart*, we needn't all face challenges that might cost us our lives. I strongly advise: do not take on such hurdles unless there is no other choice!

Assignment: week 4. Some people, whether or not they put it into words, think of initiation and walking the shamanic path as equivalent to coming to power. Yes!

Training and gathering information are not the same as coming to power. Write that last statement in your workbook. Then when you have a chance, write your thoughts about it as part of writing your own bible. A reminder: you need write only a line or two. More is not always better.

Sometimes instead of more training, one needs absorption, practice, application, and further personal growth. Without the latter, one cannot grow in spiritual *or* magical power. And all of that *is* training, whether or not people view it that way.

Shamans train because we want to be filled with mana (a word for power)—power to heal ourselves and others, the mana of celebration, love, and joy. We want the power of having control over our own life, which is not the same as forcing our will on another person.

Glamour can "sell" a person false power, but when you seek that illusion you are robbed of true potency. Glamour tempts you when you see your teacher or role model or successful best friend lit up with tremendous mana by their style of magic or their involvement in making pots, taking astrology lessons, or line dancing. The mana rises off them like steam as they get tremendous satisfaction from their activities. It is easy to feel your own style of magic, of involvement in taking cooking classes, giving tarot readings for friends, or practicing ballet, is secondrate by comparison. Don't think that way. You want *power*, the real thing.

So imitate not by doing the exact activity they do, but by imitating them in spirit. What draws you to their activity is likely not the activity itself but how it lights them up, the power it gives them. So imitate them authentically and embrace their wisdom, not by copying their actions, but by doing what lights *you* up.

Mana is also the word for the living matter out of which all things are made. Everything is alive; even a rock is made of living power, mana. There is power in everything. If you know this, you need not feel that you can gain strength only from someone else's lifestyle. Through your own choices, inclinations, and tendencies, as well as through celebrating every part of the world that surrounds you, God offers you all the power you could ever imagine:

Assignment: during week 4, do the following ritual twice.

RITUAL

Gaining the Power of Life

This ritual feels really good!

Life offers us great power. There are endless sources of it. One need not dominate others to gain power, one can have one's own means to gain it. Joy fills you with energy. In a museum, when you are awed by a painter's skill and imagination, you feel saturated with electricity. Power is gained by giving birth to a child. The sense of accomplishment one gets after paying off debts is pure mana.

Step 1. Choose something in your life that has made you feel powerful. Perhaps it is a moment of joy or courage or a particular achievement. Perhaps it is how you feel when dancing or when teaching math. If you can think of only minor moments of feeling strong, that is a great place to start. You will learn to feel stronger as you travel along your shaman's path. If you can't think of a moment, choose a power you would like to attain: perhaps confidence, joy, or victory.

Some people might feel powerful when they control others, like their employees. They are deluding themselves. True power is not about dominating others. Or about controlling God. If the way you feel strong is by ruling someone other than yourself, or if you refrain from striving toward power because you think it requires dominating someone, this ritual will help you find real power instead.

Step 2. Imagine you feel the way you felt at that moment of power (or how you would feel if in step 1 you chose a power you've no experience with). Perhaps you imagine your body feels tingly or that you feel self-esteem. Perhaps you visualize joy sweeping through your chest. Perhaps you imagine a feeling of gratefulness for your blessings. (Gratitude truly fills one with mana.) Or you imagine you feel competent or victorious. Or you feel a quiet serene happiness.

Step 3. Take a moment to dwell on and enjoy this feeling of mana.

Step 4. When you are as full of power as you possibly can be, and your visualizations of the various forms of power are as good as they can get at this point in your training, make a request of your self: "Oh, my instinctive, intuitive self, divide this energy." I will explain that request anon. (Uh-oh, all my time travel back to the Renaissance is showing!)

Step 5. Send the power upward in an act of imagination, being aware as you do so that it goes to the god within you as well as the God and Goddess. Do not choose how much you send up. Instead, leave it to your unconscious to choose the amount. Your unconscious knows how much to send and how much to hold back so that no part of your physical or ethereal body gets drained of mana.

You might ask, "How can one imagine sending without imagining how much?" After you do the related homework a few times, you will get it and be ready to "send" during the initiation.

This sending feeds mana to the Gods inside and out, gives them power to bring into being that which you have visualized. Therefore the visualization is not just an experience in ritual but manifests once the rite is over, bearing fruit in your life after the rite.

Whenever you do "Gaining the Power of Life"—not the initiation version that you will learn later but this earlier version—check in at the end to see whether the power gained is more than you can contain. If so, add steps 4 and 5. This keeps you from getting overloaded and frying your energy circuits. It also completes a circuit: the Gods give you a gift, then you share it with them. Often these added steps are a potent, necessary energy working. After a while one gets a sense of when and how to send the extra power.

However, if the mana gained is not more than you can contain, you need not add steps 4 and 5. They become optional, and if you don't use them the Gods find other ways to manifest that which you have visualized.

Sometimes, along with the energy you feel inside you, extra energy automatically comes into the vicinity in which you are working. If this happens you will find yourself, geometrically speaking, at the center of this power. This is a natural, lovely gift. When you check in, see if there is such power. If so, send it up when, and in the same manner in which, you send up the internal excess energy. It is not safe to leave it untended. And sending it not only is a pleasurable experience but also makes the rite even stronger.

It might be hard for you to think logically at the point you are full of power because it can feel so, so good. You might want to throw caution to the wind and forget to send the power or act rashly in a ritual or a mundane way. This may be especially true the more you progress, because things just feel better and better. Using logic in the middle of a rite, or at any time one feels extreme pleasure or hope, joy, or the like, does not end the pleasurable feeling. Logic heightens it. It grounds pleasure into reality. Don't say, "Oh, I don't want to *think*." Instead, know that bringing your whole being into a wonderful moment—bringing logic and emotions and everything else together—helps you to gain full power and pleasure. And it does so in a way that makes life and magic safer. This is true in ritual and at any time you are tempted to throw caution to the wind and forsake logical action or thought.

This culture tells us repeatedly that pleasure is wrong and that we should instead focus only on logic and work. When we find joy it is easy to believe that the exact opposite of the prevailing inhibiting bias is correct. It is easy to think, "I will forsake mediocrity and chase danger, which is so tantalizing." A shaman knows better and knows also that the higher we fly, the more we need to stay grounded, and the more grounded we are, the higher we fly. If we are to walk between the worlds, we must keep our feet on the ground.

Assignment: week 4, optional. In your journal answer this question: What magical and/or mundane experience(s) gives you mana? What experience(s) that you've not had yet might give you power? Pursue one such experience instead of seeking power outside yourself.

Table of Assignments

Do these assignments during the tenth month, except where otherwise specified:

The first week:

- Acquire more training than has been given by this book if you deem it necessary. Time parameters are explained more clearly in the lesson itself, because you only *start* this daunting assignment now; it is a lifelong assignment! pg. 229

The second week:

- Find one thing inside you that makes you want to walk away from following through on a specific project that you are close to finishing. Pray about the inner block: "Mother, if you deem it best, remove this block to love, joy, protection, power, and serving others." pg. 232
- Find one inner block that makes you want to refrain from completing this training. Apply the above prayer. pg. 232

You may need to discuss either of these assignments with a Good Faerie.

The third week, then for as long as you practice shamanism:

- Ask this question: Are my spiritual and magical practices improving my mundane life? Keep in your life folks who will tell you when your life is getting off track. pg. 233

The fourth week:

- Perform "Eagle Birth." pg. 233
- Write "Training and gathering information is not the same as coming to power" in your journal, then write your thoughts about it. pg. 241
- Use the ritual "Gaining the Power of Life" twice. pg. 242
- Optional: In your journal answer this: What magical and/or mundane experience(s) gives you mana? What experience(s) that you've not had yet might give you power? Pursue one such experience. pg. 245

The Wisdom of the Ancestors

Assignment: during week 1, do the following ritual.

RITUAL

The Wisdom of the Ancestors

INGREDIENTS

- One might need the same snack following the ritual as described in "Eagle Birth." I strongly emphasize food, since, as said earlier, eating can bring us from magical realms and altered states back into our bodies and the mundane awareness needed to function well and happily on *this* plane.

In this exercise, one "talks" or otherwise communicates to one's ancestors according to whatever bloodline was discovered earlier in the lessons. So if you found in the bloodline exercise that your blood is that of a star, you would call on your ancestors, the Stars. If you have no bloodline(s) that you know of, you will be shown how you can still do this rite.

In the following ritual, one's ancestors guide one's pursuit of the gifts of one's bloodline and offer direction about anything else, mundane or spiritual, in one's life. The ritual may be a visit with an ancestor or ancestors. (Note: I will generally use the plural *ancestors* during the rite for simplicity's sake.) Like most of the training's rituals, this spell can be used over and over for the rest of your life. "The Wisdom of the Ancestors" ritual can forever be used not only to find wisdom when pursuing your special gifts but also to gain insight into any of life's opportunities and challenges.

Don't forget to add the new part of "The Magic Formula."

Step 1. Invoke your ancestors. In other words, if you found in the bloodline exercise that your blood is that of a Viking, invoke your ancestors, the Vikings.

Some ancestors, such as rocks, are present on the embodied plane. Some, like mermaids, perhaps were never embodied. And some ancestors, like the ancient Vikings, have passed on. You invoke *the spirits* of your ancestors.

Never demand their presence. Invite courteously. If they do not come, don't worry. They might be on a picnic (a little joke to take the pressure off you). It is not only rude but dangerous to try to force ancestors or any other spirits to come to you; never do a rite in which a spirit comes to you other than of his own volition. Once a spirit arrives, make requests, not demands. If a spirit is strong enough to help you, he has enough power to hurt you and might do so if you try to force him to do as you want. Even if your petition is reasonable, a spirit might have a good reason not to do as you wish: spirits have their own lives and agendas and might have priorities other than yours that are beyond your ken.

Step 2. The ancestors visit you. You may get a picture of ancestors in your mind or sense the presence of one being or experience ancestors in some other mystical way. Or you may feel nothing at all. It is all good, and the latter possibility does not mean no one came at your invitation; you simply might not realize an ancestral visit is happening.

Step 3. Ask, "What is my next step in my process toward initiation into my bloodline?"

Step 4. Be open to their answer, which can come in any form. It might come as words in your head, or you might see a single ancestor make a gesture or a group perform a rite. A symbol might appear in your mind. Perhaps the answer will come later through a synchronicity. (Reminder: synchronicity is a so-called coincidence that seems a sign, lesson, or opportunity from God.)

Step 5. Ask if there are any other things your ancestors want to convey to you: guidance about any issue in your life, anything they need for themselves, any gifts they have for you, and so forth. "Listen" for their response.

Step 6. Thank your ancestors for their help and the time they took to just plain old visit.

This rite *must* be preceded by "The Magic Formula" and followed by grounding.

Eat if needed. Often food is needed when this rite is first done.

It is invaluable to write down what you've gained in this rite.

Act on whatever guidance you received. If the guidance makes no sense or puzzles you in any other way, pray to God that you become more clear, and/or ask a Good Faerie for his or her thoughts.

Since steps 3 and 4 directly involve guidance regarding bloodline issues, those steps can be eliminated when you instead want guidance about issues other than bloodline. But for this immediate assignment, do include those steps.

Dealing with the magical realms is in some ways like dealing with the mundane world: one looks for nice people but might have to deal with bad people. In this rite, it is possible for a bad spirit to arrive accidentally. Don't expect this to happen any more than you would expect a jerk to approach you when you go for a run in the park, but be prepared just in case it does. If an evil entity arrives, end the visit. Do so however feels safest and most effective. For example, a courteous request can be sufficient. If you need to get rude, do so; don't be a doormat for spirits any more than you would be for a rude bully in the park. As you tell the spirit to leave, you can also imagine a five-pointed star appearing between you and him; that is a powerful way to banish him. If you feel even more power is needed, say, "I banish you in the name of the Great Mother of All Things."

It is good to occasionally make offering to the Gods and ancestors. A bit of food and drink, not more than a tablespoon of each, is needed. A single strand of your hair. A pretty bead, flower, or whatever your imagination, intuition, or common sense tell you. Occasionally the offering should be food and beverage: spirits and Gods do need to eat! Just as shamans ask for the Gods' help, so shamans help the Gods.

Assignment: to be done during this month, starting week 1. Since we've already determined that an initiation rite is only one moment in a process, I ask that, after doing "The Wisdom of the Ancestors" ritual, you determine another rite to initiate you into your bloodline. It can take innumerable forms, depending on who you are. It needn't even be a ritualized action. Any so-called mundane act that inspires us or connects us to the deep part of ourselves or brings us into a penetrating union with the natural world or otherwise transforms us or shifts the energy of the world around us could be called a ritual. For example, someone whose bloodline is Celtic might learn to play bagpipes. Someone whose blood is the salt of the sea might briefly walk on the beach or, if they prefer a long-term process, walk on the beach once a week for a month. Or it might be a brief, overt rite, such as praying, "Goddess, please let me feel the wisdom of my ancestors in my own thoughts, feelings, and actions." In fact, if you don't want to make up your own rite, just use that prayer. Or, if you know how to create one, it could be a great big ritual with lots of props. Week one, determine one rite; then do the rite sometime during this month.

Assignment: to be done this month, starting week 1. Training does us no good just sitting on the page. It comes to life by being lived. I want to get real work done with you. So work with the material I gave you in this training in the following way. Week 1, go through the book and look for any work *you* feel is needed given the material we have covered. It needn't be a lot; just doing something once or twice is great! Perhaps do a ritual again. Or apply a theory I gave you earlier. Sometime during the month, after week 1, do the work you've determined is important. Don't try to do everything you might think is necessary. Egad! Just do a bit. We can only do a bit at a time, *no matter how important or pressing something is.*

At any stage of the assignment, you might report the work you've done to one of your Good Faeries so that they can help you come up with a good idea, critique what you've done, answer questions that have come up, or help you in any way you need at this time.

To expand a footnote in the chapter "What to Expect in This Shamanic Training": If you're hungry for more Third Road material, you can find some of it in unlikely places. I wrote an immense body of poetry, in the form of prayers, liturgy, lore, and lecture—my lectures though prose are written with poetic devises such as images and rhythm—which embodies my work as a philosopher. I've passed on this material orally since the 1980s, and adapted some of it in *Goddess Initiation* and *Be a Goddess!* Despite all the published material I have produced and will produce, I will not publish most of my work since I am committed to passing on some shamanism solely through oral tradition. But you can find much of the material I created for oral transmission, because it has come to be considered "standard" Wicca by numerous people and is therefore included in both the written and oral bodies of work of many Wiccan traditions. For example, lines of poetry I wrote, such as "A healthy priest(ess) makes all things sound" and "Your will through mine" are now thought of as standard Wiccan expressions.

I mention this because paganism is earmarked by independence. As a pagan before there were so many pagan books available, I was blessed with, and challenged by, the need to research our past as a religion and the practices of our ancestors. I was also impelled by a need to develop a contemporary religion of new, modern practices. Many pagans have done this same work. Now that this research and development of basic matters is no longer necessary—it *does* continue to be vital with respect to the issues one can explore now that the earlier work has been done—it is still necessary for some if not all of us to define, seek, and claim our own power and our own relationship with the Gods. This is part of becoming responsible for our own souls and claiming the authority needed to be of service. Doing this assignment embodies *your* independence the same way my commitment to oral tradition embodies mine.

How to Perform a Self-Initiation Ritual

JOURNAL EXCERPTS

Buddhists discuss the heart. Christians talk about the heart of Christ. Some Wiccans talk about heart, but references to heart are not a core part of pagan philosophy. I've discussed this with many Wiccans, none of whom think of the heart as a central image of pagan theology. Love, but not heart. I feel starved because of this lack. I am starting to think heart is a crucial image, one at the heart—ha!—of spiritual health.

Vision: Gentle heart. Holding power. Not grasping for, or even striving for.
   Simply, and gently, holding power.
   Soft, like relaxed hand palm up.
   Soft, like breath of child on his mother's face.
   Gentle Heart.
   Holding power with a smile.

Lady, teach me that, in meeting this day, I am meeting You. Teach me that, having reached this day, I have reached my destiny. Having come to this day, I've nowhere else to strive toward, so help me live this day attentively, according to Your will, and accept this moment, which is Your will, whether it is a day in which to be gentle or in which to fight like a mad dog; help me be mindful, in this day, of this day.

Having done an initiation doesn't mean that one has fulfilled the requirements of one's training. Initiation is only part of what the training is for. One may need the training all the more after an initiation. And training, like initiation, never stops.

If your coven has done this training with you and you want them to attend the ritual, any one of them can do the ritual parts that are not your own responsibility. For example, they can cast the circle, but only you can take your vows.

Though the initiation does not happen until the end of next month, it appears below so that you can know how to prepare for it over the rest of this month and next.

RITUAL

The Third Road Self-Initiation Ritual Script

If you can, I suggest you avoid reading the initiation script until you do this lesson. Then, if at all possible, don't spend much time reading the initiation ritual.

This exact ritual should be performed once, then almost never again. Such power is very tempting to repeat, but in fact you lose power by doing the rite more than a few times in your lifetime. While we will discuss further how the training up to and after the initiation ritual can be used over a lifetime to continually enhance and improve your inner and outer landscape, the initiation ritual below is different. I imagine that an athlete might feel quite a high when performing at an Olympic competition, but I also imagine that to do so too often would injure her and that she might never be able to compete again. So it is with this ritual. Just as that athlete can perform at peak level in many other ways, instead of only the way she performs at the Olympic competitions, so a shaman can employ and enjoy many types of peak-level power; in fact, one of the points of this initiation is to open yourself to them. But if you do the rite too much, you are closed to them and chasing glamour. And you can be seriously hurt!

This ritual script's many in-depth explanations would be distracting in the middle of the rite. Therefore all explanations not needed the actual day of the rite are in italics.

Ingredients

- Optional: Two cords, one black, one any color you want. *Each needs to be long enough so that after they have been twisted into one cord, this cord can be tied around one's waist. These cords can be made of any material. Do not twist the two cords together until the designated moment mid-rite.*

Initiates of many Wiccan traditions have cords. This twisted cord of two colors is a symbol of The Third Road self-initiation (as opposed to the green cord designating The Third Road initiation that is passed down from a teacher and, of course, involves a different script). The black symbolizes the invisibility of some powers. The word love is not the same as love. True power is often unseen. The cord color of your choice represents your particular bloodline, often an invisible power that no one knows but you. Such invisibility denies hierarchy yet ensures quality.

My self-initiate cord is red and black. I wanted to make all Third Road self-initiate cords the same, because I thought that would make us all equals. I thank my initiate Steve Tiongco for arguing against that idea, helping me see that, though my intention was good—I wanted to avoid unhealthy hierarchy—my proposed means was misled. Choose a color to designate your bloodline. Choose white or any other color you want if your bloodline is unknown to you.

- Optional: A third cord of any design, also to be worn about the waist, perhaps independently of the twisted cord.

When I was just about to start writing this book, my initiates initiated me. They did not even know yet what type of book I was writing! One of them, Steve Tiongco, decided I needed another initiation. I thought an initiation was a silly idea but went along with it because I love him so much and it was clearly very important to him. It seemed a symbol for him more than for me. Was I wrong! The long period leading up to the rite was a time of profound change and challenge. The initiation was happening whether I did a formal ceremony or not. I was lucky to have someone in my life who knew I needed a rite to aid me through life's trials. When the ceremony was over I realized I had passed through a gate and needed to serve the community in a new way. In addition, the fears I had of a difficult year ahead abated because at the end of the initiation ritual I looked around at a room full of my initiates and remembered I was not alone in my trials. I had community.

In some ways, I do not like going through initiations. It is hard work, and I hate to face my challenges. But the challenges are there running my life whether I face them or not. The only way not to be controlled by them is to face them and get on with it. And lo, suddenly, you're happy!

When I dressed for the ritual, the trickster in me took over and I wore quite an outfit, including an absurd belt I had bought years before in a punk shop: leather and studded with small skulls from one end to the other. I've been known to show up for rites in some wild outfits. God knows what possesses me.

I call the belt absurd, but it is also beautiful. By wearing bones and skulls, shamans hold sacred the cycles of life and death soon to be discussed in this chapter.

When I met Steve for my initiation, I quipped that the skull belt was the cord for my new initiation. I forgot my joke, but Steve remembered. Since he was my initiator, I later asked him if the new initiation (or new phase of initiation) bestowed a cord. He said, "Don't you remember, you already have it, your skull belt?" Then, while writing this chapter, I thought, "Oh, right, I am going to tell people what cord to wear, and give them no freedom of design? Me, who couldn't even show up at her own initiation without wearing a jokester costume?"

Enjoy your third cord; make it silly, or beautiful, or both; wear it alone or with your other cord; weave all three cords together; wear it around your waist or hair; make a new one each week of fresh flowers; do as you will. Put it on before, after, or at any point during the initiation.

- Water and optional salt or incense (for purifying space)
- Optional: Incense or scented water to charge space
- Optional: Anything needed for "Your Own Section," should you choose to include that, should be on hand.
- Cakes and Wine

Cakes and Wine is a term many Wiccan traditions use to denote a sacred feast, eaten when the ritual is almost over; it is part of the rite. We pagans celebrate our lives as sacred, so we celebrate our meals as sacred.

Wine is not to be taken literally for Third Road rituals. In The Third Road, we almost always avoid alcohol in our rites. Many ancient documents in which the word wine is used in sacred context have been mistranslated; often the actual substance referred to was not wine but milk, a sacred substance because it is of a mother. The subtle sexism of this translation has immense ramifications politically and magically.

Third Roaders do not need alcoholic wine to loosen up; we have Third Road magic to do that. And most of us have discovered that alcohol actually dulls the magic that happens in a Third Road rite and can even make the rite dangerous. But it is a personal choice. Some shamans enjoy wine as part of a rite. However, you cannot know what you are missing unless you experience Third Road magic done without alcohol. Then you can make a real choice because it is an informed one.

"Cakes and Wine" can be anything from a snack to a full-blown meal, but usually it includes both food and drink. In this initiation, it should be a full meal, prepared beforehand so that it is ready to eat during the ritual. By full meal, I do not mean you need to cook. One should not have to do a lot of cooking and culinary cleanup the day of one's initiation. It could be more like what one would eat at a picnic, such as fruit juice, a loaf of bread, cheese, and carrot sticks. If you want more, you might add dried fruit, cold cuts, mixed nuts, celery sticks, and olives. It should be wholesome food. A sugary dessert is fine as long as the rest of the meal is good, solid, healthy food.

People assume I am a vegetarian. I'm a steak-and-potatoes, lobster-dipped-in-butter, cheese-omelet sort of woman. It is up to a shaman whether she is vegetarian or a meat eater. Different body types and lifestyles demand different diets. Some people are vegetarian for sound political reasons. Both my acupuncturists told me I need red meat in my diet. It felt good to have my choice affirmed. I feel sluggish and tired when I don't eat meat. Others feel sluggish and tired when they do.

A farmer told me that when he was a child his family would kill one of their sheep every year for food. Whatever day the family planned to do this, all the sheep would go to the end of the field, far from the farmhouse. Then one sheep would part from the pack and walk toward the house. The animal had offered itself, a holy sacrifice, to feed the family. When the fish I am buying at the fish market is pulled live from the tank, I silently thank it for the life and nourishment it sacrifices that I might live. I try to eat meat from animals who were treated well while they were raised. When I die, my body will feed the plants and microorganisms where I am buried. All things feed one another. "Cakes and Wine" is indeed a sacred part of a ceremony.

Preparation

Though discussed now, there is no reason to start preparation until the first week of next month.

Decide if there are ancestors, other than bloodline, you want to invoke at the ritual. Perhaps a famous role model of yours who has passed on (and who, unbeknownst to you, might be bloodline).

Is there is a specific deceased relative(s) you want to invite? This is part of bloodline we have not discussed until now. As a child, you might have had a favorite great-aunt who encouraged your wild streak. Or perhaps you've heard stories of a relative generations back, tales that inspired you and made you hope that a little of her or his vivacity and courage has passed down to you.

Maybe pick a patron goddess for the initiation, a goddess you have special feelings about or with whom you identify. One way to find such a goddess would be to research mythology and Wiccan books.

You may want to listen to or sing "Love Is the Magic" from my musical album. It is a poem I wrote describing a vision I had of shamanism's core mysteries. I set the poem to an upbeat tune because, though the piece is about death, death is part of life's cycles and thus part of the cycle of joy. Death is a core part of our religion: like the grain that dies at the harvest to be baked into bread that gives us life, the losses we suffer—death of a romance or dream or job or loved one or physical capacity—are all gates into new joys, though it often seems that can't possibly be the case. So this song about life's cycles of death and rebirth can be heard joyfully. Death, literal or figurative, brings renewal. I also chose to write an upbeat tune to help myself (and you) build power and confidence, courage and vigor to face life's—and initiation's (false differentiation but you get my point)—challenges.

You will also face challenges as part of your preparation, and these we will address later.

Ritual Script

"The Magic Formula" is changed for this ritual. However, this adaptation can be used for any rite.

Before the ritual there should be a ritual bath for self-purification. Do the first two steps of "The Magic Formula" (breathing exercise and pre-ritual cleansings) in a bath or shower. You can add salt to the bath as a purifying agent.

Some of the following parts of the script are valuable, important rites unto themselves. They will be explained as such.

Purifying a Space

It is necessary at some point, whether now or years from now, to start keeping your ritual space—as well as your living space—psychically cleansed.

One does so by using the following practice on a regular basis: burn sage, frankincense, or sandalwood in the room you are doing ritual in, or sprinkle water with a pinch of salt in it about the room. You can use a nominal amount of water instead of leaving saltwater stains on your furniture and walls.

"Purifying a Space" is a spell that can be done without "The Magic Formula."

One way to use the spell regularly is to add it occasionally to your "Magic Formula." One would cleanse the space after doing a pre-ritual cleansing of one's self. For most folks, it is too much and unnecessary to spiritually cleanse their space each time they do "The Magic Formula."

Casting Circle

Cast a circle by performing "The Mother's Cloak." You might want to paper-clip the page it is on to find it easily mid-ceremony. Make the "Protection Bubble" part of "The Mother's Cloak."

Charging a Space (optional)

Charging a space is along the lines of charging a battery. Burn an incense that smells lovely or that has special meaning to you or that you feel evokes power. Or sprinkle scented water about that has any of the qualities just mentioned. Perhaps rose water is your skin conditioner, and you splashed it on your face one night before you went for a walk on the beach, and, strolling along in the clean, salty air, your feet pressing into moist, soft sand, you felt enormously serene and at one with nature. And ever since, whenever you smell roses, you remember that peace and sense of union with Mother Earth. Well, a *space* in which rose water is strewn becomes *charged* with that sweet memory.

If in "Purifying a Space" you used incense, use water to charge; if you used water to cleanse, use incense to charge. *"Charging a Space" can be done as a rite unto itself, without "The Magic Formula," to add power and pleasure to any event. It can also be done to the same purpose before any rite, as part of "The Magic Formula."*

Ancestors

Say, "I invite the ancestors of The Third Road, people of the Faerie Faith. I also invite the ancestors of my bloodline." You may invite the ancestors of your bloodline whether you know who they are or not. You may also add an invitation to any other ancestors you decided to invite during your preparation. Remember: any presence you want at this ritual should be requested, not demanded.

Guardians (optional)

Invite any special spirit helpers, Faeries, angels, and the like that you have worked with previously and whose presence you want at this ritual. *Determine whom to invite by deciding if traits a spirit has shown in the past—for example, a reassuring, loving presence; wisdom; a sense of wonder and inspiration she always bestow upon you when she visits; a protective power; an ability to open you to the exhilarating beauty of life; a sense of playfulness—would be useful or enjoyable at your initiation.* Name the spirit or spirits you want present, then say, "I invite you and ask for your help, guidance, and protection."

Invocation of the Goddess and God

Do the invocation as instructed in "The Magic Formula."

The Goddess Speaks

She asks certain things of you in this rite. You can either imagine Her saying the following lines, say them to yourself, or have a coven member say them. The script will often include something like, "The Goddess says, . . ." Treat all such passages as instructed in this paragraph.

The Goddess tells you, "Declare yourself the Goddess's priest(ess)."

Answer, "I declare myself the Goddess's priest(ess)."

The Goddess says, "Declare your intent as the Goddess's priest(ess)." Answer with your intent as the Goddess's priest(ess). You needn't plan your answer. It will come at the moment needed in the initiation.

The Goddess challenges you, "What powers have you shown to make you worthy?"

Show healthy pride by listing at least one magical and one mundane achievement of the past year. Or list many. You may also include achievements over your lifetime.

"What offerings do you bring me to show you worthy?"

Relist those same achievements, because you are the most important offering. Then you may add any offering you choose, or none. Perhaps list inner virtues and talents. You might say, "I give you these virtues and skills. Use them as you will." If you are a dancer, you may want to dance for the Gods right then and there. Or offer a candle that you light in praise of Her. Or offer a commitment to be more self accepting, heal a broken relationship, or get more involved in political action. Or offer a beautiful feather or stone.

"You have declared yourself my priestess, walking The Third Road, with the words of the Eagle.* It will cost. Contemplate the price that may be exacted, and be willing to pay it."

Take a moment in which to contemplate that price.

---

*A way to interpret "walking with the words of the Eagle": I am an eagle; this initiation script is a poem I wrote; thus you walk with the words of an elder. Also, my poetry comes from the Goddess—the Great Eagle—so you walk with God's words.

Vows

After each vow the Goddess presents, respond with something like "I do so vow" unless instructed otherwise. The vows are a bit hard to understand if you see them as black and white. For example, the first vow might seem odd since you do not know all other Third Road travelers. Or a vow to uphold members of all craft traditions might seem wrong since not all people of any religion are ethical. Vow in the spirit of the vow. The Goddess asks you:

"Do you vow to support, uphold, and protect the other travelers of The Third Road, with perfect love and perfect trust?"

"Do you vow to support, uphold, and protect *all* your craft brothers and sisters?"

"Do you vow to uphold the craft and The Third Road?"

"This is a fearsome path. The Third Road is wild, its laws are not the laws of society and humankind, love is answered with love, but betrayal by avalanche. It has not the dangers of civilization; it is kinder. It has not the safety of civilization; it is more dangerous. Arrogant foolishness and lack of respect have no place on this journey. But the Mother of us all welcomes the errors and follies of your true heart's endeavors. Do you vow to walk The Third Road? Do you dare to walk The Third Road? Are you firm enough to say yes? Because it would be better to rush upon a blade and perish than to venture further with fear in your heart."

The response to this whole last paragraph is the classic Wiccan phrase, "Yes, in perfect love and perfect trust." *Another classic is the above, "It would be better to rush upon a blade and perish than to venture further with fear in your heart."*

"Vow according to the following. Now secrets of the Art will be yours, perhaps told you by other witches, and surely revealed to you through your own eyes and heart. Share them with care because Mysteries spoken can be lost forever. Share them with care because power spoken can be lost forever. Share them with care because lives are destroyed when information is given to the arrogant. Or to those not yet ready because of lack of training or purification. Share them with care because power is dispersed through chatter. Never diminish your power and knowledge, never think less of your power and knowledge by thinking that it is easily gained by another without their labor and readiness. Others must cleanse and work as you have, or else the Mysteries that you live naturally are dangerous for them. Such is the power you have gained. Share them with care because you are responsible for what is done with what you share. Share them with care because one should never give information to those who would disdain or misunderstand it. Share them with care or dishonor the Lady and weaken the craft. Do you vow to act according to these instructions?"

"Do you vow, however, that if a person comes to you needing information about our religion and ritual, you will not deny them, if at all possible? And that you will do your best to determine the proper course of action, conferring with an elder if possible?"

"Vow that you are both your own and mine. Life has its meaning that you cannot escape, even should you ignore these meanings. I offer you freedom, with which comes great joy."

Recite: "Should I break this or any of my oaths made today, may my heart know the sorrow I would thus cause others and may my weapons turn against me."

The Goddess says, "The cost to travel The Third Road is yourself—everything you are. You must be simply and joyously yourself. And you must always honor your power, never trivializing it through loose lips, never desecrating the altar your body is. These are the costs, and as your power grows, so does this cost, and so does the penalty for misuse of power—a (wo)man uses the power given or it turns on her/him."

Your Own Section (optional)

It's up to you what you do here. Affirm primary truths, ask for specific powers, chant, make another offering, use "The Wisdom of the Ancestors" ritual, do whatever you want. In the thirteenth month's lesson ahead is the "Gentle Heart Ritual." At the beginning of the section "How to Perform a Self-Initiation Ritual" I shared the journal entry that "Gentle Heart Ritual" is based on, in part to show you how you can make a visualization out of your own visions. Perhaps in this section of the initiation, you can take a core vision you had or a poem you wrote and make it into a visualization. Such creations can, among other things, bring us back again and again to core truths of our own and help us live them, at times when an intellectual remembering alone does nothing. Remember not to include others in your visualizations. Perhaps you would prefer to express a core truth in another way, such as drawing a picture, sweeping a floor, or arranging flowers; these are all rituals (more about that later).

In a bit, there will be helpful hints about how to create the sort of ritual section that is described above.

Core Mysteries

The Goddess says, "These are the three mysteries: love, death, and re-birth."

Walk in a circle from the north to the east, then south, then west and then north again. Then, moving in the same direction, spiral inward until you are in the center of your space. If the space is small it will be more the suggestion of a circle and spiral. Once you are in the center, the Goddess says,

Now is the time, between time.
Deeper into your center.
Yet ever moving out,
be you now.
Be you now!

If your coven is present, they should know beforehand that they now leave the room silently, speedily, peacefully. If there is only one room, have them sit silently without contacting you in any way, with their backs to you so that they cannot see what you do. This is time for you to be alone. *Do not plan this section. Be open and see what happens. Do not worry about this section. Initiation is a mystery; something will happen. Any of your decisions should be made right then, not beforehand. You might find yourself talking to a spirit that appears during this time alone or medi-tating or singing or spinning or shouting or . . .*

More Mysteries

If you have a bloodline cord, wrap it about one ankle. Wrap it around and around so it does not drag or trip you when you move. Then tuck the end in so it stays in place (you may want to tie it first). *You should not cinch it unpleasantly tight! There is no cruelty in Third Road initiation ceremonies; they are caring, loving rites. The cord wrapping is done in that spirit.*

The Goddess says of you, "Not bound, but not free."

Reminder for those doing this rite with a coven: your coven has left; there are none present to recite the Goddess's parts, which must now be recited by Her in your imagination. (If you are doing the entire rite alone, you've already been applying your imagination that way.)

Directional Powers and Gifts

She continues, "From each corner my garden brings gifts—to make you a shaman, witch, priestess, child of mine. From the east let My powers of light and dark run through you."

Face east. Take a moment. *You might experience something, but I won't say what, because I don't know! You will experience whatever is right and special for* you.

"From the south let your witch's name be heard."

Face south. If you don't feel, hear, or otherwise sense the name, that's fine. Maybe it is not important for you. Or not yet. You can even choose your magical moniker before the rite and simply recite it at this moment. Maybe long after the rite, the name will pop into your head or you will consciously choose one after much thought. Perhaps you've long had a name you want to keep. The name can be used publicly, shared secretly with a few people, whatever.

"From the west, may you better understand your death."

Face west, take a moment.

"From the north, may you learn secrecy. You shall need now this northern gift."

Face north, take a moment.

"To the center, and may you find your God."

Do what you will. If you chose a patron goddess, as discussed earlier in the "Preparation" part of the ritual script, take time with Her now.

"As you have vowed, you will deny no one this power should, hopefully after conferring with an elder, you deem that person is needful of it. However, always keep in mind that the most important way to pass this power on is simply by using it in your own life and letting the ways of your daily mundane actions exude love, kindness, tolerance, compassion, and power to those about you."

The Ancestral Line

If you are using cords, remove the one on your ankle, twist it together with the black cord, then tie the resulting cord about your waist. Or if you've a third cord that you want to weave with the other two, you can do that weaving now.

Then the Goddess says, "From time's beginning my children have come to me in love. I have in return given them my love and power. So this passes down to you now. And it is this power that will help you in your life's trials."

Pray now: "I request of the Lord and Lady and my ancestors that I more fully come into my bloodline and the line of The Third Road."

Holding one end of the cord (if you have one), perform "Gaining the Power of Life," adapted as follows. (You might want to put a paper clip on the page with that rite so that you can easily find it during the initiation.)

After you've done "Gaining the Power of Life" in the usual manner to gain a strong sense of inner power, but before the sending up of power, continue "Gaining the Power of Life" by adding a new power: the mana of being a Third Road initiate:

Step 1. The power of a Third Road initiate is to be Her child, always humbly in her care, fully protected in all your days, loving yourself, faults and all. That power is also having protection for the work ahead, and by that I mean the lifework, not just the work of the initiatory rite . . . Dwell on all that's been written in this step, one power at a time, and as you dwell on each power, feel it, as described, come into you.

Step 2. That power is also to be Her priest(ess), wielding great cosmic forces, able to live a moral life. Dwell on this description, feeling all parts of that power as just described come into you, one at a time.

Step 3. A Third Road initiate gains *this* power: to be of a line of shamans who have set their visions on the stars. These are the spirits who came to me, Francesca, as my then-unknown ancestors, to give me the power that this rite now passes to you. It is a line of brave, unique seekers, mystics and wild folks, spiritual outlaws and healers. A community in which are many who usually seek alone, each with their own bloodline. A family of love and power. Feel all parts of that power and responsibility as just described come into you, one at a time, dwelling on each then feeling it come into you.

Now, continue with "Gaining the Power of Life" by dividing and sending as usual. Don't forget, sometimes along with acquiring internal power, you will be surrounded by external power. Check for it; if it is there, send it up.

Another Grounding

The coven can return now. They may need to do the grounding.

You should feel filled with power, but if it still feels like too much so that it is unpleasant or more than you feel you can handle, kneel, then lower yourself until your head and forearms are on the ground, and let the excess energy drain into the earth. If you cannot take that posture, hold out your hands, palms down, and let the energy drain out through your hands into the earth.

This grounding is a useful psychic exercise whenever one feels overloaded. Henceforth, when you check in after a ritual to see what grounding you need, see if you need this.

Acknowledgment: You Are God

Goddess says, "Be thou a (wo)man now, in full, yea, in truth thou be a (wo)man now. You are the Goddess's beloved. Know and be Her lust.

As you bed, each time you bed, know you are Her, moving closer to Herself."

"You are a Faerie priestess, a child of God. You are a witch of The Third Road, Path of the Art. The rite is done. So be it!"

Cakes and Wine

Bless the feast before eating. The blessing can take any form. Here is one:

Holding the beverage or one of the beverages to be served, say, "From the mother comes milk, and in it is our own soul. Thank you, Mother."

Holding the food or one of the foods to be served, say, "Our God dies to be born again. And so we are fed with this cake. Thank you, Father."

Enjoy eating, alone or with your coven.

Usually, when Cakes and Wine occurs in a ritual, a tablespoon of food and of beverage is set aside for the God and Goddess. In this ritual, you may want to offer more, the equivalent of a small snack for you. In any case, in your initiation also set aside at least a tablespoon of food and beverage for the ancestors, and if you invited guardians, do so for them as well. *Occasional food and beverage for both Gods, ancestors, and spirit helpers is a good thing; Victor taught me that they need the food, literally. I agree.*

The above "Cakes and Wine" blessing can be used in your other rites if you so choose, whether eating a snack or full meal. Or use the blessing and make a food offering when not doing a rite but simply sitting down to breakfast or enjoying a snack at the beach or at any other time you take in food and drink.

Devocations

Say, "I thank the ancestors of The Third Road, people of the Faerie Faith, and the ancestors of my bloodline for all your help." (You may add, "I thank [insert name(s) of other ancestor(s) if you invited them] for all your help.") Then say, "Hail and farewell."

If you invited any spirits as guardians, say, "I thank you for your help, guidance, and protection. Hail and farewell."

Devoke the Goddess and God as done in "The Magic Formula."

Open Circle

After opening circle, don't forget to do your usual grounding. If ever you'll need it, this is the time.

Some people who go through a Third Road training eventually claim their own power by creating their own material. For some, that is part of bringing one's work as a Third Road initiate to fruition. However, in doing so one must keep to one's initiate vows: "Now secrets of the Art will be yours . . . revealed to you through your own eyes and heart. Share them with care. . . ." You see, though The Third Road was a construct derived from *my* research, I *still* ran it by Victor for years. And I am grateful for that; it made me a safe teacher. Not a *perfectly* safe one, but reasonably safe. I am sure there are still things wrong with the curriculum that I hope time will reveal and change. Our branch is not the same as some branches of Wicca, which are easier to transmit safely. Your own material might be the same if you are the sort of independent wild one that tends to study with me.

Assignment: optional; starting week 3, do all or any of the following.

1. Use "Purifying a Space" one to three times before the initiation (reminder: initiation happens, at the soonest, at the end of the twelfth month, so these assignments can be done into next month) so that you are used to it when you do it in the initiation and have it as part of your general repertoire of spells.
2. Use "The Mother's Cloak" one to three times before the initiation.
3. Use "Charging a Space" one to three times before the initiation.

Some of the assignments needed for the initiation, such as choosing what you will state as your accomplishment(s) during your initiation, will be delayed until next month.

Assignment: during week 4 or later. While everyone should read this assignment as part of their training, the assignment is only for those who choose to have "Your Own Section" in the initiation.

Though the initiation ritual that I wrote is amazing in its capacity to deliver all I have said an initiation can give—false modesty does a shaman no good!—you may prefer to add a part. Certain powers can be gained when you create ritual yourself. On the other hand, do not feel your initiation is any less worthy or that you are any less a shaman if you do not do this section. We all have our challenges, our powers, our strong points.

I used every internal resource I had to create this script, trying to ensure that you have all the initiation benefits possible. But later, if you want, you can create an entire initiation on your own.

After all, initiation never stops. Gaining the underpinning of psychic skills and selfhood that this training and initiation offer can prepare you to write your own later if you so choose. Having had the experience of the initiation in this book, and lived with the results for a year or two, you may be in a better position to write another all on your own if you want. But to write your own without face-to-face help and without having experienced this one first might not be good research on your part. In the same way that Wicca 101 is not the same as Third Road 101, so this Third Road self-initiation ceremony is not the same as others, and the only way to gain its benefits and know the difference is to do the ritual and live with the results for a good long time, which provides a strong backdrop for later scripts.

But, in The Third Road oral tradition (as opposed to that taught through a book), some of the most powerful self-initiations have been written only in part by the student.

It takes a tremendous commitment and an act of courage to do *Goddess Initiation*'s training and initiation rite; there is no way to describe such a great exertion of self, expression of self, examination of self, and care of self as anything other than self-initiation. I hope you are proud of that.

If you decide to write your own after having done the one in this book, *Be a Goddess!* has a lesson about creating rituals. Also browse through the rest of both this section and *Goddess Initiation*—both rituals and lectures—looking specifically for ideas, cautions, considerations, and relevant guidelines you might apply or adapt when writing a ritual.

Here are a few thoughts about creating "Your Own Section."

It can be simple or elaborate, one minute or twenty minutes.

Should you choose to finish training in a year and a month's time, you have almost two months to write your part. I've given you that amount of time so that you don't need to hurry or worry, not so that you can do three times as much as is necessary and be miserable with a time-consuming, anxiety-producing task in which you sweat blood and work yourself to the bone. No, this should be an easy pace, no rush, no pressure.

Of course, that doesn't mean it might not be tremendously hard for some folks. If you are facing challenges related to a traumatic event, past or present, and you want to create this section to heal, you may face difficulties. Working toward initiation is a healing time, and healing can bring up intensely painful feelings. You might have to do purification rites to move through blocks or get cheerleaders or other support. If you are trying to face down trauma, don't be too ambitious. Do a bit of trauma-related work in the initiation, and be proud of that. For example, instead of using "Your Own Section" to triumph completely over the trauma, fashion it so that it focuses on only one thing in yourself that needs healing. And if you want to use the section for overcoming trauma yet you feel bad because such an idea is too overwhelming, guess what? The initiation as is, without "Your Own Section," is designed to heal the soul of trauma! You needn't add a thing. After all, the ancient shamanic initiation constituted a psychic healing of a greatly traumatized soul.

Any words you write for a ritual needn't be what others might think of as professional quality; they needn't be fancy or what others might think of as special. Nothing more is needed to make them special than that you write them yourself. Honest! *Nothing* more. And you can even ask someone to guide you step by step through the writing. Though no one but you can do the work that the universe assigns you, the universe never asks you to do your work unaided and unsupported.

If you come to me for counseling, in your appointment I might give you esoteric advice or mundane information, or I might give you a ritual for self-healing to take home with you, or I may do one with you then and there. Or I may tell you to wash your dishes! It is all ritual because it all moves energy. The crucial factors in a *good* ritual are addressed by this question: Does the ritual or action or event or poem *move energy in a relevant and useful way?* And that, my dear, is one of the most important things a shaman knows about magic. Whatever you do that usefully moves energy is valid in "Your Own Section." You can sleep during that section if that is what you need! Sleep, eat, dance, paint your face. Or do overt ritual.

Here are a few questions to ask yourself: Are there primary truths in your Book of Shadows that you want or need to affirm in your initiation? What do you think is needed in the rite that is missing?

You might research ideas of things to do in that section through:

- *Books.* Wiccan books, Faerie tales, fantasy novels.
- *Psychic perception:* Do you have divination skills you can use for guidance about creating "Your Own Section"? If you have a spirit guide, you can talk to her about how to create it as well. Or ask your ancestors.
- *Oral tradition.* Find a consultant, perhaps a metaphysical shop owner, Wiccan elder or peer, professional or nonprofessional psychic.
- *Your Book of Shadows.* You may want to refer back to your writing, since it is your bible, and draw on a part or parts of it. One way to do this is to recite one of your entries in the ritual. But your writing might also be used as a consideration, a springboard, a starting point from which you create something that is not a recitation of an entry or even an adapted recitation. For example, an entry saying that you always feel courage and trust in God when dancing might encourage you to dance in your initiation. Or an entry saying that your whole life is improved whenever you use herbs or learn about them or talk to them might inspire you to offer herbs to God during the ritual.

Don't forget to rely on your Good Faeries if you want critiques on what you are preparing or if you need moral support.

What Challenges Must Be Faced Before Initiation?

JOURNAL EXCERPT

> *A vision the day after initiation: My dragon is coiled about me. I sleep, with my new senses, a child. There's fire within the coil. It's like a scene from a movie—a primitive landscape, caveman era, a child shaman, and as this child sleeps, snow-like substance descends from the sky. It is not a cold substance. Stones dance in a circle inside the dragon coil, and around the child. The child wakes and says, "Sshh," and the stones stop. But they remain alive, aware. The child leaves the coil, to explore the real world. She goes into water, to play.*

This chapter answers the question, "What challenges must be faced before initiation?" My answer: you've likely already faced them, and I will list them below.

Most people have no idea how much they've accomplished until at least a year after the fact. They may not see that the purification and empowerment spells in this training, committing to this training, and following through on all the lessons are challenges that earn initiation. This training makes you grow, and that is what an initiation challenge is about.

Initiation challenges may not be very flashy. Power is often invisible. The real challenges are not necessarily about endeavors that would look dramatic if portrayed in a movie episode. The real challenges constitute the frightening journey inward to face the self, with all one's faults and glories.

Let's further delineate the shamanic challenges that occur before initiation. To do this, I will establish false categories—each will overlap the others—but the categories provide a jumping-off point.

First, there's the training itself. We already talked about that, but let's touch on a different aspect of it: *magical* training. Just as a martial artist practices to pass his test for a black belt, one has to train to cultivate one's magical skills. Reading this book and doing your assignments—the training—bears mention as an actual magical challenge.

Regarding the training, in terms of magical, spiritual, and mundane development: never forget that initiation is not a moment in time. (I've said that enough now in this book that it should be indelibly printed on your soul. So roll your eyes and groan at hearing it one last time. Well, maybe I'll remind you once more later!)

Then there are the challenges that life itself gives us, such as pursuing a career choice, giving birth, losing a good friend, being gossiped about. Again, the training and life are not separate. (I had to get that in one last time, also!)

Any challenge met bestows power. Your challenges and the powers they bestow should be geared toward what is needed to meet your specific life goals. (One's lifework need not be what one is paid for; it can be, for example, one's volunteer work. And one may have several lifeworks.)

I will define initiation in a textbook sort of way now because your analytic mind is ready. Up to now such analysis could have too easily blocked your powers. An initiation is a rite or event that can: transform the recipient; begin a new phase of the recipient's life; empower the recipient; and/or recognize the achievements of the recipient. As such, there are many types and forms. For instance, the first menstruation is an initiation for a young girl into a phase of womanhood. Almost any kind of Wiccan initiation encompasses all the possibilities listed and deepens and empowers the practitioner's experience of magic and relationship with the Gods.

So, you successfully meet a challenge encountered while striving toward a goal, then you undergo an initiation that recognizes the power gained by triumphing over such a challenge. And the initiation also confers power needed to work further toward the goal.

So whatever gate you are going through—the gate into becoming a professional musician or the gate into being a professional musician more serenely or the gate into being a professional musician more profitably—determines what challenges you must meet. Do not see the challenges of other people as more important. Singing in front of others may not be your challenge if you don't want to be a performer. Holding silence may be your challenge. Or it may be something that is tangential to both.

Another example: I am out of the broom closet myself. But I never "out" anyone else. When I call a Wiccan on the phone I do not leave an explicitly pagan message on their answering machine. Such news, if overheard by an unsympathetic landlord or mother-in-law, could cause someone to lose custody of her children. It is important to be brave about one's religion, but that is a moot point when it comes to outing folks. Often, people of color and other disenfranchised groups have fewer resources to withstand the impact of religious discrimination and may be more likely to be attacked since they're perceived as having fewer defenses. As to those who *seem* more able to withstand the rigors of being outed: any individual may be dealing with mitigating factors that are invisible to most other people. So I cannot make a choice for someone else. Perhaps another person's bravery regarding her religion is to dare to practice it secretly, when those near her would be horrified to learn of her religion. Besides, being out of the closet might get in the way of someone's lifework: if one wants to be a teacher, perhaps there are reasons one could not do so effectively if everyone knew one was a witch.

As I wrote earlier, several years ago my life was threatened while I was doing community service. I had to contact the district attorney's office, keep a witness with me for safety, and perform other time-consuming tasks. But I kept working in close proximity to the man who persecuted me. I try not to run from the tasks the Mother asks of me, and she wanted me in that arena. I barely knew the person who threatened me, but from what I observed I saw that he was dangerously unstable mentally and, in his insanity, thought a death threat would slow down my work. I suspect he thought he could get away with bullying a woman. He didn't get rid of me. The point I am making is that I don't let anyone push me around, but my car does not have a bumper sticker saying "My other car is a broom." I choose my battles, and so should you. I am willing to be killed in the line of duty if my Gods deem it so, but only doing the service I feel is mine to do. I am not willing to be killed on the road by some nut who sees my bumper sticker and decides to blow my head off. Yet I diligently support and praise folks who have the bumper stickers. Such openness can be a great way to educate, and I am honored to support anyone who wants to take this kind of risk. The point is: just as I believe it is a personal choice to be out or not, and to have a Wiccan bumper sticker or not, so I believe we must choose our challenges according to the goals we choose.

When I choose my battles and challenges, I can be of the most use to the community that *I* can be. Instead of having a Wiccan bumper sticker, I educate folks of all religions by doing pastoral counseling for them: they experience a witch doing good for them and realize we are not bad.

Challenges that are minor for some are major for others. Don't compare yourself. For some, a real challenge is phoning a college to ask for a catalog so that they can return to school to pursue the career of their dreams. The first step of making a phone call to the college can be blocked by years of cultural programming that tell a person to forsake her dreams. The real challenge can be asking the question "Am I happy?" Or "What do I want to do with my life?" Or "What inside me is blocking my sexuality?" If you've done this training, you've faced such challenges. So you'll probably be ready for the initiation at the end of next month.

Don't think, "Oh dear, I want to be a veterinarian; do I need to finish school for that before my initiation?" No. If, in this training, you were brave enough to ask yourself what you want to do with your life, and you work through some inner blocks regarding that—perhaps blocks to hearing your inner voice a bit better or blocks to trusting your desire to serve animals medically—and maybe take the risk of telling a friend your dream of going to veterinarian school, then you've already faced challenges aplenty.

Even if you don't know what your lifework is yet, healing yourself of a few of your wounds might have been your challenge. Challenges vary not only from person to person but also from one stage of life to another. And since the training adapts itself to whatever level of experience you have and whatever goals you are traveling toward, having done the training you know you've most likely passed the challenges. I say *likely* because, finally, only you can know for sure.

You needn't get all the power you will ever need before doing your initiation. That ritual bestows power as well. And challenges and their resulting power continue after initiation; that's the nature of being alive.

How can you tell if you're ready for initiation? When I give a Third Road initiation (as opposed to one of my students doing a Third Road self-initiation), I rarely decide on my own who's ready. It is hard to decide. So I discuss it with other Third Road initiates. You might have to decide alone, though. Give the decision your best shot, and trust God.

One of my students seemed ready for me to initiate, but several initiates felt we might want to delay a bit, that it might be too much for the student in question at that point in time. He was an alcoholic who had just sobered up. He and I sat down, and I left the choice to him: Did he feel initiation would strengthen his new sobriety or distract him from the intense focus he so needed to learn how to stay off alcohol? A Third Road initiation is loving and healthy but can bring up feelings or cause big life changes or bring in a lot of power or speed up growth. So it might be too much to deal with when getting sober, or it might be a big help when getting sober. I told that student what I tell you: it's up to you; if you feel you're ready, do it!

To plan and prepare forever and not follow through with doing can be a trap. This is true not only of initiation but of anything in life. I am learning to drive. It is definitely one of the few mainstream American initiations. I am realizing that after finishing my written test, taking driving lessons, and receiving my license, I won't know how to drive! No one does at that point. It is a crazy but necessary proposition; you get on the road only mildly in control of a lethal weapon and hope for the best. This is the only way to finally learn to drive. I am stunned and gratified to realize this! Because in the same vein, one must do one's best with one's lessons and then learn by actually doing, and in many of life's situations, doing that is a high risk! Do the best you can in preparing for your initiation, writing your part, and facing challenges. Then humbly start the initiation ceremony knowing you'll fall far short of your goals.

This is part of how you learn to be the Goddess's child instead of only her priest—by trusting her to pick up the slack and then going for it!

This model of not preparing too long for initiation but jumping in, somewhat sink-or-swim, is demanded in a great many of life's situations. If you use this model for everyday living, you have gained another ability to help you follow your star.

You may want to bring your thoughts about challenges and whether you are ready to a Good Faerie—even if your ideas are in the form of vague notions, half-formed queries, or relentless confusions. One reason to do so, despite how unclear your thoughts might be, is to get help shaping your ideas better. With help, we often see that we are far more ready than we think.

Table of Assignments

Do these assignments during the eleventh month, except where otherwise specified:

The first week:
- Perform "The Wisdom of the Ancestors" ritual. pg. 247
- Determine a rite that will initiate you into your bloodline, then do the rite sometime over this month. pg. 250
- Start this month-long assignment this week: look through the training material up to this week's assignment. Work with that material according to the full parameters as given in the eleventh month's lesson. pg. 250

The third week; optional:
- Use "Purifying a Space" one to three times between now and, at the earliest, the end of the twelfth month. pg. 268
- Use "The Mother's Cloak" one to three times in the same wide range of time. pg. 268
- Use "Charging a Space" one to three times in the same wide range of time. pg. 268

The fourth week or later; optional:
- Create "Your Own Section" for the initiation. You have at least two months in which to do this assignment. pg. 269

Celebrating Your Work

Though the celebration I have in mind is done after the initiation, I discuss it now in case you need a month's lead time to invite guests.

When I give a Third Road initiation, there is always a celebration afterward. It is never a big event; in fact, usually it is very casual. But it is important that it happen, and that it happen for you. Celebrate after your initiation. It is your due. You need it. And it *is* part of the ritual.

The celebration should take place somewhere other than where the initiation was held and be very low key with only a few people attending. The new initiate should not drink alcohol, and the others drink only a minimum so that there is a grounding influence.

Often, those of us attending the initiation will go out to dinner, perhaps meeting our significant others at the restaurant. It is a quiet event, no big hoopla. But there is something special about it, and it helps bring the new initiate back to earth, or keep them on earth in the first place, after what is often a surprisingly life-changing rite.

Eating out is not a substitute for Cakes and Wine. At Third Road initiations we often eat two meals: Cakes and Wine, then dinner out immediately afterward. Initiations leave us famished, so we need a whole meal right then and there. Eating a large repast as soon as the rite is done also is necessary to bring our psyches back from the other realms. It seems that the initiation food does not have food's usual effect on our physical bodies, because eating a second meal immediately afterward does not feel like overindulgence.

I suggest your celebration not be the wild sort of event I enjoy so much at other times, such as going out dancing or attending a Gay Pride parade or Mardi Gras. I *am* a wild woman, *and* I have learned that there are times to let the energy settle down so that it can root deeply. The result: I get to be even wilder later! I can enjoy greater self-expression and fuller ecstasy down the line because I become more present in my body, more attuned to subtleties, more alive and true to myself. Restraint does not always stifle ecstasy; it often increases ecstasy!

(An aside that is core to shamanism: practice restraint not only out of ethical considerations but as a means to ecstasy; restraint is also a magical technique in that it helps you safely meet wilder and wilder powers while drawing on those powers to enormous advantage.)

I suggest you don't try for a deep celebration: no moonlit walks on the beach or séances. And avoid huge crowds or other stirring situations. Enjoy a simple event with a few people; it works.

If you have no one with whom to celebrate, you can still do it. For example, take yourself out to eat, or shop in a laid-back little store for a gift for yourself—not a metaphysical store, and not a metaphysical gift. I want you in a very mundane situation.

You may want a day off after the initiation to rest a bit after such a major event.

Self, and Cosmos as Self

JOURNAL EXCERPTS

> *Victor told me whenever I think of my depression to see the Great Eagle, but not to see it too clearly yet. And to give that depression to the Great Eagle. (Great Eagle is a Native American term, and can be viewed as deity or the sum total of all things.) Then he told me a pre-initiation story: a boy saw the Great Eagle and screamed, "I don't want to be devoured." The Great Eagle screamed to him, "I don't want to be devoured." The boy then realized he was talking to himself and to the universal consciousness of which he is a part.*

> The following entry was written the day before Brigid, a Celtic holy day (February 2) that celebrates Brigid, Goddess of metalsmithing, healing, and poetry.

My fire whispers inside me, under the ashes of my past. I have been doing dark rituals to heal myself. There are explosions of my soul, solar explosions, soul explosions, heat is being generated through me. I create, for the sake of creating, poems, dances, parties, lovers, not with purpose but because I am a God. There is purpose to my creations.

Men whisper to me their secret powers. I have longed for this. They show me their sorrows. I have longed for this. Women share their sister powers. I have longed for this: their sparks and their sparseness. We are, all together, uncovering our history and our future, in an orgy of street dancing, in a holy terror as we fearfully, bravely hope for lovers, in a terror of undiminished dreams, in a terror of proud realizations and embittered spirit, in a smoky room where a woman finally lifts her head to tell me, tiredly, "I have lost trust of men."

This is my sacred vision, and it is really happening, right now. My life and vision: one and the same.

The power of Wicca as a religion rests on the fact that we are *all* priests. An initiate, or anyone on the path, must constantly remember that action makes a priest: if you act as a priest, you are one. A title or rite doesn't make you one; *no one can say you are not a priestess just because you haven't gone through an initiation!*

As priests, each of us has the responsibility and joy to serve land, community, and Gods, while honoring the dictates, beauty, and fulfillment of our own spirit.

Assignment: week 1. Below is a breakdown of the above statement into specific duties and a few more thoughts, adding up to four items. Write down your thoughts about each item, even if it's only one sentence for each.

1. Duty to self, honoring the dictates and beauty of one's own soul.
2. Duty to community: each of us has the responsibility and joy to serve community. *Community* denotes *all* community: human, animal, mineral, as well as family and friends. (*Mineral* might seem

weird, but a shaman discovers rocks to be friends who are alive, conscious, and needing our care.) Duty to coven does not exempt you from duty to biological family or community. Neither does duty to the larger community exempt you from duty to family. One has health only if one is helping others, *both* those near and dear and those less close. A man I knew thought community consisted only of his friends, those who ate at his table. He thus neglected anyone not of his social class. This caused an enormous void in his life and in his being.

3. Duty to know the other as self, including community as self, cosmos as self, family as self, all others as self.

4. Duty to integrate care of self (duty #1) with care of others (duty #2).

Assignment: week 1. I want you to know *yourself* as Goddess by honoring the self, others, and cosmos as Goddess and God. I refer to *Goddess and God* here both in terms of their individual selves as deities and in terms of the love between them. One way to know yourself as the Goddess is this assignment: find one of your inner blocks to being of service, and use one of this training's cleansings on it. Maybe try "Gaia's Touch": in step 5 of "Eagle Birth," you were taught to cleanse yourself of an inner block by sending it down to the earth. This technique is a ritual unto itself, called "Gaia's Touch," and it can be used to cleanse away any inner blocks, is easily and quickly performed, and can be found by name in the table of rituals.

The Third Road is a mystical tradition where one's perceptions endlessly expand to encompass all of creation. Because of this, one can get too out there, in many ways. So there are limits to seeing the cosmos as self. Without some boundaries one will run into problems. Someone once said that Faerie Tradition is for people with boundaries. I agree. An example:

A while back, a prominent Christian leader attacked me viciously and repeatedly in a public forum. He criticized me in a very personal way, decrying my character and making false accusations. Should I state the actual accusations, it might make clear who the attacker was, and I am committed to protecting him, as you will see.

I ignored the attacks. Then a friend of his wrote me asking me to continue to stay mute, explaining that the offending party was very stressed and perhaps heading toward a breakdown, and his friends were concerned. They felt a counterattack might do him a great deal of psychological harm.

I carefully worded my response because the friend seemed honestly concerned, and, since he barely knew me, I imagined he had taken a real risk in writing me; he had no idea how I might respond. I wanted him to see that I understood his concern and supported him in it:

> You are right to ask me to be kind when another person is suffering. Nor do I want to inflict suffering on someone who needs compassion. But I have easily made no response, cruel, mild, or otherwise, public or private. If I got nasty whenever anyone said the sort of thing he said, I wouldn't be much of a healer or leader, and I wouldn't be able to take being in the public eye the way I need in order to do the healing and teaching I am committed to doing.
>
> On the other hand, one's right to their own process, whether that process is about getting money, or having a nervous breakdown, stops at the point when their (metaphorical) fist is about to hit my (metaphorical) face. I do not accept abuse no matter the reason.

Since the attacker's fist was not anywhere near my face—nowhere near—I could assure the friend I had no need to reciprocate. Mind you, the assaults were quite vicious, but they really couldn't harm me.

Had the fist come near, I would have stopped it. The point I am making is that in response to the actions of others, we can protect ourselves no matter what they are going through. In this case I was able to be sensitive to the attacker as long as in doing so I did not let him hit me with his fist. And I was able to offer his wonderful friend high praise for trying to take care of a fragile loved one. I had boundaries, and I recognized the limits of seeing the cosmos or other as myself. We can't give to others when we are drained dry or crippled from abuse.

My protecting the attacker did not infringe on my boundaries. At other times I might shout from the rooftops the name of someone who is abusing me. When appropriate, I would blatantly point out a person hurting a loved one. Boundaries are about knowing what works when.

A second point is implicit in this story. When you strive for excellence, others will attack. It is hard to ignore attacks. Let me reassure you: no matter how threatening a person may seem at the moment, his fist is usually not close to your face. But it is hard to see that in the middle of being menaced. Please get input from a Good Faerie when you think you need to respond to an attacker. Most of the time it only feeds the fire, but it is difficult to know when and how to do otherwise. Holding silence is powerful at such a time. And such silence is an important boundary for those who practice Faerie magic to learn, for many reasons. Silence can be an antidote to the unhealthy ego inflation that might occur when unnecessarily responding to an attack. Silence does not mean a retreat into isolation: talk with friends about the attacker, but hold silence about the problem in other arenas.

Seek with Science and Passion; Some Last Thoughts Before Initiation

I told the following to a student after I had given her The Third Road initiation: "Regarding initiation, Let the Goddess Herself judge worthiness. No person needs sanction to face the Deities, and no one needs to stand between a seeker and God, nor between a seeker and life's challenges.

"Ultimately, no initiation given by another person is needed to make each and every lover of the Mother a priest and teacher to the community; any person may teach themselves the Mysteries if they only seek with science and passion; and we are all priests of our own souls and to the community, Gods, and land."

Here are more thoughts relevant to the final leg of a shamanic journey:

- *Don't delay initiation just because there is more work to be done.* Earlier when explaining that initiation never stops, I mentioned three initiations: one from Victor Anderson, The Third Road initiation that is given to a person by another person, and a

Third Road self-initiation, each part of a larger whole. The three events took place over time. It is impossible to take care of all initiatory issues on one leg of your journey. There will be more to do later. In fact, I can add many initiations to those three: learning to drive; facing the necessity of promoting my books if they are to get into the hands of those they might help; getting married; getting married again (a little joke, but a second marriage is definitely an initiation different from that of a first marriage); making a nice home for myself; writing this book; calling myself a poet. Each item involved facing tremendous inner and outer change; items that might be minor for some—such as promoting books or making a nice home— were major for me. Each time one grows and faces inner and outer challenges, it can be called an initiation. In some ways I hate to use *initiation* that loosely, but it makes a vital point: an initiation is not a moment in time. The real hullabaloo is the work before and after the initiation, the challenge to keep on growing and moving toward one's ideals. Don't make such a big deal out of one ceremony that you forget: no initiation ritual relieves one of having to continue their spiritual work; one mustn't refrain from initiation just because one hasn't conquered or accomplished everything one needs to conquer or accomplish for all one's initiations.

- *Creating my self-initiation was a process,* and the process of working toward an initiation can last for many years.
- *You will learn what you do well if you only try to do something, anything!* You needn't know that much to be initiated. You know *something,* then initiate, and from the initiation you learn much more—so much more, in fact, that you might see how little you knew before.
- *It is common for a person to sabotage themselves when close to their initiation.* Ensure that you follow through all the way by not being a perfectionist; by getting pep talks; by praying for strength and guidance, and then by being open to them.

- *Watch out for wild goose chases,* a particularly insidious form of self-sabotage. It is easy at this point in your journey to go off on a tangent instead of continuing on toward the finish line.

  Quitting a job, fighting with a lover, taking offense at something that usually wouldn't bother you, studying another religion, starting work on another initiation—doing any of these things at this point in your training can be a sign of growth. But doing them can also be self-sabotage: avoiding the growth and power that come from finishing a process, whether it's shamanic training and initiation or completing a college degree or even cleaning one's home. Avoidance needn't be intentional; one often does it without realizing it.

  There are many reasons we defeat ourselves in such ways. To name a few: fear of losing friends or a marital partner if we're successful; low self-esteem; belief that with power comes corruption. These inner blocks to completion can be unconscious.

  Antidotes to wild goose chases include meditation and prayer, which can be applied many ways, including asking for clarity in prayer. One might then meditate in hopes of an answer. An example of meditation: one can clear one's mind by doing "The Goddess's Face," reading it slowly while dwelling on each part of it, really feeling the words, maybe even imaging oneself feeling as carefree and unworried as the ritual's words suggests. Then sit for a moment, quietly waiting for an answer. If the answer does not come right then, the cleared mind—even if it's cleared for only a moment after "The Goddess's Face"— makes it more possible for an answer to come to you later, perhaps at an unlikely moment, such as while you're in a store, being handed your credit card back after a purchase. Other antidotes to wild goose chases are self-examination, feedback from Good Faeries, and cleansing away the inner blocks that drive us to distract ourselves from our goals.

Assignment: weeks 2 and 3. Do "Gaining the Power of Life" three times during week 2, then once more during week 3. Do not use the version I created for the initiation. Instead, use the earlier, usual version.

Assignment: start week 2 or later. As long as it is done before the initiation you can work on it up to—or even start it on—the day of initiation. Decide what you are going to proclaim in pride during your initiation. What thing or many things will you name in your proclamation of powers gained, challenges met, achievements made? What inner gifts will you announce as worthy to give to the Gods? If it is one thing that covers everything, great. Or you can make a list.

If you get stuck, look into yourself to see if you've a block to healthy pride. Or a block to completing the training or reaching one of the mundane or spiritual goals you are working toward. If so, do one of the book's cleansing rites.

You have lots of time, so there's no hurry. This assignment might take only a few minutes. Be gentle with yourself concerning what you feel you must proclaim. You needn't have climbed Mount Everest. If fear kept you from checking your breasts once a month for lumps as doctors recommend, and you did it for the first time this month, that is something to be proud of and an inner gift to offer. If you have taken the first hard step of telling someone you think you might want to go back to school (write poetry, come out of the closet, run for office), you can proclaim and offer that. Maybe a spell you did worked really well; that is an accomplishment, as is any improvement in your magical skills. Or maybe you were a whiz at seeing folks get fed a decent meal in the middle of a political meeting last week. Perhaps you cooked your first really tasty meal for yourself instead of only cooking nice meals when there was someone other than yourself to cook for. Or if you are very devoted to Her, that is a wonderful offering. Remember, initiation never stops. And when we offer what we have done and who we already are, we become inspired. Pride in whatever steps we take and whatever positive traits we have, no matter how small they seem, motivates us to accomplish more. Besides, taking such little steps is the way the greater part of our whole journey is taken!

Above I asked what you will announce as *worthy* to give to the Gods. Do not be put off by *worthy*. It is not used to intimidate you and make you think less of yourself. Nor am I implying that you must slave away to be deserving. Quite the opposite: I want you to realize how very worthy you already are and that there are things about you that you might not think too much of yet but that are in fact a credit to you; you will learn that deep in your heart if you proclaim them as such before God.

Assignment: week 3. Do the following ritual.

R I T U A L

A Spell to Get Just About Anything

INGREDIENTS (OPTIONAL)

- Clothes in which you can dance
- Drum(s); this includes any percussion instrument, whether conga, finger cymbals, or oatmeal box filled with beans that one can shake like a rattle
- A bonfire or fire lit in the fireplace
- Flowers

This is a spell for material gain. I hope assigning it now drives home the point that here, close to the gate to new power and renewal of self, one should not forget that one of the reasons we are on this earth is to revel in the amazing abundance provided us. Through "A Spell to Get Just About Anything," one can gain almost any of life's goodies, from a new dress to a better job.

Step 1. Choose one thing you want to wish for yourself in this ritual, such as a new lover, money, good sex, or a better apartment. Though once in a while it is okay to wish for a lot all at once, at this stage in your training wishing for only one thing will be more powerful and effective and is a better means of building magical skills. You can always do the spell again and again to gain a lot of goodies.

Step 2. Chant for the earth to be healed: "Mother Earth, we pray: be whole, be fulfilled, be joyous." Repeat this chant over and over (as always, you can do it silently). You may want to dance and/or drum while chanting. I've done this ritual on a beach dancing and chanting around a bonfire. (I *am* a pagan! And living in San Francisco, the pagan capital of the U.S., I can *occasionally* do that sort of thing without a passerby saying anything more than "Can I join in?") If you prefer, you can dance in front of a lit fireplace.

Step 3. Continue to chant until your wish for the earth's healing is as fully made as you can make it—at least at this point in your training. You may, for example, perceive psychically that the earth feels happy and whole.

You might have a very good feeling from having done the chant. We are all parts of the earth, so we are all healed in doing this chant.

If you've gained any good feelings or any perceptions of the earth feeling good or the like, keep in touch with them as much as you can during the next step.

Step 4. Make a prayer for your personal wish (that which you decided upon in step 1): "Great Mother, grant me . . . (name your wish)."

You can visualize your wish just before saying the prayer. In any case, it is time to add two new magical techniques to your magical tool kit. These are to be used for all wishes (spells, rituals, etc.) and visualizations.

1. When you visualize or wish, it is best, if at all possible, to focus on the ends, not the means. We did a healing on Rayette because she suffered a shattered collarbone. We did not visualize the pieces of her collarbone mended together, because someone pointed out that we did not know if the doctors were going to try to put all those pieces together. Instead we imagined Rayette doing pushups, lifting weights, and doing all the other exercises she so loved, happily and pain free. (I use Rayette's example, but spells in this book are not to be done on someone other than yourself except when specified.) Another tale: Vivian wanted to work in the music industry. Hoping to get her foot in the door, she wished to "be immersed constantly in a crowd of people" in her desired field. She ended up with a job in a restaurant frequented by the sort of people she wished to meet. The restau-

rant was always packed but was so busy and fast paced that Vivian never got to speak to her customers beyond, "What would you like to order?" Her high-powered customers were too focused on their dining partners to pay her any mind. Choose your wishes and visualizations carefully. The very means you choose can cancel out the end you had in mind. Vivian's job at the restaurant could have magically preempted a job in a private recording studio, where there were no crowds, hence few distractions to keep a top musician from noticing Vivian's talents.

Don't get morbidly fearful now, thinking, "Magic is too dangerous." The rule I've given you is a simple rule for living on the mundane plane as well. One can often preempt one's goals through the wrong means. A woman who wants more attention from her husband won't get it by nagging him about it. He'll tune her out more than ever. We should do our magic with the same common sense with which we should live life.

2. Always add to any spell: "Goddess, may my wish come true if it is your will. May my spell come to fruition in a manner that is for the greatest good of all." No matter how badly we want or need something, no matter *how* right it feels, God knows best. And since She's not a punishing, mean-spirited god, you needn't fear that She will spitefully keep you unhappy. Since She is so caring and attentive, you don't have to fear Her overlooking your needs. From now on, before doing any rite, one should cleanse such fears in the preritual cleansing. Look for such blocks whether you think they might be there or not. If new ones appear when you actually start the prayer, send them down into Mother Earth.

As to the greater good of all, you must mean this when you say it. *Always,* in pre-ritual purification, check to see if you have blocks to saying it sincerely. Some people believe that praying "for the greater good of all" implies they cannot compete for a job or a home purchase or in sports. There is nothing wrong with healthy competition. It is okay, and in fact good, to compete on the mundane plane for a job or in a basketball game. And in a competition someone often loses. It is great to wish for a certain job that you want or to wish that you'll win an Olympic gold medal. But there is no place in life or in magic for an attitude some people think is implicit in competition: "I don't care who loses out (or gets hurt) in order for me to win" or "I don't care what damage happens to others along the way as long as I achieve my goal." If you pray for the greater good, the "loser" will get the prize he really wants, and folks affected along the way by your striving will also get what they need.

Using the pre-ritual purification so that you are genuine when you say "for the greater good of all" may not be sufficient. When you are just about to say that phrase, if you discover you are still insincere, send the block(s) to sincerity down to the earth.

When we did this ritual at the beach, we each threw a flower into the ocean at the moment of the prayer. It is an optional, lovely way to make this wish. You might do a variation by throwing a flower into the fireplace.

Step 5. Send power upward if that is necessary, as you would in "Gaining the Power of Life." Henceforth, when doing a spell, check in to see if power—internal and external—needs to be sent at spell's end.

Review all of "A Shaman Is a Healer" before doing this ritual so you know exactly how to leave details to God in the healing part of this ritual. The same review is needed should you use "A Spell to Get Just About Anything" as a love spell. The relevant instructions can be found throughout that section. Here is extra information about leaving the details to the Goddess when you do a ritual to gain a lover:

Do not cast the spell on a specific person. A real love spell, like real love, is not about controlling another person! Instead, do a spell asking for God to send you the person that *She* deems would make you the happiest. Simply ask, "Mother, send me the (wo)man of my dreams, the person *you* know will make me as happy as I can possibly be."

No matter how much I say the above, people respond by shaking their heads side to side, explaining why they are the exception who needs to cast a spell that manipulates a specific someone. I don't think they realize they are suggesting control. My suspicion is that people who aren't usually controlling lose their common sense when doing magic, especially love spells. Most of us, however sane we are, become a little unhinged when it comes to love. Let's look at some of the statements I hear from people who try to justify controlling another human being for the sake of romance:

- "Since we used to be together, it is not immoral to do a spell that makes him come back."
  Answer: "There is a reason you broke up. Besides, 'makes him come back'? No matter what, you shouldn't control another human being."
- "I know if he just noticed me he would realize we are meant for each other."
  Answer: "Would you walk up to someone on the mundane plane and force their head to turn toward you to look at you? That is what you will be doing if you magically make him notice you. Besides, no matter what, you shouldn't control another human being."
- "I only want to make him call me; that's not so much to ask."
  Answer: "That is still controlling him. No matter what, you shouldn't control another human being."

These are only a few examples of the blind spots people have when it comes to controlling someone in a love spell. I have deleted a huge number of e-mails, each with a new reason the sender needs a controlling love spell, and each requesting yet another variation on the specific influence the spell should have on the person desired. Thus am I convinced the impulse to control another person for love is an amazingly strong force in us humans, not to mention one that we consistently deceive ourselves about. I imagine you might come up with variations yourself. But no matter the reason, no matter the degree, it is still controlling. And no matter what, say it with me, boys and girls, you shouldn't control another human being. Sigh, I wish it were not true, there is this really cute guy and . . .

Now, that doesn't mean you can't get all excited with a love spell. Have a fun time with it. You can make your prayer with great relish and giggles. (I think I'll take my own advice here. My, that idea just lit me up; excuse me, I'll be right back, I'm going to do a noncontrolling love spell and giggle. Okay, I'm back. I feel much better now!) You can enjoy anticipating the outcome once you've done the spell.

You can make a list of everything you want, all the traits of the perfect mate for you. That is great fun and effective magic, though be sure to end the list with "May my mate appear to me with all the traits in this list, if it is your will, Goddess. If you know better, I look forward to your choice. You know what personality in a mate would make me the happiest."

Since the urge to control in a love spell is so prevalent and difficult to recognize in oneself, one must search oneself, in the pre-ritual purification, for anything that would make one even *tend* to be controlling of another person. Make this self-examination whether you think such a trait exits in you or not. In just about any of us, there are impulses to control others for the sake of love, and those impulses are often hidden or very subtle. Make sure there is no unconscious control that will affect the spell adversely, not to mention boomerang back at you. Wiccans of most traditions believe in the law of threefold return, which states that anything you do comes back to you three times over. Any control of another person means you are three times over in their control.

Invisible Power, the True Magnificence

Invisible power: there is the invisible power of knowing God, and of serving Her. Both of these can be visible or invisible. Often what is important is unseen. There is the invisible power of serving as well as the invisible power of community. My initiate and pal Ian Anderson (no, not the well-known musician, but the lesser-known musician and gifted writer) says that two people having coffee at each other's kitchen tables is community. Yes! That is invisible.

Power can be obscured in the attempt to gain prestige and titles. Someone can be more invested in becoming able to say "I am an initiate" than in the lessons the ocean offers. Or take Jarred, who thinks he displays wisdom when constantly telling others at parties everything he has read about shamanism, but who misses the opportunity Hallie has.

No one sees Hallie in her home all day as she takes care of her two small children. But she has the chance to be surprised by the authority found in a moment so utterly quiet and piercingly bright that only great sacrifice—or a miracle—could have birthed it.

Some invisible powers cannot display themselves through titles and should be talked of only in certain ways. For example, there are powers that must remain so invisible that I will only hint at them in this section.

Secret, invisible, hidden. These words are often equated with shades drawn and doors and minds locked to provide an opportunity for shameful conduct or unhealthy family behavior that continues unabated in tortuous isolation. These are not invisible powers, mystical secrets, hidden gems. Nor are these the same as discretion, privacy, humility, love, inconspicuous peacefulness, unobtrusive self-worth, or innocent strivings toward God.

Each of you, Third Road priests (if you are trying to move toward self-love and God and choose to call yourself a Third Road priest, you are one right now), brings your own unique and very special magic to The Third Road, making our magic and our community what it is! This is a tradition that we can only create by each of us following our own star, a star we may barely see ourselves, let alone be able to show to others. This is a tradition we can only make survive if we all are priests, which may often mean just getting the dishes washed instead of doing something overtly pagan or priestly.

The point of a Third Road training is to wake up a person's cells so that he manages his mundane life and magic in his own unique and often invisible way. I love that we all can be concealed warriors in unique priesthoods. That is the essence of this tradition. The invisible, indefinable tradition.

All Third Road shamans take an unseen journey, the ultimate journey, into the self, perhaps without drums or chanting out loud or moonlit forests or memorization of ancient gods' names. Do not compare yourself to others because you do not have their outward trappings. If someone writes poems or teaches Wicca publicly or reads tarot cards or wears a ritual robe or has a teacher or reports "We drummed for ten hours until we could clearly visualize the underworld* and find our totem animals there"—and you do not, *do not invalidate yourself*. I love drums, chant out loud, write poems, teach Wicca publicly, read tarot cards, wear ritual robes sometimes, have drummed and then gone to the underworld to meet an animal spirit, and *am* a teacher. So I am not denigrating such. They have power for me. But I am also a semirecluse, which means much of my magic, service, relationship with God, and other parts of my life are invisible. Trappings do not always indicate what one might imagine they do. I know people whose outer trappings and more obvious actions are like mine, but their power, style, actions, goals, morals, and so on are very different.

One's external trappings may indicate the means that God has given one to take one's life journey, but they may not reveal to others one's inner and outer journey. Your outer trappings may not indicate yours. All you need know, instead of how you compare with others, is that finally there is no shamanic journey more profound, deeper, and authentic than facing your inner demons, knowing yourself, and finding your special gifts so that you can serve yourself and others. This is the truest journey to the underworld, the journey into yourself, into the often hidden part of you where many of your inner blocks as well as many of your talents and powers reside. This is the most important underworld, deep within you, the most trustworthy realm of power; it is you.

Faeries are invisible. I have barely mentioned them in this book, though their magic is invisibly throughout. This is the real Faerie power. Shhh. Now go and be silent!

Assignment: though the ritual below is given now, so as to appear in the context of its accompanying lecture, perform it during next month's week 1. This will be right after your initiation. It will bring power to your initiation.

---

*The underworld is an alternate realm where shamans find power.

RITUAL

The Invisible Heroes

Mothers, quiet friends, wives, fortune tellers, office assistants. There are so many who do so much that is not acknowledged. I had a therapist, Mavis, who was able to deal with this complex mind of mine over twenty years ago, guiding me when I was so hell-bent on self-destruction that people were taking bets on me. I ask a ritual of you now; give thanks to an invisible servant, someone who helped you.

There might have been someone in your past who climbed down into your well with you as Mavis did with me. By *well* I mean a time of crisis, perhaps depression or hopelessness, overwhelming fear or bewilderment. No matter how hard you have worked to come to power and how much you have accomplished through your *own* effort, if you've ever been in a deep well, it is likely someone climbed in with you to help you out. And in doing that, they suffered, made sacrifices, and worked very hard in ways you may not see.

Maybe this person did a small act, but it meant a lot to you. The cashier, Leotia, at a nearby supermarket is always very nice to me, smiling, asking how I am, and speaking to me in a very caring way. She sees me a few minutes at a time, maybe one to three times a week, but once when I was in a well, those few minutes meant a lot to me. Leotia is raising a daughter alone, and, for all I know, she may hate her job. What does it cost her to dole out such warmth and kind smiles all day to so many customers, no matter what she is feeling like? Wow! What a hero!

No one really knows how much hardship is endured to help someone out. Wells are often hidden—sometimes an unhealthy invisibility, unlike the special invisibility spoken of earlier—and the helper may be the only other person who sees the well. People often ignore the fact that friends, family members, and co-workers are in crisis. Or perhaps the person being helped is too ashamed to tell anyone but the helper. Or is so befuddled that she does not see the cost that her helper pays. Or upon leaving the well wants to leave it all behind, including any memory of what help she received.

Perhaps a well is not relevant to you. Maybe your assignment is to thank someone who did unheralded work, such as cooking, cleaning, or typing, work without which a project of yours could not succeed.

Call up a person who helped you in a less visible way, or write her. Tell her you thank her, that you owe a lot to her, and that you realize how much she did. You will make someone's day. Such people are the invisible wonders of the world.

Please don't insist instead, "But she was paid to help me." You don't know how often she might have wept worrying about you or lost sleep frantically strategizing for your well-being. Don't say, "But of course my *mother* helped me." A mother is a human being with all the concerns, needs, and attributes of any other human, and if she did something special, it is because she was a special person and should be acknowledged as such.

You might offer praise such as, "I am forever grateful: you facilitated an immense healing in me. You have an enormous gift for healing," or, "When you coached me to play high school softball, the confidence you helped me find made it possible for me to try to go to college," or, "You have been an invaluable business mentor. Your savvy insights have made a world of difference in my professional success." You might feel that you are admitting to not being as good as the one you praise. This is not so. We *all* need help as we stumble along this road called the human journey, all of us magnificent and divine, awe-inspiring and remarkable, despite—and often because of—the immense wounds and shortcomings we all have.

No one can be powerful without help. The even more powerful people are those who admit others helped them.

I am doing the above assignment by dedicating this lesson to Mavis and Leotia, then showing them this chapter. Mavis and I almost never talk now, but I will always be grateful and honor her amazing talents.

Some invisibilities should not exist. Earlier I wrote that honoring all sources is part of how we honor Mother Earth and ancestors. This is a radical notion nowadays. Some white supremacists are actually *angered* at the idea that Africa might have been the origin of human life. We are destroying another source: our mother, the Earth. We forget we owe her for all our food and the fulfillment of *all* our other needs. Everything we use—food, clothing, gasoline, air, even plastic—comes from her. Third Road initiate Molly Carter says that folks don't even remember that eggs come from chickens but think that they come from egg cartons!

Mothers are also our source; they bring us all into this world. But though often spoken of with high regard, they are not always treated so. A large section of the homeless population is typical American moms. Once their families were raised and their husbands were nursed through old age and death, such average homemakers often found themselves uncared for, falling through sexist, financial loopholes because American finances are constructed to follow the husband and father, not the wife and mother, through life. You might find this impossible to believe, far-fetched. The mind can barely grasp something comparable to "That's my mom on the street" or "That could be me in twenty years." We want to think that couldn't happen to us or to those we love. We want to believe in a better, safer world than that. We can create that kind of world if we face the problems that exist and the reasons for them.

Many other moms are abandoned alone in nursing homes. I recently visited a friend of mine, an elderly grandmother, in a nursing home. When I arrived she said that she was in tremendous physical pain and that the staff would not listen to her when she told them so. She is a quiet, self-effacing woman who would not complain if you stuck a pen in her eye! So I realized her pain must be quite severe, and I was appalled to hear that her complaints were being ignored. When she described her symptoms, even I, a person with no medical training, could see that her life was endangered.

I asked a staff member to get a doctor. The staff member told me he would relay the message to the doctor. I insisted the doctor come immediately. When the doctor arrived, he talked to me instead of my elderly friend. I told him that she was perfectly capable of telling him her problems. He then listened absentmindedly to her complaints, paying them little mind. I explained that she was neither senile nor prone to unnecessary complaints and that, if she was so much as mentioning pain, there must be a serious problem.

Over the next few days, the test that I insisted on made clear that my friend had a life-threatening infection, one that had been not only ignored but also exacerbated by conditions that, even before my visit, my friend had frequently requested be changed, to no avail. We could not find another nursing home to move her to for a while. For the next few weeks, it took my continuing insistence, combined with a lawyer's, as well as daily visits from friends and relatives to see she got the care she needed. My friend was lucky: she had people who loved her and could fight for her care. But, though there are good nursing facilities, I learned over those weeks that neglect is rampant, and often patients with no visitors are seriously mistreated because the staff is not accountable.

Let's talk about oral tradition in terms of its source. An oral source is no less worthy of acknowledgment and attribution than one that is written down. Oral tradition is not limited to what is formally passed down from shaman to student. Whenever anyone *speaks* of her life philosophy, her ideas on child rearing, her solutions to marketing dilemmas, and so forth, she is participating in oral tradition. Women enjoy oral tradition when one mother tells another, "I just figured out how to diaper the baby, even when he will barely lie still. This is what I do . . ." or when a woman explains to her newly married granddaughter, "I finally learned that the best way to deal with my husband when he is irritable is to . . ." It is oral tradition when a husband, stumped by a work problem, gets ideas from his wife over breakfast. Material in oral tradition is often transmitted in everyday circumstances—standing in line for a movie or while lovemaking or sitting in a class listening to another student—and in a casual manner, like the flippant remark made as one walks out the door, the quick aside, or the "Hmm, honey, this is just an idea, but maybe your project at the office would succeed if you . . ." No matter the place and style in which the material is transmitted, it may be the result of years of research and development.

Not every person thoroughly analyzes the things they see throughout the day or bothers to give life a lot of thought, but many people do, gaining wisdom during the same sort of everyday circumstances in which they will later pass that wisdom on. If an oral source is "just" one's wife (barber, secretary), it is hard for some folks to recognize that their wife's (barber's, secretary's) research and development might have taken place every single day as they observed the world around them on the way to work, eating in restaurants, caring for their children, or waiting on tables. *Research and development* might seem too big a term for that, but I trust the data arrived at when one lives daily life with awareness. Because it can constitute an amount of work equaling that of formal researchers, its fruits should be attributed.

Denying sources or keeping them hidden—whether Africa, mother, father, Mother Earth, oral speaker—is a wrong invisibility. It weakens one's magic, self-realization, and control over one's life and breaks the link of power between oneself and Mother Earth as well as between oneself and one's ancestors. And it can deeply hurt others.

Assignment: lifelong; do as needed.
1. Honor source: speak of them as such so that they are no longer invisible. And tend them.
2. Honor yourself as source: sometimes tell someone your process in getting to where you are, or in saying what you said. If no one is available, occasionally write it down in your journal. I will make something visible about myself to give you an example. This is hard to write. I should tell you why. Then maybe some reader will feel supported to get something off her chest should she need to in order to honor herself as source. I fear I will be perceived as being stuck-up. Deep down, a part of me still believes that a woman should never say how hard she worked to do something.

    Having gotten that off my chest, I can honor myself as source: someone once said he was confused by phrases that sounded ancient coming out of my mouth, and yet they were my own original compositions. I explained that I studied poetry and worked hard learning to focus so that when I try to orally convey my thoughts about God, magic, and life, those ideas—whether expressed through poetry or prose—easily take the form of improvised rhythms, images, even subtle rhymes. To convey any sense of my thoughts about God, magic, and life without rhythm, rhyme, and image seemed impossible to me. I worked as hard to develop the skills of a poet as some folks work for their college degrees so that I could apply that know-how when speaking in prose.

There, now that I took the risk of bragging, I hope it helps you do it yourself!

Ana and Arddu

Ana—the aged face of the Goddess, Crone, and Wise Woman—and Arddu, the winter King, are also the Gods of death, teachers both. Until we face death, we cannot face and know life. There are many little deaths—call them sacrifices, some voluntary, many not—that when faced squarely bring us lessons and power. Victor taught me to pronounce *Arddu* as "Ar'zee," almost rolling the *r*.

Women should not have to give up so much to raise their children, but in this society many must. And do. And thereby they gain lessons and power. One such lesson is that self-sacrifice can bring self-fulfillment. Ana and Arddu's lesson.

One gives up time to help a friend and thus learns that through service comes happiness.

Though it is false humility to feel one should always go uncredited for one's work, there are endless times when one cannot get the credit one deserves. After acknowledging one's anger and other upsets (instead of suppressing them or feeling ashamed of them), one must then sacrifice those feelings by no longer dwelling on the outrage and need for recognition. Without that sacrifice, one suffers needlessly from lack of peace of mind. With that sacrifice, one learns to find happiness despite one's circumstances.

Another example of sacrifice: we may lose a marvelous opportunity that by all rights should have been ours. No matter how holy it is to fight for our betterment and rights, life will throw us repeated curves. And when we cannot prevent losing what is rightfully ours, we can sacrifice it in exchange for whatever lesson that sacrifice brings.

Sometimes a sacrifice is almost unbearable. A crippling injury. The loss of trust when someone on whom you relied heavily betrays you deeply. Our Gods do not torture us to teach us. But when true horrors do occur, sometimes we can survive whole only if we wrest a lesson from the sacrifice. But if we cannot, God will not punish us. I will shame no one if a devastating loss is too great for them to learn from. How can I know if God wants all tragedies to be lessons? I cannot. I can only be a guide when a person seeks a lesson in their losses. Or help them see the lesson. Or be a comfort when no consolation, no meaning, seems possible.

This all might make the following ritual sound more fearsome than it need be. This is a ritual for guidance. There need not be tragedy for one to seek guidance. This ritual can just as much be about facing life's little challenges when everything is going well. One may need guidance about how to hold one's temper on the commute to work, because without that sacrifice one might end up grumpy the whole day. Arddu and Ana also give guidance about things other than sacrifice. They offer wisdom about anything under the sun. The only thing to fear is this: if we do not learn life's lessons and wisdom through gentle means, life has a way of giving us harder ways to learn those lessons and wisdoms. Ana and Arddu will teach gently only if you will learn from gentle lessons.

Assignment: week 3, optional. Do both or either of the rituals below:

RITUAL

Ritual of Ana, the Wise Crone

Step 1. Invoke: "Great Mother, in your aspect as the Crone, Ana, come to me. I want to visit with you because I seek guidance."

Step 2. Notice the darkness of the mind's eye, that darkness that is automatically present when you close your eyes.

Step 3. See, feel, sense Her presence however you choose. That might mean imagining Her appearing in the darkness of the mind's eye as if a projection on a movie screen, perhaps as an elderly, heavy-set woman, Her grin so wide that it lifts Her round cheeks until they almost hide the good-natured mischief glistening in Her dark wise eyes. Perhaps, you build further on this image, and She exudes a sexiness that refutes the belief that older women lose their sex appeal. On the other hand, you might visualize Her as an aged woman with shrewd, bright blue eyes, gray hair down to Her knees, and a dark robe covered with stars. This figure may be leaning over Her wizened staff, inspecting a tree's old, gnarled roots. Or create your own visualization on the movie screen in your mind. If you choose to visualize Her, you might want to add one trait or aspect at a time so as to build a strong image, layer by layer.

Or be open and see if She appears on the screen on Her own, looking however She chooses to appear.

Or ignore the screen and see if you simply get a sense of someone's presence or hear Her words.

Or . . .

Step 4. Visit. Maybe ask questions. Be open to Her guidance, in whatever form it takes.

Step 5. Devoke: "Crone, Ana, I thank you for your visit and help. Hail and farewell."

Ritual of the Winter King, Lord of the Hunt, Arddu

If you do this second rite and not the first, read the first to get a firmer sense of magical instructions.

Step 1. Invoke: "Crone, Ana, come to me. I would visit with Arddu because I seek His guidance. Come be our safety, our guide, our love."

Step 2. Notice the darkness that is automatically present when your eyes are closed.

Step 3. See, feel, sense Her presence however you choose. This can be for a mere split second.

Step 4. Invoke: "Winter King, Shepherd of Souls, Lord of the Hunt, Arddu, come to me. I want to visit with you because I seek guidance."

Step 5. Feel His presence however you choose. Or let Him appear or communicate with you as *He* will. You might imagine Him appearing in the darkness of the mind's eye as an elderly, lanky man, leaning against an apple tree, eating an apple from the tree of knowledge, with a mischievous grin, still a rake at His age! Or you might visualize Him in the same manner that I suggested you may imagine Ana: aged with shrewd, bright blue eyes, gray hair down to His knees, His dark robe covered with stars, as He leans over His wizened staff.

Step 6. Visit with Him. Maybe ask questions. Be open to His guidance, in whatever form it takes.

Step 7. Devoke: "Ana and Arddu, I thank you for your visit and help. Hail and farewell."

Zap, You're a Shaman

Assignment: week 4. Do the initiation!

Assignment: week 4. The day after your initiation, read the three paragraphs below, reciting the third paragraph—my personal prayer—as a prayer for yourself. Repeat this procedure two more times this week.

This Faerie initiation bestows its own sacred duties and powers and has its own challenges. An initiate of this rite has undergone vigorous training, has faced the dangers of our ways bravely, and has the right to be enormously proud of his cord.

But keep in mind, your training never stops.

I pray for the humility to know that no matter how long I train, no matter what challenges I conquer and rites I undergo, it is only through greater training and suitable living that I may become able to fulfill all obligations and gain all powers and joys of the Faerie priesthood. All obligations, powers, and joys: an ideal no one can ever reach.

Table of Assignments

Do these assignments during the twelfth month, except where otherwise specified:

The first week:
- Optional: If you want guests to attend the celebration that will follow your initiation and need to invite them this far in advance, do so. pg. 278
- Optional: Start working on any of the suggestions in the section of "The Third Road Self-Initiation Ritual Script" called "Preparation." pg. 257
- Write down your thoughts about duty. pg. 280
- Find one of your inner blocks to being of service, and cleanse it away with one of this training's purification rituals. pg. 281

The second week:
- Perform "Gaining the Power of Life" three times. pg. 286
- If you choose, you can start this assignment later: decide what you are going to proclaim during your initiation. pg. 286

The third week:
- Do "Gaining the Power of Life" once. pg. 286
- Use "A Spell to Get Just About Anything." pg. 287
- Optional: Use "Ritual of Ana, the Wise Crone." pg. 301
- Optional: Perform "Ritual of the Winter King, Lord of the Hunt, Arddu." pg. 301

The fourth week:
- Enjoy your initiation! pg. 303
- The next day, read the three paragraphs indicated by the lesson's text, reciting the third paragraph as a prayer. Repeat this procedure two more times within the week. pg. 303

Lifelong; done when needed:
- Honor and tend your sources. Honor yourself as a source. pg. 299

So What if You're an Initiate? Go Wash Your Dishes and Call Your Mother

Since The Third Road initiation never stops, let's talk about where you go from here. The following is initiate's work. It is simple; in fact, some of it is material that beginners can use, but it takes on other dimensions after initiation and so becomes far more powerful. Some of this work must be done immediately after initiation for your well-being, and *all* of it is part of your total initiation. To think the work is finished once the rite is over and title is gained is to defeat yourself spiritually, mundanely, and magically; and you will miss opportunities to increase your power.

Assignment: for the year after the initiation, keep an occasional eye to *post-initiation grounding,* a term I use to designate work that is not usually referred to as grounding. Part of your post-initiation grounding is keeping your feet under you as you go about your daily life. Initiation, and the shamanic path before and after, can cause psychic breakthroughs, mystical revelations, and other rewarding marvels. These wondrous and intense gifts from God are so compelling that they can make one forget the equally important, unobtrusive virtues such as patience, tolerance, humility, and trust in God. These spiritual basics are less glamorous and more difficult to face, yet without them we find ourselves filled with superiority, condemnation, and bitterness—which are not spiritual—as well as unnecessary amounts of frustration, discouragement, and exhaustion.

Daphne: An Exhausted Mystic Finds Spiritual Relief

Daphne, a talented Third Road initiate, came to me for counseling because she couldn't find it in herself to change her exhausting lifestyle. She is a technical writer and explained, "It always feels impossible to meet my deadlines. I want to do good work, and there is never enough time. I work far too many hours but still don't have the time to do the amount of revision necessary." She added that her job included many other responsibilities. "So, quite bluntly," Daphne complained, her shoulders drooping almost as much as her weary voice, "I'm pretty exhausted right now."

I offered my intuited perceptions: "Some of your extreme fatigue is for another reason. Everything your husband does drives you crazy, and you're more exhausted by that than by your job. If you practice patience at home, and pray for tolerance, a great deal of your exhaustion will leave. Your husband is no worse than anyone else, but the less you practice patience and tolerance, the worse his typical human flaws seem to be and the more they drain you. Your ego has convinced you to focus only on fascinating metaphysics and the more interesting parts of self-help, instead of those seemingly hokey basics like faith, trust, patience, tolerance. You are walking on the airy clouds of metaphysics twenty-four hours a day instead of visiting them periodically to inspire and nourish you before returning to earth, where you actually live your day."

Once Daphne found peace and rest at home, she had enough energy to fight her workaholic tendencies on the job.

Daphne and I share a flaw with many mystics: the tendency to forget the "hokey" basics then suffer for it, feeling put upon and drained, tormented by our indignation at the world around us. It is the nature of being human to forget spiritual basics and forgo their salving, peace-giving nourishment; mystics just have their own style of forgetting.

Humility is key: it impels us to maintain the spiritual basics. No matter how far you advance, keep humble. If you do something better than others, you still do not have the right to judge them. And more to the point, in thinking yourself superior, you likely are not seeing your own faults. A truly spiritually superior person defers the "right" to condemn and replaces it with compassion for people's shortcomings.

Humility also keeps one from expecting too much of oneself. Daphne's arrogance led her to believe she was capable of accomplishing more at her job than was humanly possible, at the risk of damaging herself.

Post-initiation grounding also includes handling the issues discussed in the ninth month's lesson, "How to Avoid Dangers and Problems Before, During, and After Initiation." Look at that chapter again so that you do not wander off on a wild goose chase or otherwise get off track.

Another post-initiation grounding is to make sure you can safely and comfortably channel and use the energy you bring in on a psychic level—the pure life force. To do this, keep using a wide variety—a true cross-section—of exercises and concepts in this book, including the ones that don't appear to be related to the psychic realm but seem concerned only with ethics or daily mundane life; they are all related. If you ever feel energetically uncomfortable or distressed, discuss it with others to find yet more solutions.

One can't ever list all forms of post-initiation grounding. You are unique; there are as many ways things can go awry as there are ways to have a car accident on the way to a party. But you can be guided through your post-initiation challenges and be shown any potential problems you might have overlooked. Just keep up contact with Good Faeries and elders, if the latter are available, discuss with them your life both magical and mundane, call on professionals—whether shamanic, psychological, or medical—when needed, and you will be fine.

Gentle Heart, Palm Up: Self-Love

Assignment: week 2, do the following ritual two times. Reminder: This, and the rest of the chapter, is initiate work.

Gentle Heart Ritual

Step 1. Visualize your heart as a gentle heart . . . holding power . . . not grasping for or even striving for, but simply and gently holding power.

Step 2. Imagine your heart soft, like a relaxed hand, palm up . . . soft, like the breath of a child on his mother's face.

Step 3. Imagine your gentle heart . . . holding power with a smile.

I use this rite for many reasons. It gets in touch with my true self when I am lost in false ego, fear, or worry. It is also good when the pressures and unfairness of modern life seem to have me by the throat; the exercise may not seem an antidote, but try it!

Assignment: week 2, say the prayer below two times. This prayer is derived from one of my journal entries. The above heart ritual stems from another of my entries. You can find both entries in the eleventh month's lesson; I placed them together because the two are related. One way to experience how they are related is by doing both assignments in one week.

LADY, TEACH ME MY DESTINY

Lady, teach me that, in meeting this day, I am meeting you. Teach me that, having reached this day, I have reached my destiny.

Having come to this day, I have nowhere else to strive toward, so help me live this day attentively, according to your will, and accept this moment, which is your will, whether it is a day in which to be gentle or in which to fight like a mad dog; help me be mindful, in this day, of this day.

Whatever you do, wherever you do it, love yourself. Constant caring for yourself is needed, not only when ill but always, because you are alive and want to stay alive. Feed yourself good food and good times with the tenderness of mother to child because all day and always we remain children to the Mother as well as soldiers in battle, Her soldiers.

The alarm clock rings, you get up, your sleepiness undimmed while dressing, then you take a dazed bus ride to your job. Love yourself throughout, before and after, in any way you can.

You wash a floor. Then you wash more: diapers, clothes, little faces. Love yourself throughout, before and after, any way you can.

You are short on money, so you walk home, a tired walk. So eat something wholesome, and love yourself, love yourself, love yourself.

Death eventually pulls us all down into the dirt. If we have fed ourselves with good food, kind thoughts about ourselves, and caring attention to our own needs, we will fearlessly greet death, who will smile and bless us as we relish Her.

Let love from the very air constantly fill you. Otherwise, when death—and its younger sister, those daily deaths, the inescapable sacrifices that life demands of us—comes to take you, you will not recognize Her as a friend who offers solace. Instead you will think death is an enemy, who will triumph over you though you run in fear.

Constant need is not inappropriate. Appetite, gargantuan appetite, is not inappropriate. Always be vigilant; ask yourself without cease, "What do I need now to love myself?" and later, "and *now* to love myself?" then again, *"now,* to love myself?" This is only the average human need.

I've met an aspect of God whom I call Green Leaf Father. He is present in every leaf and in every atom of every moment; and every atom in the world around us is Him taking care of us.

Optional assignment: Recite the following whenever you wish.

GREEN LEAF FATHER

Our Good Father, Potent One, Lord of Life and of Living,
God of the dark night's green leaf,
I feel you, feel your pulse in every atom of this moment,
and I know that even you, God of life, need feeding.

May I feed you now, feed life now,
for we feed gods or they die.

Help me feed the god within myself,
now and now and now,
and so feed you.

Death can pull us down into the dirt too early.
If I am fed, then instead
you, God, and the Little Death rejoice entering me, my lover,
and our joining.
We are intoxicated with God-life, peace, sexpeace, life.

If you have no beloved or are celibate, the prayer is still relevant; the lover can be metaphorical, though in fact it needn't be, since the whole cosmos is always your lover and beloved. *Little Death* is the French expression for orgasm.

There is a belief in the New Age movement that we cause our own illnesses through improper attitudes and by not facing—and not healing—our emotional pain. So, for example, anger might cause a bladder infection, or one might suffer a back injury because one has repressed one's memories of being molested as a child. Though this New Age viewpoint has validity and can be a profoundly effective approach to healing, it is oversimplified, overused, and often misapplied. Often, it is exercised when a day in bed and compassion would be the better cure; I do not like to see an ill person beat themselves up with trumped-up shame for having caused their own illness. Routine courtesy long ago set the commonsense standard that if one has a cold, you offer them compassion and a hankie to blow their nose. I want people to do the same for themselves.

Susun Weed's book *Healing Wise* suggests that we not confront an illness with the New Age question "why?"—"Why do I have this illness? In what way am I falling down on the job in terms of staying emotionally healthy and thus causing my physical illness?"—but instead use illness as a chance to nurture ourselves. This is great! My reaction to my recently sprained ankle was, "I am a passionate person who throws herself into life. The flip side of that coin is that sometimes I overdo it. I would rather be passionate and overdo it than lack enthusiasm. I will try to act more reasonably on my enthusiasm but won't beat myself up for loving life and living it fully." And thus I feel really good about myself. That is self-love.

Love every part of yourself no matter what it is. Love yourself no matter *what* you do. Love heals. Hate of self does not. Find a million ways to love yourself, and use them constantly, from bubble baths to warmly greeting the inner blocks that you hope to be rid of; from acknowledging how wonderful you are to not rudely chastising yourself for mistakes; from doing a rite in which you imagine the Goddess fills your heart with Her love for you to loving all parts of the self, even those that are "bad."

Assignment: week 3, optional. It can take a long time to learn to love oneself. And, like much of what I've taught you, self-love is not an assignment to be done only one week. If you wish to be happy it is to be done as long as you live. But if you feel your self-love is not what you would have it be, pay special attention this week to loving yourself in whatever way or ways you choose.

Assignment: week 4. Do the following ritual of love for self and others.

RITUAL

Heart Holding

Step 1. Imagine that you are holding yourself in your own heart. If you become stumped by questions and details like "How can I hold myself *in my heart* when my heart is *in me?*" or "But the whole of me is bigger than my heart?" draw on the creative and mystical side of you. That part of you readily grasps profound experiences that aren't really logical but that nevertheless make odd, intangible sense.

Step 2. Bit by bit, add the earth with all its creatures to your heart.

Step 3. Maintaining the above images, hold yourself in the heart of the Goddess and God.

The pre-ritual cleansing for "Heart Holding" should remove thoughts about and inclinations toward controlling others as well as preconceptions about what others need. For example, you may think that well-being for all creatures implies physical health. Not so. Or you may assume that, since affliction can help one grow whole, well-being necessitates great suffering. Not so. The Goddess alone knows how much suffering, bounty, pleasure, and pain each being needs. Look for biases in either direction—toward the good life or toward suffering and pain. Those are not the only possible biases; examine yourself to discover any other biases you hold. Make a self-examination as delineated in this paragraph even if you think you don't need it.

This rite is central to shamanism and spirituality: this rite is love.

This exercise is good to perform when you're depressed, self-absorbed, or so angry about someone that you become distracted from your goals. You can also benefit from this ritual if the magnitude of your anger at a person is helping him manipulate you. I do not use the term *self-absorbed* in an accusing or judgmental way but as a practical description of completely legitimate feelings; for example, the loss of a loved one and the inevitably deep grief that follows can so easily overwhelm *any* person that she can't get past them. Or perhaps she heals from the loss, but pain somehow continues to cling like a wet, dismal garment. This rite offers relief.

If you attempt "Heart Holding" and feel you're not ready for it yet, continue to do "Gentle Heart Ritual" one to three times a week, even if doing so extends well past this thirteen-month training, until a trial run of "Heart Holding" makes you feel its time has come.

By the way, I'm not knowledgeable about Buddhism, but I seem to remember a Buddhist practice in which one holds others in one's heart.

Seven-Hour Orgasms

I once mentioned that I used to have seven-hour orgasms. Needless to say, I've gotten quite a few queries on how to do that and bewilderment because no one could find directions for a seven-hour orgasm in any lesson I taught.

All is not lost! I'll let you in on a secret: though I don't ever give explicit instructions for seven-hour orgasms, if one uses this training or the one in *Be a Goddess!*—or better, both trainings—one has the initial building blocks for seven-hour orgasms.

Remember, all tools for sexual abundance are not obvious as such. And that will continue to be true nine years from now, when you'll be well on your way to seven-hour orgasms (should you want them). One reason this is so is that we achieve orgasm as a complete being. When you are free in your soul, you are free to have outrageously ecstatic sex.

The seven hours is something one builds up to (and it's fun to practice, so I expect you to work very hard at your lessons). Also, think of it as the sexual Olympics in that you may never make it to the big event, but you'll be in great shape and feeling *really* fine from the training.

More on Where to Go from Here:
Tools for Living

You've learned all the rituals in this magical cookbook! (Well, a few more are to come.) Now you can whip up something anytime you want. Milk the material, both the book's rites and lecture material, for all it is worth by applying it, applying it, applying it: practice, not learning or theory, is the key to happiness! One wins the Witch of the Week award by being happy and serving others!

Learn additional ways to apply the tools taught in this training. Be creative about it. Often folks have many spiritual tools but either forget to use them or don't realize all their uses. It seems the way humans are made. It is a lifelong process to learn how to apply your tools. We're starting now!

Assignment: week 4, tell a Good Faerie something in your life to which you wish you could apply your shamanism but don't know how. That person might help you apply what you have learned. For example, if you have been trying unsuccessfully to get pregnant and don't see how to apply shamanic tools to either increase your chances of pregnancy or accept that you cannot, perhaps your Good Faerie will say, "Try the one spiritual tool that always works: trust in God."

Shamanism is not solely for problem solving. Shamanism also helps one take advantage of opportunities. Let's say you want a position that has just opened up at your place of employment. Your Good Faerie might suggest you visualize yourself working at that job.

A long-range function of elders and peers is showing you ways to apply your tools as well as reminding you to do so when you've fallen off track.

"Kissed by a Star: A Spiritual Cleansing" is an all-purpose spell that can be used in the future whenever inner problems or turmoil keep you from achieving goals or finding inner peace. All through your life, forever more, you have an effective tool! Don't try to remove all blocks at once. It takes time to grow and change. Pace yourself gently.

Never stop purification work. Without ongoing cleansings of the things inside us that keep us from our happiness, destiny, peace of mind, equilibrium, and power, we cannot stay on our path, be happy, and serve well.

As you continue the exercises and use the theories in this text, your magical skills will become refined and your spirituality will improve, both of which in turn will make your spells more effective.

Goddess Initiation is designed so that after having done the program, its rites and ideas can be used at deeper and deeper levels. In other words, the more you grow as a person and magician, the more impact the tools have. If you continue along The Third Road, do reread non-ritual parts of this training. New aspects of it will be revealed, which are necessary to staying on track as well as following your star. Perhaps open the book at a random page and see what the Goddess wants you to read. If down the line you do the whole training again, it will be very different and much richer. I have several times retrained myself—or been trained by others—from the ground up.

The reading list at the back of this book is more than just a list of books. It offers suggestions for moving further along one's path. One way to continue your training in Third Road shamanism—or to get more spiritual tools whatever path you choose to pursue—is through *Be a Goddess!*, which develops aspects of The Third Road not developed as fully in this text. If you are committed to shamanism as a lifelong path, *Be a Goddess!* also adds further lessons on that; for example, it will explain additional ways to bring the dream into the waking mind as well as further guidelines about how Third Road contradictions can be acted on in a lifetime commitment.

By now you know I do not suffer from false modesty; this training provides a lot of tools! But a book cannot be a comprehensive system. If you need more, on any leg of your spiritual or mundane journey, seek it. For example, if you experience psychic trouble, call on a witch, shaman, or psychic.

The personal attention and fellowship that are important and integral parts of Wiccan training have no substitutes. A teacher is vital for many.

Self-Styling

To whatever degree is appropriate for you, The Third Road is a path you blaze yourself. This might seem a contradiction since The Third Road is a path one is *taught*. But my goal with a student is often to help him fully believe what he already knew before he ever started training with me!

Finding your own style of living and thinking implies awesome responsibilities: that we each become informed and educated enough to make well-considered moral and lifestyle decisions; and that we achieve spiritual and emotional integrity so that our decisions are made from a place of spiritual and emotional wholeness. Otherwise our spiritual beliefs easily become justifications and tools for denial while we do things to hurt ourselves and others. This wholeness means purification rites, dialogue, and maybe therapy. A shaman faces personal challenges instead of being "too holy" to need improvement or be criticized.

It can be hard to be open to other people's ideas, but it is necessary. Draw on all sources to continue to develop your unique way of looking at the world. For example, you might study different religions.

If you so desire, continue to develop and discover the gifts of your bloodline, private mythology, and personal magic. You might repeat relevant assignments or find new ways to pursue these avenues.

Adapt material—whether learned in this book or elsewhere—as needed. Doing so correctly requires hard work, dedication, imagination, and boldness, but it can be part of bringing one's Third Road initiation to fruition. Wait at least six months after your initiation before you adapt Third Road material. For one thing, I want you to live with the results of the material awhile so you are better informed about the material before adapting it. Even planning adaptations any sooner than six months from initiation—whether you execute those plans now or later—will distract you from absorbing the full power and transformations of your year long training and initiation.

If you adapt Third Road material, do so as a scientist. Adapt carefully, bit by bit, studying the results, so that you can see what works and what doesn't. Get feedback on your adaptations. Perform the original forms occasionally both to gain their benefits and to discover experientially if you have left something crucial behind in your adaptations or if further adaptations are needed. All of this paragraph's instructions are relevant to the theories in the training.

Some Third Road students prefer to do things by rote; they don't want to individualize their magic. That choice is valid and, in fact, a way to individualize one's magic. Everyone is different.

In a Fey-spirited life, anything spoken or explored is relevant. Nothing is irrelevant to the advanced Fey shaman. It is all grist for the mill, all power to fuel one along The Third Road. Whether you are dealing with Faerie myths and lore, herbal medicine, herbal magic, sacred sex, community service, frustration with a poorly paying job, a colicky infant, thwarted romance, or a messy divorce, it is all part of your training, your spirituality, your growth, your magic, and your power. The point of shamanism is to live *your* life, not be led away from it.

Assignment: optional; done when you wish. If one refuses to be a mindless follower, one must not expect a teacher with all the answers. Write about that, and talk with a Good Faerie about it. Then write and talk about what is missing in this training for you so that you know where to go from here. You need not leave *this* tradition to find your own answers. Instead, you can be supported by this tradition to find *your* truths. Completing this training makes it that much easier to find them.

You might also consider, write about, and talk about the following question: What physical and emotional environment might you create to facilitate your finding your primary truths?

Assignment: done throughout your life. Once in a while discuss and perhaps write about the following, which we've talked about a lot but need to reconsider now and again: What are the responsibilities of someone who follows their own style? What are the responsibilities of an initiate? What are *anyone's* spiritual responsibilities? In addition to considering aspects of these issues we've already touched on, you might also dwell on: rigorous commitment, willingness to labor, and finding the rites, spiritual attitudes, and mundane skills necessary to fulfill your responsibilities.

Here is an optional rite to help you as you continue your work.

RITUAL

How to Meet a Faerie

Use this rite for guidance, inspiration, power, camaraderie, and the sheer joy of the visit.

The guidance of Faeries has its place. My friend Grace once told me that she could not find her airplane ticket. She thought the Fey Folk had taken it, for whatever reason, and asked me to tell them she needed it back. Faeries may not care whether you make your airplane flight; they have their own priorities, which can often defeat your goals. Always check out their input with a down-to-earth human.

Don't take this rite lightly. The Fey Folk are wild, and their integrity is so strong and unusual that you must be careful with them. However, if you approach one correctly, she or he can be an honorable, powerful, and delightful friend and ally. If you find you cannot handle the power of this rite, courteously end the visit.

In this rite, it is possible, though unlikely, that a bad Faerie (they do exist) or a negative entity other than a Faerie might accidentally come. If this happens, remember: instructions for banishing bad spirits are in "The Wisdom of the Ancestors" ritual.

Step 1. Focus on the darkness of the mind's eye, the darkness that's automatically there when your eyes are closed.

Step 2. See that darkness filled with a glowing green, a Faerie green, a magic glow.

Step 3. Feel that magic, green, Fey glow start swirling around you . . . bathing you in its beauty . . . bathing you in its magic.

Step 4. Enjoy drinking in that magic for a minute.

Step 5. Let that Fey power feed you . . . cleanse you . . . and give you things you need . . . Let it work its magic on you.

Step 6. Into that green mist, call out for a friend. Don't demand a visit, for we do not control the Fey Folk. Invite with warmth, courtesy, goodwill, and good cheer.

Step 7. Greet and welcome your visitor with dignity and courtesy . . . Ask her name and her need of you. If no name is given to you, usually you should end the visit. When you meet someone on the physical plane who will not tell you their name, something is usually awry, right?

Never lightly make an agreement with a Faerie. They take commitments seriously. They are also tricksters, who often have an unusual view about what life should be like. You may not want the same goals as they. Even if what they offer seems to perfectly satisfy a long-unfulfilled dream, it can be best to think about it before proceeding. You can visit again later.

It is time-honored wisdom: do not partake of Faerie food or drink.

Step 8. Visit. If you fall asleep, your visit might happen on an unconscious level, so you would still need the following steps upon awakening.

Step 9. If you would like, ask your visitor for something you need.

Step 10. Offer thanks for the visit and for any help you were given. At this point it may be appropriate to give or promise a gift, for example, a bit of food and drink left out one night.

Step 11. Perhaps this spirit will become your friend for a while or even a lifetime. You can use this ritual to visit again. But for now say, "Farewell."

This is one exercise after which you *must* ground.

This ritual, since the day I constructed it, has proven to be an exercise that, though many people enjoy performing, many others undertake without results. The latter folks might experience nothing or might encounter an amount of mental distraction that is unusual for them, a degree so overwhelming that it is impossible to do the ritual at all. Or images come to mind that are too troubling. Or maybe mundane interruptions occur over and over, and they seem more than coincidence.

None of this surprises me. I published "How to Meet a Faerie" on my Web site because the Fey Folk wanted this information available, but I've always realized that not everyone really, deep down, wants to, needs to, or should meet a Faerie. This ritual isn't for everyone. Neither is strawberry ice cream! The Goddess creates adventures for all of us, tailoring each saga to the individual to whom She gives it. Of course, as with any spell, success with "How to Meet a Faerie" might simply be a matter of time and persistence. But if you decide, whether after many attempts or one try, that your style isn't in keeping with this rite, don't be discouraged or feel you are not up to snuff. Pat yourself on the back for self-knowledge and wisdom. Then go enjoy the adventure that *you* are equipped to be a triumphant hero in, safe and joyous.

Table of Assignments

Do these assignments during the thirteenth month, except where otherwise specified:

The first week:

- Starting week 1, and continuing throughout the year after the initiation: tend to post-initiation grounding. pg. 305
- Do the ritual "The Invisible Heroes." pg. 294

The second week:

- Do "Gentle Heart Ritual" two times. pg. 307
- Say the "Lady, Teach Me My Destiny" prayer twice. pg. 308

The third week; optional:

- Pay special attention this week to loving yourself in whatever way or ways you choose. pg. 311

The fourth week:

- Enjoy the "Heart Holding" ritual. pg. 311
- Enlist a Good Faerie into helping you better apply your shamanism. pg. 314

Optional:

- Recite the "Green Leaf Father" prayer. pg. 309
- Write about mindless followers and teachers with all the answers. Also, talk with a Good Faerie about it. In addition, write and talk about what's missing in this training for you so that you know where to go from here. pg. 317
- Also consider, write about, and talk about the environment you might create to facilitate your finding your primary truths. pg. 317

Done throughout your life:

- Once in a while discuss and perhaps write about the responsibilities of: someone who follows their own style; an initiate; *anyone.* You might also dwell on: rigorous commitment; willingness to labor; and the rites, spiritual attitudes, and mundane skills necessary to fulfill your responsibilities. pg. 317

Ahem! In Closing . . .

I sometimes end a Third Road group ceremony with the following prayer. As I recite it to share it with others, I experience a moment that I cherish. The prayer is personally dear to me. And so I offer it to you to end your training, if you so desire.

The prayer is suitable to end rituals, parties, or other events, or it can be said at *any* time and place just to express gratefulness and union with all beings. It can be said by anyone, with or without any training.*

PRAYER: GRATITUDE TO THE COSMOS

Gratitude to the cosmos—
swirling masses of dancers:

dancer atoms
dancer gases
dancer people
dancer animal people
dancer rocks
dancer of endless possibility
dancing emptiness
dancing reaches
and dancing arcs of outer space
dancing of all things that have ever been
and will ever be.

Gratitude to the cosmos
and blessings.

Thank you for sharing these lessons.

~~Your humble servant,~~

Your not-so-humble Fey Sorceress,
truly committed to being your servant,

Francesca De Grandis

---

*"Gratitude to the Cosmos" is after Gary Snyder's "Prayer for the Great Family," which in turn is after a Mohawk prayer. See Snyder's book *Turtle Island*.

Supplementary Magical Resources

One lively session of counseling (or call it spiritual guidance or shamanic counseling) furthers one's inner and outer goals. In a short, effective *series* of sessions, I guide you in a personalized journey toward self-realization, spiritual fulfillment, and prosperity. One-time or ongoing counseling also provides professional support for any of your needs, including your training in *Goddess Initiation*. Shamanic counseling is suitable for people of all religions and can include soul-healings. I counsel people all over the world by phone. Go to www.well.com/user/zthirdrd/psychic.html or call (415) 750-1205.

For weekend-long and more extended Third Road® shamanic trainings in the San Francisco Bay Area, visit www.well.com/user/zthirdrd/Wicca7.html, or contact me at the above number or at PO Box 210307, San Francisco, CA 94121. A Third Road weekend training creates self-healing, abundance, and empowerment.

The bulk of my courses are taught in the San Francisco Bay Area. Visit www.well.com/user/zthirdrd/francescadcal.html for events outside California.

Enjoy the benefits of Third Road training wherever you live with TeleFDG, shamanic telephone seminars. All you need is your telephone. Ask for TeleFDG information at the above phone number or postal address.

Go to www.well.com/user/zthirdrd/WiccanMiscellany.html to view *The Wiccan and Faerie Grimoire of Francesca De Grandis*. A grimoire is a book of magical knowledge. My on-line grimoire provides *general* shamanic information (which complements my professional services)—for example, Wiccan networking and magical reading lists—and has links to Web sites that offer such information. My grimoire also is a potpourri of rituals, articles, links, and other useful magical sundries. Go there to learn how to be on my e-mail list to receive new rituals, announcements of upcoming books and workshops, and newsletters.

If you are looking for more resources to supplement this book, I regret that I'm unable to make referrals regarding teachers (covens, Third Roaders, Wiccan-friendly therapists, and so forth) in your area, but simply surf from my links page to others sites, and find what you want. I created a Web site to give you free research resources. Use them vigorously; you will find your answers and power. Trust your ability to research! To search for your own truth is to gain power.

Circle Guide to Pagan Groups offers a listing of stores, centers, networks, and more in the United States and internationally. Contact Circle Sanctuary, PO Box 219, Mt. Horeb, WI 53572 USA.

To purchase magical incenses and oils and ritual accouterments, write to Astral Sea, Ltd., PO Box 228, Salem, MO 65560, or call (800) 732-1734. Ask for their catalog.

My musical album *Pick the Apple from the Tree* reflects the diverse wonders of shamanism: the album's spiritual lyrics and music have a wide emotional and musical range, from a cappella Celtic-style ballads to a straight-ahead jazz blues to a comedic rock 'n' roll tune. The title song is a samba, and its lyrics are a version (albeit somewhat irreverent) of what Eve *really* said to Adam. One person jokingly called me "a pagan lounge act." Use mail, phone, or fax to order *Pick the Apple from the Tree:* Serpentine Music, PO Box 2564, Sebastopol, CA 95473; (800) 270-5009 (phone); (800) 207-3869 (fax); $16 each CD, $11 each cassette, plus $4.50 shipping for the first item, $1 for each additional item (U.S. funds only); California residents please add 7.25% sales tax. Check, Visa, or MasterCard accepted.

Go to WyldWytch's Web at www.wyldwytch.com or to http://BeAGoddess.listbot.com to subscribe to the on-line *Be a Goddess!* discussion group. You'll have access to connection with like-minded fey-spirited souls. You need not have read *Be a Goddess!* to enjoy the list. Address any queries directly to WyldWytch.

Earlier, I stated that sacred sexuality must go hand in hand with safe sex. The shaman is practical: his education is inclusive, touching upon all that he needs to be happy. For information about how to practice safe sex and protect yourself or partner from herpes and other sexually transmitted diseases, call the CDC National STD and AIDS Hotlines at (800) 342-2437 or (800) 227-8922. Or go to their Web site: www.ashastd.org. Their services are free and confidential.

Magical Reading: Recommended Books About Shamanism, Self-Help, and Great Sex

The training in *Goddess Initiation* has no required reading, but many of my students are voracious readers. Here are texts that might help you further your work in *Goddess Initiation*. Many books on this list are relevant to initiatory phases of life, such as menopause, illness, and death.

Some books below are not *overtly* shamanic. An everyday cookbook might be more relevant to me spiritually than a book that has *Goddess* in the title. I'm drawn to books that, no matter what their titles suggest, hold the gemlike core of magic, personal growth, or spiritual depth. The texts below can enrich your wanderings along the Faerie highways and byways.

Space limits the number of books below. Go to www.well.com/user/zthirdrd/F_D'sbooks.html for more suggested reading.

People of the Earth: The New Pagans Speak Out, by Ellen Evert Hopman and Lawrence Bond (Rochester, NY: Inner Traditions, 1996), is an extensive collection of interviews with pagan leaders and teachers.

Margot Adler's *Drawing Down the Moon: Witches, Druids, Goddess-Worshippers, and Other Pagans in America Today* (rev. ed., New York:

Penguin, 1997) has provided a fun peek into paganism for many people. Margot is brave, warm, and generous.

I recommend Victor H. Mair's translation of *Tao Te Ching,* written by Lao Tzu (New York: Bantam, 1990). The various translations of *Tao Te Ching,* which holds core teachings of Taoism, might as well be translations of completely different texts. I like Mair's sense of this ancient Chinese philosophy's relevance to modern living.

Jambalaya: The Natural Woman's Book of Personal Charms and Practical Rituals, by Luisa Teish (San Francisco: HarperSanFrancisco, 1988), is rooted in Lucumi, an African-based religion. The book honors the past and brings Lucumi into the present with a feminist sensibility and the high integrity for which Luisa has gained so much respect.

Religion Without Beliefs: Essays in Pantheist Theology, Comparative Religion, and Ethics, by Fred Lamond (London: Janus, 1997), conveys a precious, personal vision of Wicca. That vision is different from mine; diversity is wonderful. Gerald Gardner, one of the founders of the Goddess movement in the early 1900s, trained Fred, now a Wiccan elder. Fred's longtime love of the Goddess makes this book worth reading.

Medicine Woman, by Lynn V. Andrews (San Francisco: HarperSanFrancisco, 1981), is an autobiographical novel, a fun, exciting, and easy read, and an authentic portrayal of the shamanic journey.

Sanctuary: A Tale of Life in the Woods, by Paul Monette (New York: Scribner's, 1997), is a must-read for anyone who believes, as I do, that (to quote my own book *Be a Goddess!)* "Faerie magic is not a poetry on the page but a living breathing poetry . . . the poetry of waking each morning to the Mother's embrace, the Art of walking with Her on the way to work." Monette's book holds not poems but a ninety-five-page story that touches the heart of love for self, community, and planet. Faerie-tale-like beauty!

Spiral Dance, by Starhawk (rev. ed., San Francisco: HarperSanFrancisco, 1989), offers a feminist approach to magic. She agrees that the text is not a Faerie Tradition how-to. I suggest it here because it has material from Victor Anderson's Faerie Tradition in it. Maybe more important, this woman walks her talk! I also recommend it to round out the material in *Goddess Initiation:* in the old days I occasionally sent my students to classes in Reclaiming (Starhawk's tradition)—and Reclaiming students came to my classes—because the two traditions complemented each other and, to quote a Reclaiming elder, "dovetailed." Reclaiming focused on groups and the political with an eye to the personal, whereas I focused more on each person's self-healing and individual growth, with sensitivity to race, gender, class, and the like.

The Celts believed that the food we harvest is the body of our male God who thus sacrifices his life that we may be fed. Since Wicca is a way of life, and one of the profound Celtic mysteries is that food is the body of our Father, I suggest *The Self-Healing Cookbook,* by Kristina Turner (Grass Valley, CA: Earthtones Press, 1988). Described as a "primer for healing body, mind and moods with whole natural foods," this book teaches readers a relationship with food that is self-nurturing, self-loving, and gently transformative.

Aradia, written by Charles Godfrey Leland (Blaine, WA: Phoenix Publishing, 1998), originally published in the 1800s, is a Wiccan classic. Italian witchcraft! It's one of my favorites.

A poet is a lover of the Goddess, even when he doesn't know it! Lew Welch was a Beat poet. His *Ring of Bones: Collected Poems, 1950–1971* (Bolinas, CA: Grey Fox Press, 1973) is "nonpagan" but expresses the essence of what I try to teach.

The Tibetan Book of Living and Dying, by Sogyal Rinpoche (San Francisco: HarperSanFrancisco, 1992), challenges the Western tendency to ignore death and ignore the dying. The text brings comfort and spiritual vigor to the dying and their bereaved.

Spiritual Cleansing: A Handbook of Psychic Protection, by Draja Mickaharic (York Beach, ME: Samuel Weiser, 1982) not only provides the cautions necessary for safe practices but also offers information on incenses for happy parties and other important magical needs. Draja knows her stuff!

Post-Porn Modernist: My 25 Years as a Multimedia Whore, by Annie Sprinkle (San Francisco: Cleis Press, 1998), has some gems in it. Its two pages titled "Annie's Sex Guidelines for the 90s, or You Can Heal Your Sex Life" are worth the price of the book. It's an intelligent text on one of my favorite topics: sex! And if Annie ain't spiritual, no one is.

Prayer Is Good Medicine, by Larry Dossey, M.D. (San Francisco: HarperSanFrancisco, 1996) addresses real issues about prayer. Substitute the word *spells* for some of what he says, and you have good magical instruction as well! Dossey answers questions like: Why is prayer not to be used in place of concrete action? Do you need permission to pray for someone?

Prayers for Healing: 365 Blessings, Poems, and Meditations from Around the World, edited by Maggie Oman (Berkeley: Conari Press, 1997), has page after page of rich worth, and represents a diverse cross-section of spiritual paths.

Healing Wise, by Susun S. Weed (Woodstock, NY: Ash Tree Publishing, 1989), is imperative reading for any woman who wants to own and control her own body, health, and destiny. The theory underpinning my book—a great deal of which is not discussed in the text—and the theory in hers have a lot in common. Susun will help you make your illness a growth experience, which is what initiation is all about.

Menopausal Years: The Wise Woman's Way, also by Susun S. Weed (Woodstock: Ash Tree Publishing, 1992), is essential reading and provides alternative modalities for health and healing that are needed when a woman navigates the puzzling maze of menopause.

Mother's Nature: Timeless Wisdom for the Journey into Motherhood, by Andrea Alban Gosline, Lisa Burnett Bossi, and Ame Mahler Beanland (Berkeley: Conari Press, 1999), is a must for expectant and new mothers, offering wisdom from a wide variety of perspectives—from such figures as Adrienne Rich, the Dalai Lama, Ursula LeGuin—as well as birthing and fertility customs from around the world. I wish this book had existed when I had my daughter way back when, in the early feminism of the sixties. When I conceived I understood the profound importance of the maternal state, but everyone else treated it as a minor event. I was "just a pregnant woman," leap by huge leap relegated to the second-class citizenship of wife and mother. Everyone's lack of wonder over birth and motherhood confused me. All this was one of the first ways my feminist consciousness developed as I understood how greatly the world demeans women. This book, which would have been an antidote, honors divine motherhood and mirrors back to pregnant women and new moms the goddess within, and thus would surely help a woman use pregnancy as initiation.

I discussed *Games Mother Never Taught You,* by Betty Lehan Harragan (New York: Warner Books, 1977), in the seventh month's lesson. The book is out of print, but I so strongly believe in it that I recommend it constantly anyway. Over 1,000,000 copies were printed, so it is easily available. Many bookstores will search it out for you.

If you wonder where to go after (or before) you read *Goddess Initiation,* my *Be a Goddess! A Guide to Celtic Spells and Wisdom for Self-Healing, Prosperity, and Great Sex* (San Francisco: HarperSanFrancisco, 1998) complements and furthers the work in *Goddess Initiation.* Each book explores different aspects of Goddess Spirituality and The Third Road. *Be a Goddess!,* with its focus on training in magical skills and personal growth and its Third Road perspective, will help you continue your self-empowerment.

If you like the focus on magical technique in *Goddess Initiation* and *Be a Goddess!* and have trained with both books, I suggest that you follow through by living with their material for a while. Then, for more lessons of a purely *magical* nature, try Franz Bardon's *Initiation into Hermetics* (Salt Lake City: Merkur Publishing, 1999). Like *Goddess Initiation* and *Be a Goddess!,* it offers extensive magical training. Face-to-face tutelage is always preferable, especially with the advanced magical arts, but Bardon created one of the best *written* magical trainings available: an exquisite course. One must have compelling ambitions to be a magician par excellence in order to pursue Bardon's daunting training. Also, it is pure magic as opposed to the integration of magic and everyday life typical of Third Road lessons, so keep in touch with Good Faeries during Bardon's course to keep your feet on the ground.

Acknowledgments

To all who diligently critiqued this manuscript: your excellent input made an enormous difference; I alone am responsible for the book's faults.

My test readers, Anith, Carl McColman, Mildred Fernandes, Jeff Lind, Kristen O., Michael Thorn, Vanna Z. Red, Thom Fowler, Kirsten Soler, Michael Tsongas, and Fred Lamond, told me when the manuscript was boring, confusing, or otherwise problematic. My early students, Kathleen Marshall, Steven Tiongco, and Jane Lind, now elders, checked the manuscript for spiritual and magical flaws. Sara Shopkow copyedited the book proposal.

Harper San Francisco: My editor, David Hennessy, was a perfectionist (in the best sense of the word) on all aspects of this project. Margery Buchanan's performance is far above and beyond the call of duty. I've been blessed with friendships with remarkable people. I consider Margery and David two of them. Terri Leonard, Jim Warner, and Priscilla Stuckey: you do great work. Exceptional work is not exceptional when it comes to Harper: *everyone* has been amazingly excellent on this project!

I owe much to Victor and Cora Anderson as my teachers and spiritual parents. My anthropology and poetry professor, Kush, gave input in the early Third Road days about the material I created. As a teacher, he helped me trust what I already knew and convinced me that I am a good writer. He gives support when I moan, "Woe is me, the sky is falling in!"

The work and friendship of my agents, Elizabeth Pomada and Mike Larsen, make all the difference professionally and personally. They give fastidious attention to all of publishing's exhausting, important minutiae. Their enthusiasm keeps me going. They've prodded, even confronted, me when I needed it. I try to emulate their business skills and spirituality and that of Mark Chimsky, still my publishing mentor and friend.

Jim Hoggs gave permission to misquote his letter to me. If you're someone to whom I *wrote* a letter, from which I excerpted something for this book: thank you for your kind ear.

To my readers (some of whom honor me by considering me their teacher) and my in-person students: my work continues only because of your support and your love. I especially thank Sara Robinson and Dawnwalker.

My dearest Phoebe Wray is doubly precious because she listens when I grumble about my hard day writing and calls back later to complain about her *own* publishing trials.

To "Hobbits" and my other friends who keep me sane enough to write and are so much fun that I stop work and go play: thank you, thank you. To the shamans, innovators, and family members who have gone before me: you are my link to my own soul. To the Staffords et al.: sincerest, maximum gratitude for the family reunion and everything else you have given me. To those in "the fellowship": you know what you've done for me! Thank you, Divine Mother and Father; you fulfill the needs of us all.